The World's Best Poetry

THE GRANGER ANTHOLOGY
SERIES I VOLUME II

LOVE

THE GRANGER ANTHOLOGY
Series I

The World's Best Poetry

The World's Best Poetry

THE GRANGER ANTHOLOGY
SERIES I VOLUME II

LOVE

Edited by Bliss Carman

GRANGER BOOK CO., INC.
GREAT NECK, NEW YORK

Copyright © Granger Book Company, Inc. 1981

LC 80-84498   ISBN 0-89609-203-8

Printed and Bound in the United States of America

TABLE OF CONTENTS.

INTRODUCTORY ESSAY:

PREFACE TO THE NEW EDITION.

THE GRANGER ANTHOLOGY, published in several multivolume series, is a comprehensive conspectus of international poetry in English designed to form the core of a library's poetry collection. *The World's Best Poetry*, in ten volumes, constitutes Series I. It covers the entire range of poetic literature and encompasses all topics and national literatures (in the best English translations) necessary to constitute a basic and inclusive poetry collection for the small to medium-sized library. Each volume contains a complete author-title index; the final volume concludes with author-title and title-first line indexes for the complete series.

The World's Best Poetry is a comprehensive and well-balanced anthology of 2,400 poems written prior to 1904 by 1,100 poets from all parts of the world; it is a superb representation of the best poetic literature of all nationalities and is an appropriate introductory series to THE GRANGER ANTHOLOGY. The scope of this series is so broad in theme and time that it might serve as a book of reference or as a comprehensive exhibit of the history and growth of poetry.

The arrangement is neither chronological, alphabetical, nor by nationality or sex of authors, but it is arranged by special subjects according to the ideas of the poets. Each volume is devoted to major topics; each volume is indexed so as to form a complete and independent work for the subject theme. The tenth and final volume of this series contains an additional 2,700 quotations from poems grouped under more than 300 headings for general topics, in addition to the general indexes for all volumes. Brief biographical notes for each poet are included.

The complete work is contained in ten volumes:

Volume I   Home and Friendship
    II   Love
    III   Sorrow and Consolation
    IV   The High Life (religious poetry)
    V   Nature
    VI   Fancy and Sentiment
    VII   Descriptive and Narrative
    VIII National Spirit
    IX   Tragedy and Humor
    X   Poetical Quotations; General Indexes

The plan of the work is simple and yet it is unique. It is distinctive in its totality, arrangement, inclusiveness, and quality of material presented.

THE FUTURE OF POETRY.

BY JOHN VANCE CHENEY.

Is the future of poetry, as Matthew Arnold prophesied, " immense "? For the answer to this very important question, we must turn to the past,—to man, his nature and his needs as there recorded. If the past answers that poetry has been of immense influence upon the life of man, we are warranted by the stability of the forces operative about us and within us, in asserting that poetry will continue to be of immense influence; indeed, we cannot, with any show of reason, come to a contrary conclusion.

What is the answer of the past? All that is written rests on oral delivery,—tradition, and the tradition was poetry; that is, the verbal expression of the fresh, astonished outlook of the child-man, an ardent utterance of matter instinct with imagination, addressed, as poetry is always addressed, to both the mind and the heart, to the intellect and to the emotions. Our history and our literature, sacred and secular, rest on folk-lore, which is always suffused with poetry, luminous with it, and on minstrelsy, which is song itself. War-songs and hymns of praise, lyric voicings of the powers and processes of nature—these lie at the bottom. The matter of our Hesiod and

ix

of our Homer belongs not to them, but to the Hesiods and Homers of others, long before them, singing in brightness so far back that it was to the gaze of ancient Greece impenetrable shadow. As it is with the writings of the Greeks, so it is with the writings of all nations; be the substance sacred or profane,—is it not all sacred?—be the form, now or hereafter, verse or prose, the original was matter of imagination, which always speaks with the accent of song. The heart of the older portion of our Bible, as of all Bibles, is poetry. It is not the priest, not the scribe, that holds us in this new day; it is the prophet, who, massing the idyllic and lyric traditions of a past voiceful with the music of youth, and touching them with the fresh, fusing fire of genius and devotion, sings the might and glory of the God of righteousness. Farther and farther we may wander away from the old concepts, but the old arc of glory bends overhead, unbroken, and the old music sounds on. Ideas change, but the first heart-gleams flash yet, the burning early words keep the first far-off splendor.

The master secret of poetry is its power to seize and keep the attention; the appeal is double, taking at once the mind and the heart, enchaining the intellect *and* the affections. An old Eastern poet is reported to have said of himself, " Saadi's whole power lies in his sweet words." There is much in the saying; for, though prose may have the substance of poetry, it can never have the music and the splendor of poetry,—the supernal charm, the rapture.

Our Bible rests largely on poetry; and as our religion rests largely on our Bible, our religion rests largely on poetry. Now, if the world has all along had a religion resting largely on poetry, we run little risk in saying that the religion of the future will rest largely on poetry. The indications are, indeed, that the world will rest its religion on poetry more heavily in the future than it has rested it in the past. Never man spoke truer words than old Homer's where he says, "Men cannot go on without the gods." The future of religion is "immense"; from this there is no escape; and poetry is, and must continue to be, the corner-stone of the spiritual building,—which is but another way of saying that the future of poetry is "immense."

But our way is not continually on the hills of religion. Beauty, in and for itself, is, perhaps, the next necessity after religion to one that would get the most out of life. We are haunted by the ideal, by the vision of perfection, by the high dream, the lustre of which, glinting down at fortunate moments, irradiates the common way of toil and care. In the region of the beautiful, the perfect, in the realm of ideality lying between man's yearning toward God and his efforts in the performance of the humblest duty,—in this wide region poetry reigns as it reigns in the realm of religion, supreme. Here, also, it is the ruling power, supplementing faith, patience, and reverence with health-giving, joy-giving beauty, spread lavishly as the sunlight is showered on the mountains and into the valleys. The

significant situations and experiences of every-
day life, the pleasing phenomena of nature, are
here woven together in imperishable melody,
which wells up hourly in the hearts of those familiar with it, dispelling the gloom and softening
the harshness that make heavy the lot of him that
knows not the " divine delightfulness " of song.
The mind, the heart, that is fed on poetry, is conscious of a perpetual influx of strength, buoyancy
and courage. The way, after all, has a thousand
flowers to one thorn, has myriad happy airs to
one wail of want, of doubt, or despair. Poetry
doth " raise and erect the mind." There is something in the very movement of the words, a " happy valiancy," which invigorates and enlivens,
makes us strong and joyous, proof against the
harassing little hurts, the stings of the gnat-
swarm infesting the general air as we journey.
Many a wayfarer, in need of a mental or a moral
tonic, would rather recall a few lines from Shakespeare, Milton, Wordsworth, or Emerson than
the gist of the longest doctrinal sermon; in pref-
erence to the battle-cry of an army of schoolmen,
would have for martial inspiration one perfect
utterance aglow with the gold of the morning of
the heart, ringing with the music of eternal
youth, the music that only the poet can wake.
Recall the farewell scene between crested Hector
and Andromache of the fragrant bosom; summon
before the mind's eye Helen nearing the wall,
shedding around her unspeakable loveliness as
she comes; look on wayworn Ulysses, striving to
clasp his shadowy mother in the dim Land of the

Dead; stand in the presence of Prospero as, laying aside his magic cloak, he turns to that whitest embodiment of innocence, his daughter, and asks,

> " Canst thou remember
> A time before we came unto this cell?"

behold in Paradise Lost the chariot "instinct with spirit," the wheels set with beryl, aflame with "careering fires,"—behold the chariot of the Most High rolling on, bearing him that stepped into it from the "right hand of glory";—let the mind fix itself for a moment on some one among the thousand thousand splendors of poetry new or old, then name another source from which the whole being can catch the exhilaration that it gives, can take the sudden strength that it imparts. There is little danger of exaggerating the resources of the poets for strength and joy. Those souls of the steadfast-looking habit, those souls that see so deep and wide, and tell what they have seen in heavenly melody,—what hallowing experience escapes them, what vision of healing beauty? The petrifaction of bodies in the grave is rare; but the petrifaction of spirits in life is common. The great preventive against this petrifaction—is it not poetry? To the poets—with the poets are included always the musical composers —we must look first, not only for the highest support and encouragement, but for the gentle ministration that is our consolation and joy through all the vast region stretching between the highland of religion and the valley of toil.

The essential features of poetry, and the old

need of it, remain; poetry endures, however, and must more and more endure, under new conditions. Questions religious, social and political are not now what they have been. Poetry recognizes this, and will recognize it more and more; or perception, and pliancy to the demand of the hour, are of the fibre of its might. There should be no fear that science will destroy poetry; poetry, though opposed to science in method, is the faithful ally of science. The thoughts of God are not internecine. The master forces of mind and heart are never at war among themselves; step by step, they push peacefully forward together toward perfection. The old poetry was given to prophecy; it had to do the work of the powers of exact knowledge. The new poetry, while it will not cease, on occasion, to anticipate the findings of science, will occupy itself mainly, it is safe to say, in warming and coloring, in transfiguring, the findings of science for the sustenance and solace, for the stay and delight, of the world.

Wordsworth foresaw the change that has come, and the greater change in waiting:—

" If the time should ever come when what is now called science becomes familiarized to men, then the remotest discoveries of the chemist, the botanist, the mineralogist, will be as proper objects of the poet's art as any upon which it can be employed. He will be ready to follow the steps of the man of science ; he will be at his side, carrying sensation into the midst of the objects of science itself."

The charm of beauty will, of itself, preserve poetry, maintain it in the old position of suprem-

acy. But it is in much more than the charm of
beauty that poetry is supreme; it is in much more
than the charm of beauty that we find assurance
that, whatever changes come, it will hold the old
place and power. Poetry deals with an order of
truth in the pursuit of which art has no rival;
it and the parent power, music, win access, by
methods wholly their own, to high and secret
places reached by no other ministrant. Besides
sharing with science dominion over man's intellect, poetry holds and must ever hold in sole
supremacy his heart, his soul. Exact knowledge
may not hope to suffice for the support and solace
of the emotions, of the affections. Exact knowledge, multiplied a thousand times, may not hope
to suffice for the future man; still will weigh
the heavy

> " iron time
> Of doubts, disputes, distractions, fears."

As science brings each noble task to a noble end,
poetry must take up the work, and carry it on to
the perfection that assures the satisfaction of the
whole man,—of the brain and the heart. The
brain may be the man,

> " And yet when all is thought and said,
> The heart still overrules the head."

For the " real beauty," and for the real might
as well, of the old poet singing before science
was, we must take him in his own field, a field
that yields a small harvest to toilers in cos-
mogony,—

"When I consider thy heavens, the work of thy fingers,
The moon and the stars, which thou hast ordained;
What is man, that thou art mindful of him?
And the son of man, that thou visitest him?"

After the astronomer has spoken, there is a word left to say,—a word in no wise conflicting, but additional and important. After science has spoken its words of analysis and explanation of the phenomena of nature, there is need of a word further,—the transfiguring word of the poet concerning the Power behind the phenomena, the Power

"Which shaketh the world out of her place,
And the pillars thereof tremble.

"Which commandeth the sun, and it riseth not;
And sealeth up the stars.

"Which alone stretcheth out the heavens,
And treadeth upon the waves of the sea.

"Which maketh the Bear, Orion, and the Pleiades,
And the chambers of the south.

"Which doeth great things past finding out;
Yea, marvellous things without number.

"Lo, he goeth by me, and I see him not:
He passeth on also, but I perceive him not."

To inquire profitably into the beauty and might that the poet rears on a foundation of science, we must come this side of Dante—Dante, who mastered and bent to his use the knowledge of his time—down to our own day, to Tennyson. Throughout Tennyson's music are plainly to be heard the undertones of science; the great facts recently unearthed, the mold of ages clinging to them, are launched, and borne along the golden current side by side with the lightest fancies. The laureate had the advantage of his predecessors, living, as he did, at a time when science could become a basis for the superstructure of imagination. We turn to him first, among his contemporaries, because he it was, in particular, that nature and training enabled to seize this momentous advantage and act upon it. The use he made of the new stock of knowledge bears out the belief that the poetry of the future will give no inconsiderable proportion of its force to the quickening, the warming, of fact, to the kindling of it into the mystic ignition the flame of which the soul loves, and moves in as in its own native element. Tennyson strengthens us in the conviction that

> " When Science reaches forth her arms
> To feel from world to world, and charms
> Her secret from the latest moon,"

the poet will give liberally of his strength toward the completion of the victory by setting the secret in transfiguring words. This will be done. It must be done, before the importance and meaning of the secret can burn into the mind and heart of the world, and so set aglow the general life. Hope and love, with the voice of music, must rehabilitate, yes, reshape and vitalize, ignite, the fact if we are not to stop with mere intellectual apprehension, if we are to pass on to assimilation, to perfect appropriation and practice.

Says Professor Shaler in his thoughtful little volume, "The Interpretation of Nature,"—

"So long as learning remains in the shape in which the investigator leaves it, it is generally useless to the un-initiated in the science. It is only when the poet does his work, when he phrases the truth in a form to appeal to the imagination . . . that the public has a profit from the inquiry."

> " Wait, and Love himself will bring
> The drooping flower of knowledge changed to fruit
> Of wisdom.   Wait ; my faith is large in Time,
> And that which shapes it to some perfect end."

Science does not speak with this accent, nor does it add this final, consummating word.

> " Let knowledge grow from more to more,"

sings the same poet, with the great facts of science in mind, then adds yet again the consum-mating word: so do we move on to

> " The closing cycle rich in good."

Firm is the faith in growing knowledge; but the end must be " rich in good." When growing knowledge leads to another goal than this, then shall it be thrust aside,—

> " Not only cunning casts in clay :
> Let Science prove we are, and then
> What matters Science unto men ? "

The immortality of life and love, the end " rich in good "—these science itself will not be per-

mitted to violate. At these its authority stops;
at these the poet makes a beginning, puts on his
prophet's robe, and presses hopefully forward.

Such, roughly speaking, is the attitude of
poetry toward science; but while bearing it in
mind, we are not to forget that the poet has,
beyond the power of summarizing and revoicing
the knowledge uncovered by others, that surpass-
ing gift, his own peculiar might in original in-
vestigation,—

> " The poet in his vigil hears
>   Time flowing through the night,—
> A mighty stream, absorbing tears,
>   And bearing down delight :
> There, resting on his bank of thought,
>   He listens, till his soul
> The voices of the waves has caught,
>   The meaning of their roll."

John Vance Cheney

NOTICE OF COPYRIGHTS.

I.

American poems in this volume within the legal protection of copyright are used by the courteous permission of the owners,—either the publishers named in the following list or the authors or their representatives in the subsequent one,—who reserve all their rights. So far as practicable, permission has been secured also for poems out of copyright.

PUBLISHERS OF THE WORLD'S BEST POETRY.
1904.

Messrs. D. APPLETON & CO., New York.—*W. C. Bryant:* "O, Fairest of the Rural Maids;" *P. L. Dunbar:* "On the Road."

Messrs. HARPER & BROTHERS, New York.—*J. A. Wyeth:* "My Sweetheart's Face."

Messrs. HOUGHTON, MIFFLIN & CO., Boston.—*T. B. Aldrich:* "Palabras Cariñosas;" *Arlo Bates:* "On the Road to Chorrera;" *Alice Cary:* "A Spinster's Stint;" *Margaret Deland:* "Affaire d'Amour;" *Bret Harte:* "Her Letter;" *O. W. Holmes:* "The Old Man Dreams;" *W. D. Howells:* "Caprice;" *J. R. Lowell:* "The Courtin'," "My Love," "Sonnets;" *C. E. Norton:* "My Lady;" *Nora Perry:* "The Love-Knot;" *E. C. Stedman:* "Si Jeunesse Savait;" *H. W. Story:* "Cleopatra;" *B. Taylor:* "Bedouin Love Song," "Possession," "Song of the Camp."

OLIVER HUCKEL, Baltimore.—*R. P. Jacoby:* "My Love."

E. R. LAMSON, Boston.—*Edna P. C. Hayes:* "An Opal."

LOTHROP PUBLISHING COMPANY, Boston, *P. H. Hayne:* "Love Scorns Degrees."

The FREDERICK A. STOKES COMPANY, New York.—*F. D. Sherman:* "Her Guitar," "On Some Buttercups."

The World's Best Poetry

THE GRANGER ANTHOLOGY
SERIES I VOLUME II

LOVE

POEMS OF LOVE.

POEMS OF LOVE.

I.

ADMIRATION.

WHEN IN THE CHRONICLE OF WASTED TIME.

SONNET CVI.

WHEN in the chronicle of wasted time
I see descriptions of the fairest wights,
And beauty making beautiful old rhyme,
In praise of ladies dead, and lovely knights;
Then, in the blazon of sweet beauty's best
Of hand, of foot, of lip, of eye, of brow,
I see their antique pen would have expressed
Even such a beauty as you master now.
So all their praises are but prophecies
Of this our time, all you prefiguring;
And, for they looked but with divining eyes,
They had not skill enough your worth to sing;
   For we, which now behold these present days,
   Have eyes to wonder, but lack tongues to praise.

SHAKESPEARE.

DAYBREAK.

THE lark now leaves his watery nest,
  And climbing shakes his dewy wings,
He takes your window for the east,
  And to implore your light, he sings;
Awake, awake, the morn will never rise,
Till she can dress her beauty at your eyes.

The merchant bows unto the seaman's star,
  The ploughman from the sun his season takes;
But still the lover wonders what they are,
  Who look for day before his mistress wakes:
Awake, awake, break through your veils of lawn!
Then draw your curtains and begin the dawn.

SIR WILLIAM DAVENANT.

SHALL I COMPARE THEE?

SONNET XVIII.

SHALL I compare thee to a summer's day?
Thou art more lovely and more temperate:
Rough winds do shake the darling buds of May,
And summer's lease hath all too short a date:
Sometime too hot the eye of heaven shines,
And often is his gold complexion dimmed:
And every fair from fair sometime declines,
By chance, or nature's changing course, un-
    trimmed.
But thy eternal summer shall not fade
Nor lose possession of that fair thou owest;

Nor shall Death brag thou wanderest in his shade,
When in eternal lines to time thou growest:—
  So long as men can breathe, or eyes can see,
  So long lives this, and this gives life to thee.
SHAKESPEARE.

THE PORTRAIT.

Give place, ye ladies, and begone,
Boast not yourselves at all:
For here at hand approacheth one
Whose face will stain you all.

The virtue of her lively looks
Excels the precious stone:
I wish to have none other books
To read or look upon.

In each of her two crystal eyes
Smileth a naked boy:
It would you all in heart suffice
To see that lamp of joy.

I think Nature hath lost the mould
Where she her shape did take;
Or else I doubt if Nature could
So fair a creature make.

In life she is Diana chaste,
In truth Penelope;
In word and eke in deed steadfast:
What will you more we say?

If all the world were sought so far,
Who could find such a wight?
Her beauty twinkleth like a star
Within the frosty night.

Her rosial color comes and goes
With such a comely grace,
More ruddier too than in the rose,
Within her lovely face.

At Bacchus' feast none shall her meet,
Nor at no wanton play,
Nor gazing in an open street,
Nor gadding as astray.

The modest mirth that she doth use
Is mixt with shamefastness;
All vice she doth wholly refuse,
And hateth idleness.

O Lord! it is a world to see
How virtue can repair
And deck in her such honesty,
Whom Nature made so fair!

How might I do to get a graffe
Of this unspotted tree?
For all the rest are plain but chaff,
Which seem good corn to be.

THOMAS HEYWOOD.

GIVE PLACE, YE LOVERS.

GIVE place, ye lovers, here before
    That spent your boasts and brags in vain;
My lady's beauty passeth more
    The best of yours, I dare well sayen,
Than doth the sun the candle-light,
Or brightest day the darkest night.

And thereto hath a troth as just
    As had Penelope the fair;
For what she saith, ye may it trust,
    As it by writing sealèd were:
And virtues hath she many mo'
Than I with pen have skill to show.

I could rehearse, if that I would,
    The whole effect of Nature's plaint,
When she had lost the perfect mould,
    The like to whom she could not paint:
With wringing hands, how she did cry,
And what she said, I know it aye.

I know she swore with raging mind,
    Her kingdom only set apart,
There was no loss by law of kind
    That could have gone so near her heart;
And this was chiefly all her pain;
" She could not make the like again."

Sith Nature thus gave her the praise,
    To be the chiefest work she wrought,

In faith, methink, some better ways
  On your behalf might well be sought,
Than to compare, as ye have done,
To match the candle with the sun.

HENRY HOWARD, EARL OF SURREY.

TO HIS MISTRESS,

ELIZABETH, QUEEN OF BOHEMIA.

You meaner beauties of the night,
  That poorly satisfy our eyes
More by your number than your light,—
  You common people of the skies,
  What are you when the moon shall rise?

You curious chanters of the wood,
  That warble forth Dame Nature's lays,
Thinking your passions understood
  By your weak accents,—what 's your praise
  When Philomel her voice shall raise?

You violets that first appear,
  By your pure purple mantles known,
Like the proud virgins of the year,
  As if the spring were all your own,—
  What are you when the rose is blown?

So when my mistress shall be seen
  In form and beauty of her mind:
By virtue first, then choice, a queen,—
  Tell me, if she were not designed
  The eclipse and glory of her kind?

SIR HENRY WOTTON.

THE FORWARD VIOLET THUS DID I CHIDE.

SONNET XCIX.

THE forward violet thus did I chide:—
Sweet thief, whence did thou steal thy sweet that
      smells,
If not from my love's breath? the purple pride
Which on thy soft cheek for complexion dwells,
In my love's veins thou hast too grossly dyed.
The lily I condemnèd for thy hand,
And buds of marjoram had stolen thy hair:
The roses fearfully on thorns did stand,
One blushing shame, another white despair;
A third, nor red nor white, had stolen of both,
And to this robbery had annexed thy breath;
But, for his theft, in pride of all his growth
A vengeful canker eat him up to death.
    More flowers I noted, yet I none could see,
    But sweet or color it had stolen from thee.

                      SHAKESPEARE.

THERE IS A GARDEN IN HER FACE.

FROM "AN HOURE'S RECREATION IN MUSICKE," 1606.

    THERE is a garden in her face,
      Where roses and white lilies blow;
    A heavenly paradise is that place,
      Wherein all pleasant fruits do grow;

There cherries grow that none may buy,
Till cherry-ripe themselves do cry.

Those cherries fairly do enclose
　　Of orient pearl a double row;
Which when her lovely laughter shows,
　　They look like rosebuds filled with snow;
Yet them no peer nor prince may buy,
Till cherry-ripe themselves do cry.

Her eyes like angels watch them still,
　　Her brows like bended bows do stand,
Threatening with piercing frowns to kill
　　All that approach with eye or hand
These sacred cherries to come nigh,
Till cherry-ripe themselves do cry.

ANONYMOUS.

OLIVIA.

FROM "TWELFTH NIGHT," ACT I. SC. 5.

VIOLA.—'T is beauty truly blent, whose red and
　　white
Nature's own sweet and cunning hand laid on:
Lady, you are the cruel'st she alive,
If you will lead these graces to the grave,
And leave the world no copy.

SHAKESPEARE.

PORTIA'S PICTURE.

FROM "THE MERCHANT OF VENICE," ACT
III. SC. 2.

FAIR Portia's counterfeit? What demi-god
Hath come so near creation? Move these eyes?
Or whether, riding on the balls of mine,
Seem they in motion? Here are severed lips,
Parted with sugar breath; so sweet a bar
Should sunder such sweet friends. Here in her
    hairs
The painter plays the spider; and hath woven
A golden mesh to entrap the hearts of men,
Faster than gnats in cobwebs: but her eyes!—
How could he see to do them? having made one,
Methinks it should have power to steal both his,
And leave itself unfurnished.

                          SHAKESPEARE.

SONG.

THE shape alone let others prize,
    The features of the fair:
I look for spirit in her eyes,
    And meaning in her air.

A damask cheek, an ivory arm,
    Shall ne'er my wishes win:
Give me an animated form,
    That speaks a mind within.

A face where awful honor shines,
    Where sense and sweetness move,
And angel innocence refines
    The tenderness of love.

These are the soul of beauty's frame;
    Without whose vital aid
Unfinished all her features seem,
    And all her roses dead.

But ah! where both their charms unite,
    How perfect is the view,
With every image of delight,
    With graces ever new:

Of power to charm the greatest woe,
    The wildest rage control,
Diffusing mildness o'er the brow,
    And rapture through the soul.

Their power but faintly to express
    All language must despair;
But go, behold Arpasia's face,
    And read it perfect there.

                              MARK AKENSIDE.

TRIUMPH OF CHARIS.

SEE the chariot at hand here of Love!
    Wherein my lady rideth!
Each that draws is a swan, or a dove,
    And well the car Love guideth.

As she goes, all hearts do duty
    Unto her beauty.
And, enamored, do wish, so they might
    But enjoy such a sight,
That they still were to run by her side
Through swords, through seas, whither she would
    ride.

Do but look on her eyes! they do light
  All that Love's world compriseth;
Do but look on her hair! it is bright
  As Love's star when it riseth!
Do but mark, her forehead's smoother
    Than words that soothe her!
And from her arched brows such a grace
    Sheds itself through the face,
As alone there triumphs to the life,
All the gain, all the good, of the elements' strife.

Have you seen but a bright lily grow,
  Before rude hands have touched it?
Have you marked but the fall of the snow,
  Before the soil hath smutched it?
Have you felt the wool of the beaver?
    Or swan's down ever?
Or have smelt o' the bud of the brier?
    Or the nard i' the fire?
Or have tasted the bag of the bee?
Oh, so white! oh, so soft! oh, so sweet is she.

                    BEN JONSON.

BELINDA.

FROM THE "RAPE OF THE LOCK."

On her white breast a sparkling cross she wore,
Which Jews might kiss, and Infidels adore,
Her lively looks a sprightly mind disclose,
Quick as her eyes, and as unfixed as those:
Favors to none, to all she smiles extends:
Oft she rejects, but never once offends.
Bright as the sun, her eyes the gazers strike,
And, like the sun, they shine on all alike.
Yet, graceful ease and sweetness void of pride,
Might hide her faults, if belles had faults to hide;
If to her share some female errors fall,
Look on her face, and you 'll forget them all.

ALEXANDER POPE.

HERO'S BEAUTY.

FROM THE FIRST SESTIAD OF "HERO AND LEANDER."

On Hellespont, guilty of true love's blood,
In view and opposite two cities stood,
Sea-borderers, disjoined by Neptune's might;
The one Abydos, the other Sestos hight.
At Sestos Hero dwelt; Hero the fair,
Whom young Apollo courted for her hair,
And offered as a dower his burning throne,
Where she should sit, for men to gaze upon.
The outside of her garments were of lawn,

The lining purple silk, with gilt stars drawn;
Her wide sleeves green, and bordered with a grove,
Where Venus in her naked glory strove
To please the careless and disdainful eyes
Of proud Adonis, that before her lies;
Her kirtle blue, whereon was many a stain,
Made with the blood of wretched lovers slain.
Upon her head she ware a myrtle wreath,
From whence her veil reached to the ground be-
  neath:
Her veil was artificial flowers and leaves,
Whose workmanship both man and beast de-
  ceives:
Many would praise the sweet smell as she past,
When 't was the odor which her breath forth cast;
And there for honey bees have sought in vain,
And, beat from thence, have lighted there again.
About her neck hung chains of pebble-stone,
Which, lightened by her neck, like diamonds
  shone.
She ware no gloves; for neither sun nor wind
Would burn or parch her hands, but, to her mind,
Or warm or cool them, for they took delight
To play upon those hands, they were so white.
Buskins of shells, all silvered, usèd she,
And branched with blushing coral to the knee;
Where sparrows perched, of hollow pearl and
  gold,
Such as the world would wonder to behold:
Those with sweet water oft her handmaid fills,
Which as she went, would cherup through their
  bills.
Some say, for her the fairest Cupid pined,

And, looking in her face, was strooken blind.
But this is true; so like was one the other,
As he imagined Hero was his mother;
And oftentimes into her bosom flew,
About her naked neck his bare arms threw,
And laid his childish head upon her breast,
And, with still panting rockt, there took his rest.

CHRISTOPHER MARLOWE.

DRINK TO ME ONLY WITH THINE EYES.

FROM "THE FOREST."

DRINK to me only with thine eyes,
　And I will pledge with mine;
Or leave a kiss but in the cup,
　And I 'll not look for wine.
The thirst that from the soul doth rise
　Doth ask a drink divine;
But might I of Jove's nectar sup,
　I would not change for thine.

I sent thee late a rosy wreath,
　Not so much honoring thee
As giving it a hope that there
　It could not withered be;
But thou thereon didst only breathe
　And sent'st it back to me;
Since when it grows, and smells, I swear,
　Not of itself but thee!

From the Greek of PHILOSTRATUS.
Translation of BEN JONSON.

EROS IS MISSING.

Eros is missing. In the early morn
  Forth from his bed the rascal took his flight.
Sweet are his tears; his smile is touched with
    scorn—
    A nimble - tongued, swift - footed, fearless
      sprite!

And he is winged; his hands a quiver bear.
  What father 't was begot him none can tell.
" He is not mine," Earth, Air, and Sea declare.
  That he 's a foe to all, I know full well.

So keep good watch : beware his snare's embrace;
  Even now his toils may in thy pathway lie.
But look, who 's that?   Ah, there 's his hiding-
    place!
  I see him, bow and all, in Chloe's eye.

From the Greek of MELEAGER.
Translation of CHARLES WHIBLEY.

A VIOLET IN HER HAIR.

A violet in her lovely hair,
A rose upon her bosom fair!
    But O, her eyes
A lovelier violet disclose,
And her ripe lips the sweetest rose
    That 's 'neath the skies.

A lute beneath her graceful hand
Breathes music forth at her command;
    But still her tongue

2

Far richer music calls to birth
Than all the minstrel power on earth
    Can give to song.

And thus she moves in tender light,
The purest ray, where all is bright,
    Serene, and sweet;
And sheds a graceful influence round,
That hallows e'en the very ground
    Beneath her feet!

CHARLES SWAIN.

TO DIANEME.

SWEET, be not proud of those two eyes,
Which starlike sparkle in their skies;
Nor be you proud that you can see
All hearts your captives, yours yet free.
Be you not proud of that rich hair,
Which wantons with the lovesick air;
Whenas that ruby which you wear,
Sunk from the tip of your soft ear,
Will last to be a precious stone
When all your world of beauty 's gone.

ROBERT HERRICK.

ROSALYND.

LIKE to the clear in highest sphere
Where all imperial glory shines:
Of selfsame color is her hair,
Whether unfolded, or in twines:
    Heigh-ho, fair Rosalynd!

Her eyes are sapphires set in snow,
Refining heaven by every wink;
The gods do fear whenas they glow,
And I do tremble when I think
   Heigh-ho, would she were mine!

Her cheeks are like the blushing cloud
That beautifies Aurora's face,
Or like the silver-crimson shroud
That Phœbus' smiling looks doth grace:
   Heigh-ho, fair Rosalynd!
Her lips are like two budded roses
Whom ranks of lilies neighbor nigh,
Within which bounds she balm encloses
Apt to entice a deity:
   Heigh-ho, would she were mine!

Her neck, like to a stately tower
Where Love himself emprisoned lies
To watch for glances every hour
From her divine and sacred eyes:
   Heigh-ho, fair Rosalynd!
Her paps are centres of delight,
Her breasts are orbs of heavenly frame,
Where Nature moulds the dew of light
To feed perfection with the same:
   Heigh-ho, would she were mine!

With orient pearl, with ruby red,
With marble white, with sapphire blue,
Her body every way is fed,
Yet soft to touch and sweet in view:
   Heigh-ho, fair Rosalynd!

Nature herself her shape admires;
The gods are wounded in her sight;
And Love forsakes his heavenly fires
And at her eyes his brand doth light:
  Heigh-ho, would she were mine!

Then muse not, Nymphs, though I bemoan
  The absence of fair Rosalynd,
Since for a fair there's fairer none,
Nor for her virtues so divine:
  Heigh-ho, fair Rosalynd!
Heigh-ho, my heart! would God that she were
  mine!

                    THOMAS LODGE.

———

DISDAIN RETURNED.

He that loves a rosy cheek,
  Or a coral lip admires,
Or from starlike eyes doth seek
  Fuel to maintain his fires;
As old Time makes these decay,
So his flames must waste away.

But a smooth and steadfast mind,
  Gentle thoughts, and calm desires,
Hearts with equal love combined,
  Kindle never-dying fires:—
Where these are not, I despise
Lovely cheeks or lips or eyes.

                    THOMAS CAREW.

TO A LADY ADMIRING HERSELF IN
A LOOKING–GLASS.

Fair lady, when you see the grace
Of beauty in your looking-glass;
A stately forehead, smooth and high,
And full of princely majesty;
A sparkling eye no gem so fair,
Whose lustre dims the Cyprian star;
A glorious cheek, divinely sweet,
Wherein both roses kindly meet;
A cherry lip that would entice
Even gods to kiss at any price;
You think no beauty is so rare
That with your shadow might compare;
That your reflection is alone
The thing that men most dote upon.
Madam, alas! your glass doth lie,
And you are much deceived; for I
A beauty know of richer grace
(Sweet, be not angry), 't is your face.
Hence, then, O, learn more mild to be,
And leave to lay your blame on me:
If me your real substance move,
When you so much your shadow love,
Wise nature would not let your eye
Look on her own bright majesty;
Which, had you once but gazed upon,
You could, except yourself, love none:
What then you cannot love, let me,
That face I can, you cannot see.
  Now you have what to love, you 'll say,

What then is left for me, I pray?
My face, sweet heart, if it please thee;
That which you can, I cannot see,
So either love shall gain his due,
Yours, sweet, in me, and mine in you.

THOMAS RANDOLPH.

PHILLIS IS MY ONLY JOY.

PHILLIS is my only joy
　　Faithless as the wind or seas;
Sometimes coming, sometimes coy,
　　Yet she never fails to please.
　　　　If with a frown
　　　　I am cast down,
　　　　Phillis, smiling
　　　　And beguiling,
Makes me happier than before.

Though, alas! too late I find
　　Nothing can her fancy fix;
Yet the moment she is kind
　　I forgive her all her tricks;
　　　　Which though I see,
　　　　I can't get free;
　　　　She deceiving,
　　　　I believing,
What need lovers wish for more?

SIR CHARLES SEDLEY.

CONSTANCY.

OUT upon it. I have loved
  Three whole days together;
And am like to love three more,
  If it prove fair weather.

Time shall moult away his wings,
  Ere he shall discover
In the whole wide world again
  Such a constant lover.

But the spite on 't is, no praise
  Is due at all to me;
Love with me had made no stays,
  Had it any been but she.

Had it any been but she,
  And that very face,
There had been at least ere this
  A dozen in her place.

SIR JOHN SUCKLING.

A VISION OF BEAUTY.

IT was a beauty that I saw,—
  So pure, so perfect, as the frame
  Of all the universe were lame
To that one figure, could I draw,
Or give least line of it a law:
  A skein of silk without a knot!

A fair march made without a halt!
A curious form without a fault!
　A printed book without a blot!
　All beauty!—and without a spot.

BEN JONSON.

***

TO THE PRINCESS LUCRETIA.

THY unripe youth seemed like the purple rose
That to the warm ray opens not its breast,
But, hiding still within its mossy vest,
Dares not its virgin beauties to disclose;
Or like Aurora, when the heaven first glows,—
For likeness from above will suit thee best,—
When she with gold kindles each mountain crest,
And o'er the plain her pearly mantle throws.
No loss from time thy riper age receives,
Nor can young beauty decked with art's display
Rival the native graces of thy form:
Thus lovelier is the flower whose full-blown leaves
Perfume the air, and more than orient ray
The sun's meridian glories blaze and warm.

From the Italian of TORQUATO TASSO.

***

MY LADY.

So gentle and so gracious doth appear
　My lady when she giveth her salute,
　That every tongue becometh, trembling, mute;
Nor do the eyes to look upon her dare.

Although she hears her praises, she doth go
  Benignly vested with humility;
And like a thing come down she seems to be
From heaven to earth, a miracle to show.
So pleaseth she whoever cometh nigh,
  She gives the heart a sweetness through the
      eyes,
Which none can understand who doth not prove.
And from her countenance there seems to move
  A spirit sweet and in Love's very guise,
  Who to the soul, in going, sayeth: Sigh!

From the Italian of DANTE.
Translation of CHARLES ELIOT NORTON.

VISION OF A FAIR WOMAN.

TELL us some of the charms of the stars:
  Close and well set were her ivory teeth;
White as the canna upon the moor
  Was her bosom the tartan bright beneath.

Her well-rounded forehead shone
  Soft and fair as the mountain snow;
Her two breasts were heaving full;
  To them did the hearts of heroes flow.

Her lips were ruddier than the rose;
  Tender and tunefully sweet her tongue;
White as the foam adown her side
  Her delicate fingers extended hung.

Smooth as the dusky down of the elk
  Appeared her shady eyebrows to me;

Lovely her cheeks were, like berries red;
 From every guile she was wholly free.

Her countenance looked like the gentle buds
 Unfolding their beauty in early spring;
Her yellow locks like the gold-browed hills;
 And her eyes like the radiance the sunbeams
 bring.

From the Ancient Erse.
ELIZABETH A. SHARP'S "*Lyra Celtica.*"

SPRING.

Now the bright crocus flames, and now
 The slim narcissus takes the rain,
And, straying o'er the mountain's brow,
 The daffodillies bud again.
The thousand blossoms wax and wane
 On wold, and heath, and fragrant bough,
 But fairer than the flowers art thou,
Than any growth of hill or plain.

Ye gardens, cast your leafy crown,
That my Love's feet may tread it down,
 Like lilies on the lilies set;
My Love, whose lips are softer far
Than drowsy poppy petals are,
 And sweeter than the violets!

From the Greek of MELEAGER.
Translation of ANDREW LANG.

SONG.

WHEN from the sod the flowerets spring,
 And smile to meet the sun's bright ray,

When birds their sweetest carols sing,
    In all the morning pride of May,
What lovelier than the prospect there?
Can earth boast anything more fair?
To me it seems an almost heaven,
So beauteous to my eyes that vision bright is
    given.

But when a lady chaste and fair,
    Noble, and clad in rich attire,
Walks through the throng with gracious
    air,
    As sun that bids the stars retire,—
Then where are all thy boastings, May?
What hast thou beautiful and gay,
Compared with that supreme delight?
We leave thy loveliest flowers, and watch that lady
    bright.

Wouldst thou believe me,—come and place
    Before thee all this pride of May,
Then look but on my lady's face,
    And which is best and brightest say.
For me, how soon (if choice were mine)
This would I take, and that resign;
And say, "Though sweet thy beauties,
    May,
I 'd rather forfeit all than lose my lady gay!"

From the German of WALTHER VON DER VOGELWEIDE.
Translation of EDGAR TAYLOR.

THE GIRL OF CADIZ.

Oh, never talk again to me
    Of northern climes and British ladies;
It has not been your lot to see
    Like me, the lovely girl of Cadiz.
Although her eyes be not of blue,
    Nor fair her locks, like English lasses',
How far its own expressive hue
    The languid azure eye surpasses!

Prometheus-like, from heaven she stole
    The fire that through those silken lashes
In darkest glances seems to roll,
    From eyes that cannot hide their flashes;
And as along her bosom steal
    In lengthened flow her raven tresses,
You'd swear each clustering lock could feel,
    And curled to give her neck caresses.

Our English maids are long to woo,
    And frigid even in possession;
And if their charms be fair to view,
    Their lips are slow at love's confession;
But, born beneath a brighter sun,
    For love ordained the Spanish maid is,
And who, when fondly, fairly won,
    Enchants you like the girl of Cadiz?

The Spanish maid is no coquette,
    Nor joys to see a lover tremble;
And if she love, or if she hate,
    Alike she knows not to dissemble.

Her heart can ne'er be bought or sold—
  Howe'er it beats, it beats sincerely;
And, though it will not bend to gold,
  'T will love you long, and love you dearly.

The Spanish girl that meets your love
  Ne'er taunts you with a mock denial;
For every thought is bent to prove
  Her passion in the hour of trial.
When thronging foemen menace Spain,
  She dares the deed and shares the danger;
And should her lover press the plain,
  She hurls the spear, her love's avenger.

And when, beneath the evening star,
  She mingles in the gay bolero;
Or sings to her attuned guitar
  Of Christian knight or Moorish hero;
Or counts her beads with fairy hand
  Beneath the twinkling rays of Hesper;
Or joins devotion's choral band
  To chant the sweet and hallowed vesper:

In each her charms the heart must move
  Of all who venture to behold her.
Then let no maids less fair reprove,
  Because her bosom is not colder;
Through many a clime 't is mine to roam
  Where many a soft and melting maid is,
But none abroad, and few at home,
  May match the dark-eyed girl of Cadiz.

                              LORD BYRON.

I FEAR THY KISSES, GENTLE MAIDEN.

I FEAR thy kisses, gentle maiden;
  Thou needest not fear mine;
My spirit is too deeply laden
  Ever to burden thine.

I fear thy mien, thy tones, thy motion;
  Thou needest not fear mine;
Innocent is the heart's devotion
  With which I worship thine.

                    PERCY BYSSHE SHELLEY.

A BUDGET OF PARADOXES.

CHILD in thy beauty; empress in thy pride;
Sweet and unyielding as the summer's tide;
Starlike to tremble, starlike to abide.

Guiltless of wounding, yet more true than steel;
Gem-like thy light to flash and to conceal;
Tortoise to bear, insect to see and feel.

Blushing and shy, yet dread we thy disdain;
Smiling, a sunbeam fraught with hints of rain;
Trilling love-notes to freedom's fierce refrain.

The days are fresh, the hours are wild and sweet,
When spring and winter, dawn and darkness
    meet;
Nymph, with one welcome, thee and these we
    greet.

                    JOHN MARTLEY.

LOVE DISSEMBLED.

FROM "AS YOU LIKE IT," ACT III. SC. 5.

THINK not I love him, though I ask for him;
'T is but a peevish boy:—yet he talks well;—
But what care I for words?—yet words do well,
When he that speaks them pleases those that hear.
But, sure, he 's proud; and yet his pride becomes
    him:
He 'll make a proper man: The best thing in
    him
Is his complexion; and faster than his tongue
Did make offence, his eye did heal it up.
He is not very tall; yet for his years he 's tall;
His leg is but so so; and yet 't is well:
There was a pretty redness in his lip,
A little riper and more lusty red
Than that mixed in his cheek; 't was just the dif-
    ference
Betwixt the constant red, and mingled damask.
There be some women, Silvius, had they marked
    him
In parcels, as I did, would have gone near
To fall in love with him: but, for my part,
I love him not, nor hate him not; and yet
I have more cause to hate him than to love him:
For what had he to do to chide at me?
He said mine eyes were black and my hair black;
And, now I am remembered, scorned at me:
I marvel, why I answered not again:
But that 's all one; omittance is no quittance.

SHAKESPEARE.

HER LIKENESS.

A GIRL, who has so many wilful ways
  She would have caused Job's patience to for-
    sake him;
Yet is so rich in all that's girlhood's praise,
Did Job himself upon her goodness gaze,
  A little better she would surely make him.

Yet is this girl I sing in naught uncommon,
  And very far from angel yet, I trow.
Her faults, her sweetness, are purely human;
Yet she's more lovable as simple woman
  Than any one diviner that I know.

Therefore I wish that she may safely keep
  This womanhede, and change not, only grow:
From maid to matron, youth to age, may creep,
And in perennial blessedness, still reap
  On every hand of that which she doth sow.

DINAH MARIA MULOCK CRAIK.

SHE WALKS IN BEAUTY.

" HEBREW MELODIES."

SHE walks in beauty, like the night
  Of cloudless climes and starry skies,
And all that's best of dark and bright
  Meet in her aspect and her eyes,
Thus mellowed to that tender light
  Which heaven to gaudy day denies.

One shade the more, one ray the less,
　Had half impaired the nameless grace
Which waves in every raven tress
　Or softly lightens o'er her face,
Where thoughts serenely sweet express
　How pure, how dear their dwelling-place.

And on that cheek and o'er that brow
　So soft, so calm, yet eloquent,
The smiles that win, the tints that glow,
　But tell of days in goodness spent,—
A mind at peace with all below,
　A heart whose love is innocent.

LORD BYRON.

SHE IS NOT FAIR TO OUTWARD VIEW.

She is not fair to outward view,
　As many maidens be;
Her loveliness I never knew
　Until she smiled on me:
O, then I saw her eye was bright,—
A well of love, a spring of light.

But now her looks are coy and cold;
　To mine they ne'er reply;
And yet I cease not to behold
　The love-light in her eye:
Her very frowns are fairer far
Than smiles of other maidens are!

HARTLEY COLERIDGE.

3

VERSES WRITTEN IN AN ALBUM.

HERE is one leaf reserved for me,
From all thy sweet memorials free;
And here my simple song might tell
The feelings thou must guess so well.
But could I thus, within thy mind,
One little vacant corner find,
Where no impression yet is seen,
Where no memorial yet has been,
O, it should be my sweetest care
To write my name forever there!

THOMAS MOORE.

TO ROSES IN THE BOSOM OF CASTARA.

YE blushing virgins happy are
In the chaste nunnery of her breasts,
For he 'd profane so chaste a fair,
Who e'er should call them Cupid's nests.

Transplanted thus how bright ye grow,
How rich a perfume do ye yield!
In some close garden cowslips so
Are sweeter than i' th' open field.

In those white cloisters live secure
From the rude blasts of wanton breath,
Each hour more innocent and pure,
Till you shall wither into death.

Then that which living gave you room
Your glorious sepulchre shall be:
There wants no marble for a tomb,
Whose breast has marble been to me.

WILLIAM HABINGTON.

TO HELEN.

HELEN, thy beauty is to me
  Like those Nicæan barks of yore,
That gently, o'er a perfumed sea,
  The weary, wayworn wanderer bore
  To his own native shore.

On desperate seas long wont to roam,
  Thy hyacinth hair, thy classic face,
Thy Naiad airs, have brought me home
  To the glory that was Greece
  And the grandeur that was Rome.

Lo! in yon brilliant window-niche
  How statue-like I see thee stand,
The agate lamp within thy hand!
  Ah, Psyche, from the regions which
  Are Holy Land!

EDGAR ALLAN POE.

ON A GIRDLE.

THAT which her slender waist confined
Shall now my joyful temples bind;
No monarch but would give his crown,
His arms might do what this hath done.

It was my heaven's extremest sphere,
The pale which held that lovely deer:
My joy, my grief, my hope, my love,
Did all within this circle move.

A narrow compass! and yet there
Dwelt all that's good, and all that's fair.
Give me but what this ribbon bound,
Take all the rest the sun goes round!

EDMUND WALLER.

THE WHITE ROSE.

SENT BY A YORKISH LOVER TO HIS LANCASTRIAN
MISTRESS.

If this fair rose offend thy sight,
    Placed in thy bosom bare,
'T will blush to find itself less white,
    And turn Lancastrian there.

But if thy ruby lip it spy,
    As kiss it thou mayest deign,
With envy pale 't will lose its dye,
    And Yorkish turn again.

ANONYMOUS.

A SONG.

Ask me no more where Jove bestows,
When June is past, the fading rose;
For in your beauty's orient deep,
These flowers, as in their causes, sleep.

Ask me no more whither do stray
The golden atoms of the day;
For in pure love heaven did prepare
Those powders to enrich your hair.

Ask me no more whither doth haste
The nightingale when May is past;
For in your sweet dividing throat,
She winters and keeps warm her note.

Ask me no more where those stars light
That downward fall in dead of night;
For in your eyes they sit, and there
Fixèd become as in their sphere.

Ask me no more if east or west
The Phœnix builds her spicy nest;
For unto you at last she flies,
And in your fragrant bosom dies.

THOMAS CAREW.

GO, LOVELY ROSE.

Go, lovely rose!
Tell her that wastes her time and me,
That now she knows,
When I resemble her to thee,
How sweet and fair she seems to be.

Tell her that 's young,
And shuns to have her graces spied,
That hadst thou sprung
In deserts, where no men abide,
Thou must have uncommended died.

Small is the worth
Of beauty from the light retired;
Bid her come forth,
Suffer herself to be desired,
And not blush so to be admired.

Then die, that she
The common fate of all things rare
May read in thee;
How small a part of time they share,
That are so wondrous sweet and fair.

EDMUND WALLER.

STANZA ADDED BY HENRY KIRKE WHITE.

Yet, though thou fade,
From thy dead leaves let fragrance rise;
And teach the maid,
That goodness Time's rude hand defies,
That virtue lives when beauty dies.

———

WHENAS IN SILKS MY JULIA GOES.

WHENAS in silks my Julia goes,
Then, then, methinks, how sweetly flowes
That liquefaction of her clothes.

Next, when I cast mine eyes and see
That brave vibration each way free,
O how that glittering taketh me!

ROBERT HERRICK.

O, DO NOT WANTON WITH THOSE EYES.

O, do not wanton with those eyes,
  Lest I be sick with seeing;
Nor cast them down, but let them rise,
  Lest shame destroy their being.

O, be not angry with those fires,
  For then their threats will kill me;
Nor look too kind on my desires,
  For then my hopes will spill me.

O, do not steep them in thy tears,
  For so will sorrow slay me;
Nor spread them as distract with fears;
  Mine now enough betray me.

BEN JONSON.

BLACK AND BLUE EYES.

THE brilliant black eye
  May in triumph let fly
All its darts without caring who feels 'em;
  But the soft eye of blue,
  Though it scatter wounds too,
Is much better pleased when it heals 'em!
    Dear Fanny!

The black eye may say,
  " Come and worship my ray;
By adoring, perhaps you may move me!"

But the blue eye, half hid,
Says, from under its lid,
" I love, and am yours, if you love me!"
Dear Fanny!

Then tell me, O why,
In that lovely blue eye,
Not a charm of its tint I discover;
Or why should you wear
The only blue pair
That ever said " No " to a lover?
Dear Fanny!

THOMAS MOORE.

BLUE EYES.

ANSWER TO A SONNET ENDING THUS—

" Dark eyes are dearer far
Than those that made the hyacinthine bell."
BY T. H. REYNOLDS.

BLUE! 'T is the life of heaven,—the domain
  Of Cynthia,—the wide palace of the sun,—
The tent of Hesperus, and all his train,—
  The bosom of clouds, gold, gray, and dun.
Blue! 'T is the life of waters—ocean
  And all its vassal streams: pools numberless
May rage, and foam, and fret, but never can
  Subside, if not to dark-blue nativeness.
Blue! Gentle cousin of the forest-green,
  Married to green in all the sweetest flowers—
Forget-me-not,—the blue-bell,—and, that queen
  Of secrecy, the violet: what strange powers

Hast thou, as a mere shadow! But how great,
When in an Eye thou art alive with fate!

JOHN KEATS.

O, SAW YE THE LASS?

O, SAW ye the lass wi' the bonny blue een?
Her smile is the sweetest that ever was seen;
Her cheek like the rose is, but fresher, I ween;
She 's the loveliest lassie that trips on the green.
The home of my love is below in the valley,
Where wild-flowers welcome the wandering bee;
But the sweetest of flowers in that spot that is
  seen
Is the maid that I love wi' the bonny blue een.

When night overshadows her cot in the glen,
She 'll steal out to meet her loved Donald again;
And when the moon shines on the valley so green,
I 'll welcome the lass wi' the bonny blue een.
As the dove that has wandered away from his
  nest
Returns to the mate his fond heart loves the best,
I 'll fly from the world's false and vanishing scene,
To my dear one, the lass wi' the bonny blue een.

RICHARD RYAN.

A HEALTH.

I FILL this cup to one made up
  Of loveliness alone,
A woman, of her gentle sex
  The seeming paragon;

To whom the better elements
  And kindly stars have given
A form so fair, that, like the air,
  'T is less of earth than heaven.

Her every tone is music's own,
  Like those of morning birds,
And something more than melody
  Dwells ever in her words;
The coinage of her heart are they,
  And from her lips each flows,
As one may see the burdened bee
  Forth issue from the rose.

Affections are as thoughts to her,
  The measures of her hours;
Her feelings have the fragrancy,
  The freshness of young flowers;
And lovely passions, changing oft,
  So fill her, she appears
The image of themselves by turns,—
  The idol of past years!

Of her bright face one glance will trace
  A picture on the brain,
And of her voice in echoing hearts
  A sound must long remain;
But memory, such as mine of her,
  So very much endears,
When death is nigh my latest sigh
  Will not be life's, but hers.

I fill this cup to one made up
  Of loveliness alone,

A woman, of her gentle sex
  The seeming paragon.
Her health! and would on earth there stood
  Some more of such a frame,
That life might be all poetry,
  And weariness a name.

EDWARD COATE PINKNEY.

MY SWEETHEART'S FACE.

My kingdom is my sweetheart's face,
And these the boundaries I trace:
Northward her forehead fair;
Beyond a wilderness of auburn hair;
A rosy cheek to east and west;
    Her little mouth
    The sunny south.
It is the south that I love best.

Her eyes two crystal lakes,
  Rippling with light,
Caught from the sun by day,
  The stars by night.
    The dimples in
    Her cheeks and chin
Are snares which Love hath set,
And I have fallen in!

JOHN ALLAN WYETH.

HER GUITAR.

By the fire that loves to tint her
　　Cheeks the color of a rose,
While the wanton winds of winter
　　Lose the landscape in the snows,—
While the air grows keen and bitter,
　　And the clean-cut silver stars
Tremble in the cold and glitter
　　Through the twilight's dusky bars,—
In a cosey room where lingers
　　Happy Time on folded wings,
I am watching five white fingers
　　Float across six slender strings
Of an old guitar, held lightly,—
　　Captivated while she sets,
Here and there, five others tightly
　　　　On the frets.

Lost in loving contemplation
　　Of the fair, shy, girlish face
Conscious of no admiration,
　　Posed with such a charming grace
O'er this instrument some Spanish
　　Serenader used to keep
Hidden till the sun would vanish
　　And the birds were fast asleep;
Who, below his loved one's casement,
　　With the mellow Southern moon
Through a leafy interlacement
　　Shining softly, thrummed a tune:

Did she answer it, I wonder?
  Did she frame a sweet reply?
Did she grant the wish made under
      Such a sky?

This I know, if she had listened
  To the melody I 've heard,
Mute confessions must have glistened
  In her eyes at every word;
And the very stars above her
  Must have whispered, one by one,
Something sentimental of her
  When the serenade was done.
For this music has but ended,
  And I leave my dreams to find
With the notes are somehow blended
  Like confessions of my mind;
And the gentle girl who guesses
  What these broken secrets are,
Is the one whose arm caresses
      This guitar.

                FRANK DEMPSTER SHERMAN.

ON SOME BUTTERCUPS.

A LITTLE way below her chin,
  Caught in her bosom's snowy hem,
Some buttercups are fastened in,—
  Ah, how I envy them!

They do not miss their meadow place,
  Nor are they conscious that their skies

Are not the heavens, but her face,
  Her hair, and mild blue eyes.

There, in the downy meshes pinned,
  Such sweet illusions haunt their rest;
They think her breath the fragrant wind,
  And tremble on her breast;
As if, close to her heart, they heard
  A captive secret slip its cell,
And with desire were sudden stirred
  To find a voice and tell!

                FRANK DEMPSTER SHERMAN.

O, FAIREST OF RURAL MAIDS!

O, FAIREST of the rural maids!
Thy birth was in the forest shades;
Green boughs, and glimpses of the sky,
Were all that met thine infant eye.

Thy sports, thy wanderings, when a child,
Were ever in the sylvan wild,
And all the beauty of the place
Is in thy heart and on thy face.

The twilight of the trees and rocks
Is in the light shade of thy locks;
Thy step is as the wind, that weaves
Its playful way among the leaves.

Thine eyes are springs, in whose serene
And silent waters heaven is seen;
Their lashes are the herbs that look
On their young figures in the brook.

The forest depths, by foot unpressed,
Are not more sinless than thy breast;
The holy peace, that fills the air
Of those calm solitudes, is there.

WILLIAM CULLEN BRYANT.

TO A LADY.

ON HER ART OF GROWING OLD GRACEFULLY.

You ask a verse, to sing (ah, laughing face!)
Your happy art of growing old with grace?
O Muse, begin, and let the truth—but hold!
First let me see that you are growing old.

JOHN JAMES PIATT.

ON THE ROAD TO CHORRERA.

THREE horsemen galloped the dusty way
  While sun and moon were both in the sky;
An old crone crouched in the cactus' shade,
  And craved an alms as they rode by.
    A friendless hag she seemed to be,
    But the queen of a bandit crew was she.

One horseman tossed her a scanty dole,
  A scoffing couplet the second trolled;
But the third, from his blue eyes frank and free,
  No glance vouchsafed the beldam old;
    As toward the sunset and the sea,
    No evil fearing, rode the three.

A curse she gave for the pittance small,
  A gibe for the couplet's ribald word;

But that which once had been her heart
At sight of the silent horseman stirred:
    And safe through the ambushed band they speed
For the sake of the rider who would not heed!

ARLO BATES.

THE MILKING-MAID.

THE year stood at its equinox,
    And bluff the North was blowing,
A bleat of lambs came from the flocks,
    Green hardy things were growing;
I met a maid with shining locks
    Where milky kine were lowing.

She wore a kerchief on her neck,
    Her bare arm showed its dimple,
Her apron spread without a speck,
    Her air was frank and simple.

She milked into a wooden pail,
    And sang a country ditty,—
An innocent fond lovers' tale,
    That was not wise or witty,
Pathetically rustical,
    Too pointless for the city.

She kept in time without a beat,
    As true as church-bell ringers,
Unless she tapped time with her feet,
    Or squeezed it with her fingers;
Her clear, unstudied notes were sweet
    As many a practised singer's.

I stood a minute out of sight,
　Stood silent for a minute,
To eye the pail and creamy white
　The frothing milk within it,—

To eye the comely milking-maid,
　Herself so fresh and creamy.
" Good day to you! " at last I said;
　She turned her head to see me.
" Good day! " she said, with lifted head;
　Her eyes looked soft and dreamy.

And all the while she milked and milked
　The grave cow heavy-laden :
I 've seen grand ladies, plumed and silked,
　But not a sweeter maiden;

But not a sweeter, fresher maid
　Than this in homely cotton,
Whose pleasant face and silky braid
　I have not yet forgotten.

Seven springs have passed since then, as I
　Count with a sober sorrow;
Seven springs have come and passed me by,
　And spring sets in to-morrow.

I 've half a mind to shake myself
　Free, just for once, from London,
To set my work upon the shelf,
　And leave it done or undone;

To run down by the early train,
　Whirl down with shriek and whistle,
4

And feel the bluff north glow again,
   And mark the sprouting thistle
Set up on waste patch of the lane
   Its green and tender bristle;

And spy the scarce-blown violet banks,
   Crisp primrose-leaves and others,
And watch the lambs leap at their pranks,
   And butt their patient mothers.

Alas! one point in all my plan
   My serious thoughts demur to:
Seven years have passed for maid and man,
   Seven years have passed for her too.

Perhaps my rose is over-blown,
   Not rosy, or too rosy;
Perhaps in farm-house of her own
   Some husband keeps her cosy,
Where I should show a face unknown,—
   Good-bye, my wayside posy!
             CHRISTINA GEORGINA ROSSETTI.

LOVELY MARY DONNELLY.

O LOVELY Mary Donnelly, it 's you I love the best!
If fifty girls were round you, I 'd hardly see the
   rest.
Be what it may the time of day, the place be where
   it will,
Sweet looks of Mary Donnelly, they bloom before
   me still.

Her eyes like mountain water that's flowing on a
rock,
How clear they are! how dark they are! and they
give me many a shock.
Red rowans warm in sunshine, and wetted with
a shower,
Could ne'er express the charming lip that has me
in its power.

Her nose is straight and handsome, her eyebrows
lifted up,
Her chin is very neat and pert, and smooth like a
china cup,
Her hair's the brag of Ireland, so weighty and so
fine,—
It's rolling down upon her neck, and gathered in a
twine.

The dance o' last Whit-Monday night exceeded all
before;
No pretty girl for miles about was missing from
the floor;
But Mary kept the belt of love, and O, but she
was gay!
She danced a jig, she sung a song, that took my
heart away.

When she stood up for dancing, her steps were so
complete
The music nearly killed itself to listen to her
feet;
The fiddler moaned his blindness, he heard her so
much praised,

But blessed himself he wasn't deaf when once her
   voice she raised.

And evermore I 'm whistling or lilting what you
   sung,
Your smile is always in my heart, your name beside my tongue;
But you 've as many sweethearts as you 'd count
   on both your hands,
And for myself there 's not a thumb or little finger
   stands.

O, you 're the flower o' womankind in country or
   in town;
The higher I exalt you, the lower I 'm cast down.
If some great lord should come this way, and see
   your beauty bright,
And you to be his lady, I 'd own it was but right.

O, might we live together in a lofty palace hall,
Where joyful music rises, and where scarlet curtains fall!
O, might we live together in a cottage mean and
   small;
With sods of grass the only roof, and mud the
   only wall!

O lovely Mary Donnelly, your beauty 's my dis-
   tress;
It 's far too beauteous to be mine, but I 'll never
   wish it less.
The proudest place would fit your face, and I am
   poor and low;
But blessings be about you, dear, wherever you
   may go!

WILLIAM ALLINGHAM.

THE IRISH SPINNING-WHEEL.

Show me a sight,
Bates for delight
An ould Irish wheel wid a young Irish girl at it.
Oh no!
Nothing you 'll show
Aquals her sittin' an' takin' a whirl at it.

Look at her there—
Night in her hair,
The blue ray of day from her eye laughin' out on
us!
Faix, an' a foot,
Perfect of cut,
Peepin' to put an end to all doubt in us.

That there 's a sight
Bates for delight
An ould Irish wheel wid a young Irish girl at it—
Oh no!
Nothin' you 'll show
Aquals her sittin' an' takin' a twirl at it.

See! the lamb's wool
Turns coarse an' dull
By them soft, beautiful weeshy white hands of her.
Down goes her heel,
Roun' runs the wheel,
Purrin' wid pleasure to take the commands of her.

Then show me a sight
Bates for delight
An ould Irish wheel wid a young Irish girl at it.
Oh no!
Nothin' you 'll show
Aquals her sittin' an' takin' a twirl at it.

Talk of Three Fates,
Seated on sates,
Spinnin' and shearin' away till they 've done for
me!
You may want three
For your massacree,
But one Fate for me, boys—and only the one for
me!

And isn't that fate
Pictured complate—
An ould Irish wheel with a young Irish girl at it?
Oh no!
Nothin' you 'll show
Aquals her sittin' and takin' a twirl at it.

ALFRED PERCEVAL GRAVES.

THE LOW–BACKED CAR.

WHEN first I saw sweet Peggy,
'T was on a market day:
A low-backed car she drove, and sat
Upon a truss of hay;
And when that hay was blooming grass
And decked with flowers of spring

No flower was there that could compare
  With the blooming girl I sing.
As she sat in the low-backed car,
The man at the turnpike bar
    Never asked for the toll,
    But just rubbed his ould poll,
And looked after the low-backed car.

In battle's wild commotion,
  The proud and mighty Mars
With hostile scythes demands his tithes
  Of death in warlike cars;
While Peggy, peaceful goddess,
  Has darts in her bright eye,
That knock men down in the market town,
  As right and left they fly;
While she sits in her low-backed car,
Than battle more dangerous far,—
    For the doctor's art
    Cannot cure the heart
That is hit from that low-backed car.

Sweet Peggy round her car, sir,
  Has strings of ducks and geese,
But the scores of hearts she slaughters
  By far outnumber these;
While she among her poultry sits,
  Just like a turtle-dove,
Well worth the cage, I do engage,
  Of the blooming god of Love!
While she sits in the low-backed car,
The lovers come near and far,

And envy the chicken
That Peggy is pickin',
As she sits in the low-backed car.

O, I 'd rather own that car, sir,
  With Peggy by my side,
Than a coach and four, and gold galore.
  And a lady for my bride;
For a lady would sit forninst me,
  On a cushion made with taste,—
While Peggy would sit beside me,
  With my arm around her waist,
While we drove in the low-backed car,
To be married by Father Mahar;
    O, my heart would beat high
    At her glance and her sigh,—
Though it beat in a low-backed car!

SAMUEL LOVER.

A GAGE D'AMOUR.

" *Martiis cœlebs quid agam Kalendis,*
——— *miraris ?*"—HORACE iii. 8.

CHARLES,—for it seems you wish to know,—
You wonder what could scare me so,
And why, in this long-locked bureau,
  With trembling fingers,—
With tragic air, I now replace
This ancient web of yellow lace,
Among whose faded folds the trace
  Of perfume lingers.

Friend of my youth, severe as true,
I guess the train your thoughts pursue;

But this my state is nowise due
        To indigestion;
I had forgotten it was there,
A scarf that Some-one used to wear.
Hinc illæ lacrimæ,—so spare
        Your cynic questions.

Some-one who is not girlish now,
And wed long since.   We meet and bow;
I don't suppose our broken vow
        Affects us keenly;
Yet, trifling though my act appears,
Your Sternes would make it ground for
        tears;—
One can't disturb the dust of years,
        And smile serenely.

" My golden locks " are gray and chill,
For hers,—let them be sacred still;
But yet I own, a boyish thrill
        Went dancing through me,
Charles, when I held yon yellow lace;
For, from its dusty hiding-place,
Peeped out an arch, ingenuous face
        That beckoned to me.

We shut our heart up nowadays,
Like some old music-box that plays
Unfashionable airs that raise
        Derisive pity;
Alas,—a nothing starts the spring;
And lo, the sentimental thing
At once commences quavering
        Its lover's ditty.

Laugh, if you like. The boy in me,—
The boy that was,—revived to see
The fresh young smile that shone when she,
    Of old, was tender.
Once more we trod the Golden Way,—
That mother you saw yesterday,
And I, whom none can well portray
    As young, or slender.

She twirled the flimsy scarf about
Her pretty head, and stepping out,
Slipped arm in mine, with half a pout
    Of childish pleasure.
—Where we were bound no mortal knows,
For then you plunged in Ireland's woes,
And brought me blankly back to prose
    And Gladstone's measure.

Well, well, the wisest bend to Fate.
My brown old books around me wait,
My pipe still holds, unconfiscate,
    Its wonted station.
Pass me the wine. To Those that keep
The bachelor's secluded sleep
Peaceful, inviolate, and deep,
    I pour libation.

                    AUSTIN DOBSON.

AN EXPERIENCE AND A MORAL.

I LENT my love a book one day;
  She brought it back; I laid it by:
'T was little either had to say,—
  She was so strange, and I so shy.

But yet we loved indifferent things,—
    The sprouting buds, the birds in tune,—
And Time stood still and wreathed his wings
    With rosy links from June to June.

For her, what task to dare or do?
    What peril tempt? what hardship bear?
But with her—ah! she never knew
    My heart and what was hidden there!

And she, with me, so cold and coy,
    Seemed a little maid bereft of sense;
But in the crowd, all life and joy,
    And full of blushful impudence.

She married,—well,—a woman needs
    A mate her life and love to share,—
And little cares sprang up like weeds
    And played around her elbow-chair.

And years rolled by,—but I, content,
    Trimmed my own lamp, and kept it bright,
Till age's touch my hair besprent
    With rays and gleams of silver light.

And then it chanced I took the book
    Which she perused in days gone by;
And as I read, such passion shook
    My soul,—I needs must curse or cry.

For, here and there, her love was writ,
    In old, half-faded pencil-signs,

As if she yielded—bit by bit—
Her heart in dots and underlines.

Ah, silvered fool, too late you look!
I know it; let me here record
This maxim: *Lend no girl a book*
Unless you read it afterward!

                    FREDERICK SWARTWOUT COZZENS.

AT THE CHURCH GATE.

ALTHOUGH I enter not,
Yet round about the spot
        Ofttimes I hover;
And near the sacred gate
With longing eyes I wait,
        Expectant of her.

The minster bell tolls out
Above the city's rout,
        And noise and humming;
They 've hushed the minster bell;
The organ 'gins to swell;
        She 's coming, coming!

My lady comes at last,
Timid and stepping fast,
        And hastening hither,
With modest eyes downcast;
She comes,—she 's here, she 's past!
        May Heaven go with her!

Kneel undisturbed, fair saint!
Pour out your praise or plaint
   Meekly and duly;
I will not enter there,
To sully your pure prayer
   With thoughts unruly.

But suffer me to pace
Round the forbidden place,
   Lingering a minute,
Like outcast spirits, who wait,
And see, through heaven's gate,
   Angels within it.
        WILLIAM MAKEPEACE THACKERAY.

II.

LOVE'S NATURE.

LOVE.

FROM "THE MERCHANT OF VENICE," ACT III.
SC. 2.

Tell me where is fancy bred,
Or in the heart, or in the head?
How begot, how nourishèd?
Reply, reply.

It is engendered in the eyes,
With gazing fed; and fancy dies
In the cradle where it lies.
Let us all ring fancy's knell;
I 'll begin it,—ding, dong, bell,
Ding, dong, bell.

SHAKESPEARE.

LOVE IS A SICKNESS.

Love is a sickness full of woes,
All remedies refusing;
A plant that most with cutting grows,
Most barren with best using.
Why so?

More we enjoy it, more it dies;
If not enjoyed, it sighing cries
    Heigh-ho!

Love is a torment of the mind,
   A tempest everlasting;
And Jove hath made it of a kind,
   Not well, nor full, nor fasting.
    Why so?
More we enjoy it, more it dies;
If not enjoyed, it sighing cries
    Heigh-ho!

SAMUEL DANIEL.

THE SHEPHERD AND THE KING.

Ah! what is love? It is a pretty thing,
As sweet unto a shepherd as a king,
    And sweeter too;
For kings have cares that wait upon a crown,
And cares can make the sweetest face to frown:
    Ah then, ah then,
If country loves such sweet desires gain,
What lady would not love a shepherd swain?

His flocks are folded; he comes home at night
As merry as a king in his delight,
    And merrier too;
For kings bethink them what the state require,
Where shepherds, careless, carol by the fire:
    Ah then, ah then,
If country loves such sweet desires gain,
What lady would not love a shepherd swain?

He kisseth first, then sits as blithe to eat
His cream and curd as doth the king his meat,
    And blither too;
For kings have often fears when they sup,
Where shepherds dread no poison in their cup:
    Ah then, ah then,
If country loves such sweet desires gain,
What lady would not love a shepherd swain?

Upon his couch of straw he sleeps as sound
As doth the king upon his beds of down,
    More sounder too;
For cares cause kings full oft their sleep to spill,
Where weary shepherds lie and snort their fill:
    Ah then, ah then,
If country loves such sweet desires gain,
What lady would not love a shepherd swain?

Thus with his wife he spends the year as blithe
As doth the king at every tide or syth,
    And blither too;
For kings have wars and broils to take in hand,
When shepherds laugh, and love upon the land;
    Ah then, ah then,
If country loves such sweet desires gain,
What lady would not love a shepherd swain?

ROBERT GREENE.

LOVE.

FROM " HERO AND LEANDER."

It lies not in our power to love or hate,
For will in us is over-ruled by fate.

When two are stript long e'er the course begin,
We wish that one should lose, the other win;
And one especially do we affect
Of two gold ingots, like in each respect:
The reason no man knows; let it suffice,
What we behold is censured by our eyes.
Where both deliberate, the love is slight:
Who ever loved, that loved not at first sight?

CHRISTOPHER MARLOWE.

LOVE AND WOMAN.

FROM " LOVE'S LABOR 'S LOST," ACT IV. SC. 3.

KING.—But what of this? are we not all in
    love?

BIRON.—Nothing so sure; and thereby all for-
    sworn.

KING.—Then leave this chat; and, good Biron,
    now prove
Our loving lawful, and our faith not torn.

DUMAIN.—Ay, marry, there; some flattery for
    this evil.

LONGAVILLE.—O, some authority how to pro-
    ceed;
Some tricks, some quillets, how to cheat the devil.

DUMAIN—Some salve for perjury.

BIRON.—   'T is more than need.
Have at you, then, affection's men at arms.
Consider what you first did swear unto,—
To fast, to study, and to see no woman;
Flat treason 'gainst the kingly state of youth.
Say, can you fast? your stomachs are too young,
    5

And abstinence engenders maladies.
And where that you have vowed to study, lords,
In that each of you have forsworn his book,
Can you still dream and pore and thereon look?
For when would you, my lord,—or you,—or you,—
Have found the ground of study's excellence
Without the beauty of a woman's face?
From women's eyes this doctrine I derive:
They are the ground, the books, the academes,
From whence doth spring the true Promethean
    fire.
Why, universal plodding poisons up
The nimble spirits in the arteries,
As motion and long-during action tires
The sinewy vigor of the traveller.
Now, for not looking on a woman's face,
You have in that forsworn the use of eyes,
And study too, the causer of your vow;
For where is any author in the world
Teaches such beauty as a woman's eye?
Learning is but an adjunct to ourself,
And where we are our learning likewise is;
Then when ourselves we see in ladies' eyes,
Do we not likewise see our learning there?
O, we have made a vow to study, lords,
And in that vow we have forsworn our books;
For when would you, my liege,—or you,—or
    you,—
In leaden contemplation have found out
Such fiery numbers as the prompting eyes
Of beauty's tutors have enriched you with?
Other slow arts entirely keep the brain,
And therefore, finding barren practisers,

Scarce show a harvest of their heavy toil;
But love, first learned in a lady's eyes,
Lives not alone immured in the brain,
But, with the motion of all elements,
Courses as swift as thought in every power,
And gives to every power a double power,
Above their functions and their offices.
It adds a precious seeing to the eye;
A lover's eyes will gaze an eagle blind;
A lover's ear will hear the lowest sound,
When the suspicious head of theft is stopped;
Love's feeling is more soft and sensible
Than are the tender horns of cockled snails;
Love's tongue proves dainty Bacchus gross in
     taste;
For valor, is not Love a Hercules,
Still climbing trees in the Hesperides?
Subtle as Sphinx; as sweet and musical
As bright Apollo's lute, strung with his hair;
And when Love speaks, the voice of all the gods
Make heaven drowsy with the harmony.
Never durst poet touch a pen to write
Until his ink were tempered with Love's sighs;
O, then his lines would ravish savage ears
And plant in tyrants mild humility!
From women's eyes this doctrine I derive:
They sparkle still the right Promethean fire;
They are the books, the arts, the academes,
That show, contain, and nourish all the world,
Else none at all in aught proves excellent.
Then fools you were these women to forswear,
Or keeping what is sworn, you will prove fools.
For wisdom's sake, a word that all men love,

Or for love's sake, a word that loves all men,
Or for men's sake, the authors of these women,
Or women's sake, by whom we men are men,
Let us once lose our oaths to find ourselves,
Or else we lose ourselves to keep our oaths.
It is religion to be thus forsworn,
For charity itself fulfils the law,—
And who can sever love from charity?

SHAKESPEARE.

AH, HOW SWEET.

FROM "TYRANNIC LOVE," ACT IV. SC. 1.

Ah, how sweet it is to love!
  Ah, how gay is young desire!
And what pleasing pains we prove
  When we first approach love's fire!
Pains of love be sweeter far
Than all other pleasures are.

Sighs which are from lovers blown
  Do but gently heave the heart:
E'en the tears they shed alone
  Cure, like trickling balm, their smart.
Lovers, when they lose their breath,
Bleed away in easy death.

Love and Time with reverence use,
  Treat them like a parting friend;
Nor the golden gifts refuse
  Which in youth sincere they send:
For each year their price is more,
And they less simple than before.

Love, like spring-tides full and high,
  Swells in every youthful vein;
But each tide does less supply,
  Till they quite shrink in again.
If a flow in age appear,
'T is but rain, and runs not clear.

JOHN DRYDEN.

WELCOME, WELCOME, DO I SING.

  Welcome, welcome, do I sing,
  Far more welcome than the spring;
  He that parteth from you never
  Shall enjoy a spring forever.

Love, that to the voice is near,
  Breaking from your ivory pale,
Need not walk abroad to hear
  The delightful nightingale.
    Welcome, welcome, then I sing, etc.

Love, that still looks on your eyes
  Though the winter have begun
To benumb our arteries,
  Shall not want the summer's sun.
    Welcome, welcome, then I sing, etc.

Love, that still may see your cheeks,
  Where all rareness still reposes,
Is a fool if e'er he seeks
  Other lilies, other roses.
    Welcome, welcome, then I sing, etc.

Love, to whom your soft lip yields,
    And perceives your breath in kissing,
All the odors of the fields
    Never, never shall be missing.

                    WILLIAM BROWNE.

LOVE.

FROM THE "LAY OF THE LAST MINSTREL,"
CANTO III.

AND said I that my limbs were old,
And said I that my blood was cold,
And that my kindly fire was fled,
And my poor withered heart was dead,
    And that I might not sing of love?—
How could I, to the dearest theme
That ever warmed a minstrel's dream,
    So foul, so false a recreant prove!
How could I name love's very name,
Nor wake my heart to notes of flame!

In peace, Love tunes the shepherd's reed;
In war, he mounts the warrior's steed;
In halls, in gay attire is seen;
In hamlets, dances on the green.
Love rules the court, the camp, the grove,
And men below, and saints above;
For love is heaven, and heaven is love.

True love's the gift which God has given
To man alone beneath the heaven;
    It is not fantasy's hot fire,
        Whose wishes, soon as granted, fly;

It liveth not in fierce desire,
   With dead desire it doth not die;
It is the secret sympathy,
The silver link, the silken tie,
Which heart to heart, and mind to mind,
In body and in soul can bind.

SIR WALTER SCOTT.

SONG.

LOVE still has something of the sea,
   From whence his Mother rose;
No time his slaves from love can free,
   Nor give their thoughts repose.

They are becalmed in clearest days,
   And in rough weather tost;
They wither under cold delays,
   Or are in tempests lost.

One while they seem to touch the port,
   Then straight into the main
Some angry wind in cruel sport
   Their vessel drives again.

At first disdain and pride they fear,
   Which if they chance to 'scape,
Rivals and falsehood soon appear
   In a more dreadful shape.

By such degrees to joy they come,
   And are so long withstood,

So slowly they receive the sum,
   It hardly does them good.

'T is cruel to prolong a pain,
   And to defer a bliss,
Believe me, gentle Hermione,
   No less inhuman is.

An hundred thousand oaths your fears
   Perhaps would not remove,
And if I gazed a thousand years,
   I could no deeper love.

'T is fitter much for you to guess
   Than for me to explain,
But grant, oh! grant that happiness,
   Which only does remain.

SIR·CHARLES SEDLEY.

IF IT BE TRUE THAT ANY BEAUTE-
OUS THING.

IF it be true that any beauteous thing
Raises the pure and just desire of man
From earth to God, the eternal fount of all,
Such I believe my love; for as in her
So fair, in whom I all besides forget,
I view the gentle work of her Creator,
I have no care for any other thing,
Whilst thus I love. Nor is it marvellous,
Since the effect is not of my own power,
If the soul doth, by nature tempted forth,

Enamored through the eyes,
Repose upon the eyes which it resembleth,
And through them riseth to the Primal Love,
As to its end, and honors in admiring;
For who adores the Maker needs must love his
     work.

From the Italian of MICHAEL ANGELO.
Translation of JOHN EDWARD TAYLOR.

SONNET.

MUSES, that sing Love's sensual empirie,
And lovers kindling your enragèd fires
At Cupid's bonfires burning in the eye,
Blown with the empty breath of vain desires;
You, that prefer the painted cabinet
Before the wealthy jewels it doth store ye,
That all your joys in dying figures set,
And stain the living substance of your glory;
Abjure those joys, abhor their memory;
And let my love the honored subject be
Of love and honor's complete history!
Your eyes were never yet let in to see
The majesty and riches of the mind,
That dwell in darkness; for your god is blind.

GEORGE CHAPMAN.

LOVE'S SILENCE.

BECAUSE I breathe not love to everie one,
     Nor do not use set colors for to weare,
     Nor nourish special locks of vowèd haire,

Nor give each speech a full point of a groane,—
The courtlie nymphs, acquainted with the moane
  Of them who on their lips Love's standard beare,
   "What! he?" say they of me. "Now I dare
    sweare
He cannot love: No, no! let him alone."
  And think so still,—if Stella know my minde.
Profess, indeed, I do not Cupid's art;
  But you, faire maids, at length this true shall
   finde,—
That his right badge is but worne in the hearte.
  Dumb swans, not chattering pies, do lovers
   prove:
  They love indeed who quake to say they love.
SIR PHILIP SIDNEY.

WHEN WILL LOVE COME?

SOME find Love late, some find him soon,
  Some with the rose in May,
Some with the nightingale in June,
  And some when skies are gray;
Love comes to some with smiling eyes,
  And comes with tears to some;
For some Love sings, for some Love sighs,
  For some Love's lips are dumb.
How will you come to me, fair Love?
  Will you come late or soon?
With sad or smiling skies above,
  By light of sun or moon?
Will you be sad, will you be sweet,
  Sing, sigh, Love, or be dumb?

Will it be summer when we meet,
Or autumn ere you come?

PAKENHAM BEATTY.

WHY?

WHY came the rose? Because the sun, in shining,
Found in the mold some atoms rare and fine:
And, stooping, drew and warmed them into grow-
    ing,—
Dust, with the spirit's mystic countersign.

What made the perfume? All his wondrous kisses
Fell on the sweet red mouth, till, lost to sight,
The love became too exquisite, and vanished
Into a viewless rapture of the night.

Why did the rose die? Ah, why ask the question?
There is a time to love, a time to give;
She perished gladly, folding close the secret
Wherein is garnered what it is to live.

MARY LOUISE RITTER.

THE ANNOYER.

LOVE knoweth every form of air,
  And every shape of earth,
And comes, unbidden, everywhere,
  Like thought's mysterious birth.
The moonlit sea and the sunset sky
  Are written with Love's words,
And you hear his voice unceasingly,
  Like song, in the time of birds.

He peeps into the warrior's heart
  From the tip of a stooping plume,
And the serried spears, and the many men,
  May not deny him room.
He 'll come to his tent in the weary night,
  And be busy in his dream,
And he 'll float to his eye in the morning light,
  Like a fay on a silver beam.

He hears the sound of the hunter's gun,
  And rides on the echo back,
And sighs in his ear like a stirring leaf,
  And flits in his woodland track.
The shade of the wood, and the sheen of the river,
  The cloud, and the open sky,—
He will haunt them all with his subtle quiver,
  Like the light of your very eye.

The fisher hangs over the leaning boat,
  And ponders the silver sea,
For Love is under the surface hid,
  And a spell of thought has he:
He heaves the wave like a bosom sweet,
  And speaks in the ripple low,
Till the bait is gone from the crafty line,
  And the hook hangs bare below.

He blurs the print of the scholar's book,
  And intrudes in the maiden's prayer,
And profanes the cell of the holy man
  In the shape of a lady fair.
In the darkest night, and the bright daylight,
  In earth, and sea, and sky,

In every home of human thought,
    Will Love be lurking nigh.

NATHANIEL PARKER WILLIS.

THREE LOVES.

THERE were three maidens who loved a king;
    They sat together beside the sea;
One cried, " I love him, and I would die
    If but for one day he might love me! "

The second whispered, " And I would die
    To gladden his life, or make him great."
The third one spoke not, but gazed afar
    With dreamy eyes that were sad as Fate.

The king he loved the first for a day,
    The second his life with fond love blest;
And yet the woman who never spoke
    Was the one of the three who loved him best.

LUCY H. HOOPER.

LOVE SCORNS DEGREES.

FROM " THE MOUNTAIN OF THE LOVERS."

LOVE scorns degrees; the low he lifteth high,
The high he draweth down to that fair plain
Whereon, in his divine equality,
Two loving hearts may meet, nor meet in vain;
'Gainst such sweet levelling Custom cries amain,
But o'er its harshest utterance one bland sigh,

Breathed passion-wise, doth mount victorious still,
For Love, earth's lord, must have his lordly will.

PAUL HAMILTON HAYNE.

LOVE NOT ME FOR COMELY GRACE.

Love not me for comely grace,
For my pleasing eye or face,
Nor for any outward part,
No, nor for my constant heart;
 For those may fail or turn to ill,
  So thou and I shall sever;
Keep therefore a true woman's eye,
And love me still, but know not why.
 So hast thou the same reason still
  To dote upon me ever.

ANONYMOUS.

LIGHT.

The night has a thousand eyes,
 The day but one;
Yet the light of the bright world dies
 With the dying sun.

The mind has a thousand eyes,
 And the heart but one;
Yet the light of a whole life dies
 When its love is done.

FRANCIS W. BOURDILLON.

O MISTRESS MINE.

FROM "TWELFTH NIGHT," ACT II. SC. 3.

O MISTRESS mine, where are you roaming?
O, stay and hear! your true-love 's coming
  That can sing both high and low;
Trip no further, pretty sweeting,
Journeys end in lovers' meeting,—
  Every wise man's son doth know.

What is love? 't is not hereafter;
Present mirth hath present laughter;
  What 's to come is still unsure:
In delay there lies no plenty,—
Then come kiss me, Sweet-and-twenty,
  Youth 's a stuff will not endure.
                  SHAKESPEARE.

PHILOMELA'S ODE

THAT SHE SUNG IN HER ARBOR.

SITTING by a river's side
Where a silent stream did glide,
Muse I did of many things
That the mind in quiet brings.
I 'gan think how some men deem
Gold their god; and some esteem
Honor is the chief content
That to man in life is lent;

And some others do contend
Quiet none like to a friend.
Others hold there is no wealth
Compared to a perfect health;
Some man's mind in quiet stands
When he's lord of many lands.
But I did sigh, and said all this
Was but a shade of perfect bliss:
And in my thoughts I did approve
Naught so sweet as is true love.
Love 'twixt lovers passeth these,
When mouth kisseth and heart 'grees—
With folded arms and lips meeting,
Each soul another sweetly greeting;
For by the breath the soul fleeteth,
And soul with soul in kissing meeteth.
If love be so sweet a thing,
That such happy bliss doth bring,
Happy is love's sugared thrall;
But unhappy maidens all
Who esteem your virgin blisses
Sweeter than a wife's sweet kisses.
No such quiet to the mind
As true love with kisses kind;
But if a kiss prove unchaste,
Then is true love quite disgraced.
Though love be sweet, learn this of me,
No sweet love but honesty.

ROBERT GREENE.

A FICTION.

It chanced of late a shepherd's swain,
That went to seek a strayed sheep,
Within a thicket on the plain,
Espied a dainty Nymph asleep.

Her golden hair o'erspread her face,
Her careless arms abroad were cast,
Her quiver had her pillow's place,
Her breast lay bare to every blast.

The shepherd stood and gazed his fill;
Naught durst he do, naught durst he say,
When chance, or else perhaps his will,
Did guide the God of Love that way.

The crafty boy that sees her sleep,
Whom if she waked, he durst not see,
Behind her closely seeks to creep
Before her nap should ended be.

There come, he steals her shafts away,
And puts his own into their place;
Nor dares he any longer stay,
But ere she wakes, hies thence apace.

Scarce was he gone when she awakes,
And spies the shepherd standing by;
6

Her bended bow in haste she takes,
And at the simple swain let fly.

Forth flew the shaft and pierced his heart,
That to the ground he fell with pain;
Yet up again forthwith he start,
And to the Nymph he ran amain.

Amazed to see so strange a sight,
She shot, and shot, but all in vain;
The more his wounds, the more his might;
Love yielded strength in midst of pain.

Her angry eyes are great with tears,
She blames her hands, she blames her skill;
The bluntness of her shafts she fears,
And try them on herself she will.

Take heed, sweet Nymph, try not thy shaft,
Each little touch will prick the heart;
Alas, thou knowest not Cupid's craft,
Revenge is joy, the end is smart.

Yet try she will, and prick some bare;
Her hands were gloved, and next to hand
Was that fair breast, that breast so rare,
That made the shepherd senseless stand.

That breast she pricked, and through that
        breast
Love finds an entry to her heart;
At feeling of this new-come guest,
Lord, how the gentle Nymph doth start!

She runs not now, she shoots no more;
Away she throws both shaft and bow;
She seeks for that she shunned before,
She thinks the shepherd's haste too slow.

Though mountains meet not, lovers may;
So others do, and so do they:
The God of Love sits on a tree,
And laughs that pleasant sight to see.

ANONYMOUS, but attributed to " A. W."

———

WISHES FOR THE SUPPOSED MISTRESS.

WHOE'ER she be,
That not impossible She
That shall command my heart and me:

Where'er she lie,
Locked up from mortal eye
In shady leaves of destiny:

Till that ripe birth
Of studied Fate stand forth,
And teach her fair steps tread our earth;

Till that divine
Idea take a shrine
Of crystal flesh, through which to shine:

—Meet you her, my Wishes,
Bespeak her to my blisses,
And be ye called, my absent kisses.

I wish her beauty
That owes not all its duty
To gaudy tire, or glistering shoe-tie:

Something more than
Taffata or tissue can,
Or rampant feather, or rich fan.

A face that's best
By its own beauty drest,
And can alone commend the rest:

A face made up
Out of no other shop
Than what Nature's white hand sets ope.

Sidneian showers
Of sweet discourse, whose powers
Can crown old Winter's head with flowers.

Whate'er delight
Can make day's forehead bright
Or give down to the wings of night.

Soft silken hours,
Open suns, shady bowers;
'Bove all, nothing within that lowers.

Days, that need borrow
No part of their good morrow
From a fore-spent night of sorrow:

Days, that in spite
Of darkness, by the light
Of a clear mind are day all night.

Life that dares send
A challenge to his end,
And when it comes, say, " Welcome, friend."

I wish her store
Of worth may leave her poor
Of wishes; and I wish—no more.

  Now, if Time knows
That Her, whose radiant brows
Weave them a garland of my vows;

Her that dares be
What these lines wish to see:
I seek no further, it is She.

'T is She, and here
Lo! I unclothe and clear
My wishes' cloudy character.

Such worth as this is
Shall fix my flying wishes,
And determine them to kisses.

Let her full glory,
My fancies, fly before ye;
Be ye my fictions:—but her story.

                    RICHARD CRASHAW.

A MATCH.

If love were what the rose is,
  And I were like the leaf,
Our lives would grow together
In sad or singing weather,
Blown fields or flowerful closes,
  Green pleasure or gray grief;
If love were what the rose is,
  And I were like the leaf.

If I were what the words are,
  And love were like the tune,
With double sound and single
Delight our lips would mingle,
With kisses glad as birds are
  That get sweet rain at noon;
If I were what the words are,
  And love were like the tune.

If you were life, my darling,
  And I, your love, were death,
We 'd shine and snow together
Ere March made sweet the weather
With daffodil and starling
  And hours of fruitful breath;
If you were life, my darling,
  And I, your love, were death.

If you were thrall to sorrow,
  And I were page to joy,

We 'd play for lives and seasons,
With loving looks and treasons,
And tears of night and morrow,
  And laughs of maid and boy;
If you were thrall to sorrow,
  And I were page to joy.

If you were April's lady,
  And I were lord in May,
We 'd throw with leaves for hours,
And draw for days with flowers,
Till day like night were shady,
  And night were bright like day;
If you were April's lady,
  And I were lord in May.

If you were queen of pleasure,
  And I were king of pain,
We 'd hunt down love together,
Pluck out his flying-feather,
And teach his feet a measure,
  And find his mouth a rein;
If you were queen of pleasure,
  And I were king of pain.

ALGERNON CHARLES SWINBURNE.

MY CHOICE.

Shall I tell you whom I love?
  Hearken then awhile to me;
And if such a woman move
  As I now shall versify,
Be assured 't is she or none,
That I love, and love alone.

Nature did her so much right
  As she scorns the help of art.
In as many virtues dight
  As e'er yet embraced a heart.
So much good so truly tried,
Some for less were deified.

Wit she hath, without desire
  To make known how much she hath;
And her anger flames no higher
  Than may fitly sweeten wrath.
Full of pity as may be,
Though perhaps not so to me.

Reason masters every sense,
  And her virtues grace her birth;
Lovely as all excellence,
  Modest in her most of mirth.
Likelihood enough to prove
Only worth could kindle love.

Such she is; and if you know
  Such a one as I have sung;
Be she brown, or fair, or so
  That she be but somewhat young;
Be assured 't is she, or none,
That I love, and love alone.

                              WILLIAM BROWNE.

A MAIDEN'S IDEAL OF A HUSBAND.

FROM " THE CONTRIVANCES."

GENTEEL in personage,
Conduct, and equipage,
Noble by heritage,
  Generous and free:
Brave, not romantic;
Learned, not pedantic;
Frolic, not frantic;
  This must he be.
Honor maintaining,
Meanness disdaining,
Still entertaining,
  Engaging and new.
Neat, but not finical;
Sage, but not cynical;
Never tyrannical,
  But ever true.

HENRY CAREY.

ROSALYND'S COMPLAINT.

LOVE in my bosom, like a bee,
  Doth suck his sweet;
Now with his wings he plays with me.
  Now with his feet;
Within mine eyes he makes his nest,
His bed amidst my tender breast,
My kisses are his daily feast,
And yet he robs me of my rest:
  Ah! wanton, will ye?

And if I sleep, then percheth he
  With pretty flight,
And makes his pillow of my knee,
  The livelong night.
Strike I the lute, he tunes the string;
He music plays, if so I sing;
He lends me every lovely thing,
Yet, cruel, he my heart doth sting:
  Whist! wanton, still ye!

Else I with roses every day
  Will whip you hence,
And bind you when you long to play,
  For your offence;
I'll shut my eyes to keep you in,
I'll make you fast it for your sin,
I'll count your power not worth a pin:
Alas! what hereby shall I win
  If he gainsay me!

What if I beat the wanton boy
  With many a rod?
He will repay me with annoy,
  Because a god;
Then sit thou safely on my knee,
And let thy bower my bosom be;
Lurk in my eyes, I like of thee,
O Cupid! so thou pity me;
  Spare not, but play thee!

THOMAS LODGE.

CUPID SWALLOWED.

T' OTHER day, as I was twining
Roses for a crown to dine in,
What, of all things, midst the heap,
Should I light on, fast asleep,
But the little desperate elf,
The tiny traitor,—Love himself!
By the wings I pinched him up
Like a bee, and in a cup
Of my wine I plunged and sank him;
And what d' ye think I did?—I drank him!
Faith, I thought him dead. Not he!
There he lives with tenfold glee;
And now this moment, with his wings
I feel him tickling my heart-strings.

Paraphrase from the Greek. LEIGH HUNT.

GREEN GROW THE RASHES O.

GREEN grow the rashes O,
   Green grow the rashes O;
The sweetest hours that e'er I spend
   Are spent amang the lasses O!

There 's naught but care on ev'ry han',
   In every hour that passes O;
What signifies the life o' man,
   An 't were na for the lasses O?

The warly race may riches chase,
   An' riches still may fly them O;

An' though at last they catch them fast,
　Their hearts can ne'er enjoy them O!

Gie me a canny hour at e'en,
　My arms about my dearie O,
An' warly cares an' warly men
　May all gae tapsalteerie O!

For you sae douce, ye sneer at this,
　Ye 're naught but senseless asses O;
The wisest man the warl' e'er saw
　He dearly lo'ed the lasses O!

Auld Nature swears the lovely dears
　Her noblest work she classes O:
Her 'prentice han' she tried on man,
　An' then she made the lasses O!

ROBERT BURNS.

PERFUME.

WHAT gift for passionate lovers shall we find?
Not flowers nor books of verse suffice for me,
Nor splinters of the odorous cedar-tree,
And tufts of pine-buds, oozy in the wind;
Give me young shoots of aromatic rind,
Or samphire, redolent of sand and sea,
For all such fragrances I deem to be
Fit with my sharp desire to be combined.
My heart is like a poet, whose one room,
Scented with Latakia faint and fine,

Dried rose-leaves, and spilt attar, and old wine,
From curtained windows gathers its warm gloom
Round all but one sweet picture where incline
His thoughts and fancies mingled with perfume.

                    EDMUND WILLIAM GOSSE.

————

LIFE.

O LIFE! that mystery that no man knows,
And all men ask: the Arab from his sands,
The Cæsar's self, lifting imperial hands,
And the lone dweller where the lotus blows;
O'er trackless tropics, and o'er silent snows,
She dumbly broods, that Sphinx of all the lands;
And if she answers, no man understands,
And no cry breaks the blank of her repose.
But a new form rose once upon my pain,
With grave, sad lips, but in the eyes a smile
Of deepest meaning dawning sweet and slow,
Lighting to service, and no more in vain
I ask of Life, " What art thou? "—as erewhile—
For since Love holds my hand I seem to know!

                    LIZZIE M. LITTLE.

III.

LOVE'S BEGINNINGS.

KATE TEMPLE'S SONG.

Only a touch, and nothing more:
Ah! but never so touched before!
Touch of lip, was it? Touch of hand?
Either is easy to understand.
Earth may be smitten with fire or frost—
Never the touch of true love lost.

Only a word, was it? Scarce a word!
Musical whisper, softly heard,
Syllabled nothing—just a breath—
'T will outlast life and 't will laugh at death.
Love with so little can do so much—
Only a word, sweet! Only a touch!

SIR JAMES CARNEGIE, EARL OF SOUTHESK.

THE FIRST KISS.

How delicious is the winning
Of a kiss at love's beginning,
When two mutual hearts are sighing
For the knot there's no untying!

94

Yet remember, midst your wooing,
Love has bliss, but love has ruing;
Other smiles may make you fickle,
Tears for other charms may trickle.

Love he comes, Love he tarries,
Just as fate or fancy carries,—
Longest stays when sorest chidden,
Laughs and flies when pressed and bidden.

Bind the sea to slumber stilly,
Bind its odor to the lily,
Bind the aspen ne'er to quiver,—
Then bind Love to last forever!

Love's a fire that needs renewal
Of fresh beauty for its fuel;
Love's wing moults when caged and captured,—
Only free he soars enraptured.

Can you keep the bee from ranging,
Or the ring-dove's neck from changing?
No! nor fettered Love from dying
In the knot there's no untying.

THOMAS CAMPBELL.

TELL ME, MY HEART, IF THIS BE LOVE.

WHEN Delia on the plain appears,
Awed by a thousand tender fears,
I would approach, but dare not move;—
Tell me, my heart, if this be love.

Whene'er she speaks, my ravished ear
No other voice than hers can hear;
No other wit but hers approve;—
Tell me, my heart, if this be love.

If she some other swain commend,
Though I was once his fondest friend,
His instant enemy I prove;—
Tell me, my heart, if this be love.

When she is absent, I no more
Delight in all that pleased before,
The clearest spring, the shadiest grove;—
Tell me, my heart, if this be love.

When fond of power, of beauty vain,
Her nets she spread for every swain,
I strove to hate, but vainly strove;—
Tell me, my heart, if this be love.

                    GEORGE, LORD LYTTELTON.

ATHULF AND ETHILDA.

ATHULF.—   Appeared
The princess with that merry child Prince Guy:
He loves me well, and made her stop and sit,
And sat upon her knee, and it so chanced
That in his various chatter he denied
That I could hold his hand within my own
So closely as to hide it: this being tried
Was proved against him; he insisted then
I could not by his royal sister's hand
Do likewise. Starting at the random word,

And dumb with trepidation, there I stood
Some seconds as bewitched; then I looked up,
And in her face beheld an orient flush
Of half-bewildered pleasure: from which trance
She with an instant ease resumed herself,
And frankly, with a pleasant laugh, held out
Her arrowy hand.
I thought it trembled as it lay in mine,
But yet her looks were clear, direct, and free,
And said that she felt nothing.

    SIDROC.—   And what felt'st thou?

    ATHULF.—A sort of swarming, curling tremu-
        lous tumbling,
As though there were an ant-hill in my bosom.
I said I was ashamed.—Sidroc, you smile;
If at my folly, well! But if you smile,
Suspicious of a taint upon my heart, .
Wide is your error, and you never loved.

                       SIR HENRY TAYLOR.

BLEST AS THE IMMORTAL GODS.

BLEST as the immortal gods is he,
The youth who fondly sits by thee,
And hears and sees thee all the while
Softly speak, and sweetly smile.

'T was this deprived my soul of rest,
And raised such tumults in my breast:
For while I gazed, in transport tost,
My breath was gone, my voice was lost.

My bosom glowed; the subtle flame
Ran quick through all my vital frame;

7

O'er my dim eyes a darkness hung;
My ears with hollow murmurs rung;

In dewy damps my limbs were chilled;
My blood with gentle horrors thrilled:
My feeble pulse forgot to play—
I fainted, sunk, and died away.

From the Greek of SAPPHO.
Translation of AMBROSE PHILLIPS.

I DREAMT I SAW GREAT VENUS.

I DREAMT I saw great Venus by me stand,
Leading a nodding infant by the hand;
And that she said to me familiarly—
" Take Love, and teach him how to play to me."
She vanished then. And I, poor fool, must turn
To teach the boy, as if he wished to learn.
I taught him all the pastoral songs I knew
And used to sing; and I informed him too,
How Pan found out the pipe, Pallas the flute,
Phœbus the lyre, and Mercury the lute.
But not a jot for all my words cared he,
But lo! fell singing his love-songs to me;
And told me of the loves of gods and men,
And of his mother's doings; and so then
I forgot all I taught him for my part,
But what he taught me, I learnt all by heart.

From the Greek of BION.
Translation of LEIGH HUNT.

FRANCESCA DA RIMINI.

FROM THE " DIVINA COMMEDIA : INFERNO."

AND then I turned unto their side my eyes,
And said,—" Francesca, thy sad destinies
Have made me sorrow till the tears arise.

But tell me, in the season of sweet sighs,
By what and how thy love to passion rose,
So as his dim desires to recognize."

Then she to me: " The greatest of all woes
Is, to remind us of our happy days
In misery; and that thy teacher knows.

But if to learn our passion's first root preys
Upon thy spirit with such sympathy,
I will do even as he who weeps and says.

We read one day for pastime, seated nigh,
Of Lancilot, how Love enchained him too.
We were alone, quite unsuspiciously.

But oft our eyes met, and our cheeks in hue
All o'er discolored by that reading were;
But one point only wholly us o'erthrew:

When we read the long sighed-for smile of her,
To be thus kissed by such devoted lover,
He who from me can be divided ne'er

Kissed my mouth, trembling in the act all over.
Accursèd was the book and he who wrote!
That day no further leaf we did uncover."

From the Italian of DANTE.
Translation of LORD BYRON.

DINNA ASK ME.

O, DINNA ask me gin I lo'e ye:
    Troth, I daurna tell!
Dinna ask me gin I lo'e ye,—
    Ask it o' yoursel'.

O, dinna look sae sair at me,
    For weel ye ken me true;
O, gin ye look sae sair at me,
    I daurna look at you.

When ye gang to yon braw braw town,
    And bonnier lassies see,
O, dinna, Jamie, look at them,
    Lest ye should mind na me.

For I could never bide the lass
    That ye'd lo'e mair than me;
And O, I'm sure my heart wad brak,
    Gin ye'd prove fause to me!

                     JOHN DUNLOP.

O SWALLOW, SWALLOW, FLYING SOUTH.

FROM "THE PRINCESS."

O SWALLOW, Swallow, flying, flying South,
Fly to her, and fall upon her gilded eaves,
And tell her, tell her what I tell to thee.

O tell her, Swallow, thou that knowest each,
That bright and fierce and fickle is the South,
And dark and true and tender is the North.

  O Swallow, Swallow, if I could follow, and
     light
Upon her lattice, I would pipe and trill,
And cheep and twitter twenty million loves.

  O were I thou that she might take me in,
And lay me on her bosom, and her heart
Would rock the snowy cradle till I died!

  Why lingereth she to clothe her heart with
     love,
Delaying as the tender ash delays
To clothe herself, when all the woods are green?

  O tell her, Swallow, that thy brood is flown:
Say to her, I do but wanton in the South,
But in the North long since my nest is made.

  O tell her, brief is life, but love is long,
And brief the sun of summer in the North,
And brief the moon of beauty in the South.

  O Swallow, flying from the golden woods,
Fly to her, and pipe and woo her, and make her
     mine,
And tell her, tell her, that I follow thee.

ALFRED, LORD TENNYSON.

SONG.

FROM " THE MILLER'S DAUGHTER."

It is the miller's daughter,
  And she is grown so dear, so dear,
That I would be the jewel
  That trembles at her ear:
For, hid in ringlets day and night,
I 'd touch her neck so warm and white.

And I would be the girdle
  About her dainty, dainty waist,
And her heart would beat against me
  In sorrow and in rest:
And I should know if it beat right,
I 'd clasp it round so close and tight.

And I would be the necklace,
  And all day long to fall and rise
Upon her balmy bosom,
  With her laughter or her sighs:
And I would lie so light, so light,
I scarce should be unclasped at night.

ALFRED, LORD TENNYSON.

IF DOUGHTY DEEDS MY LADY PLEASE.

If doughty deeds my lady please,
  Right soon I 'll mount my steed,
And strong his arm and fast his seat
  That bears frae me the meed.

I 'll wear thy colors in my cap,
  Thy picture at my heart,
And he that bends not to thine eye
  Shall rue it to his smart!
    Then tell me how to woo thee, Love;
      O, tell me how to woo thee!
    For thy dear sake nae care I 'll take,
      Though ne'er another trow me.

If gay attire delight thine eye,
  I 'll dight me in array;
I 'll tend thy chamber door all night,
  And squire thee all the day.
If sweetest sounds can win thine ear,
  These sounds I 'll strive to catch;
Thy voice I 'll steal to woo thysell,
  That voice that nane can match.

But if fond love thy heart can gain,
  I never broke a vow;
Nae maiden lays her skaith to me;
  I never loved but you.
For you alone I ride the ring,
  For you I wear the blue;
For you alone I strive to sing,
  O, tell me how to woo!
    Then tell me how to woo thee, Love;
      O, tell me how to woo thee!
    For thy dear sake nae care I 'll take,
      Though ne'er another trow me.
                ROBERT GRAHAM OF GARTMORE.

THE KISS.

1. AMONG thy fancies tell me this:
   What is the thing we call a kiss?
2. I shall resolve ye what it is:

It is a creature born and bred
Between the lips all cherry red,
By love and warm desires fed;
Chor. And makes more soft the bridal bed.

It is an active flame, that flies
First to the babies of the eyes,
And charms them there with lullabies;
Chor. And stills the bride too when she cries.

Then to the chin, the cheek, the ear,
It frisks and flies,—now here, now there;
'T is now far off, and then 't is near;
Chor. And here, and there, and everywhere.

1. Has it a speaking virtue?—2. Yes.
1. How speaks it, say?—2. Do you but this:
   Part your joined lips,—then speaks your
       kiss;
Chor. And this love's sweetest language is.

1. Has it a body?—2. Ay, and wings,
   With thousand rare encolorings;
   And as it flies it gently sings;
Chor. Love honey yields, but never stings.

ROBERT HERRICK.

AN OPAL.

A ROSE of fire shut in a veil of snow,
  An April gleam athwart a misted sky:
A jewel—a soul! gaze deep if thou wouldst know
  The flame-wrought spell of its pale witchery;
And now each tremulous beauty lies revealed,
And now the drifted snow doth beauty shield.

So my shy love, aneath her kerchief white,
  Holdeth the glamour of the East in fee;
Warm Puritan—who fears her own delight,
  Who trembleth over that she yieldeth me.
And now her lips her heart's rich flame have told;
And now they pale that they have been so bold.

                EDNAH PROCTER CLARKE HAYES.

CUPID AND CAMPASPE.

FROM "ALEXANDER AND CAMPASPE," ACT
III. SC. 5.

CUPID and my Campaspe played
At cards for kisses,—Cupid paid;
He stakes his quiver, bow and arrows,
His mother's doves, and team of sparrows,—
Loses them too; then down he throws
The coral of his lip, the rose
Growing on 's cheek (but none knows how);
With these the crystal of his brow,
And then the dimple of his chin,—
All these did my Campaspe win.

At last he set her both his eyes;
She won, and Cupid blind did rise.
O Love! has she done this to thee?
What shall, alas! become of me?

JOHN LYLY.

KISSES.

My love and I for kisses played:
  She would keep stakes—I was content;
But when I won, she would be paid;
  This made me ask her what she meant.
" Pray since I see," quoth she, " your wrangling
      vein,
Take your own kisses; give me mine again."

WILLIAM STRODE.

LOVE'S PHILOSOPHY.

THE fountains mingle with the river,
  And the rivers with the ocean;
The winds of heaven mix forever,
  With a sweet emotion;
Nothing in the world is single;
  All things by a law divine
In one another's being mingle:—
  Why not I with thine?

See! the mountains kiss high heaven,
  And the waves clasp one another;
No sister flower would be forgiven
  If it disdained its brother;

And the sunlight clasps the earth,
    And the moonbeams kiss the sea :—
What are all these kissings worth,
    If thou kiss not me?

PERCY BYSSHE SHELLEY.

KISSING 'S NO SIN.

SOME say that kissing 's a sin;
    But I think it 's nane ava,
For kissing has wonn'd in this warld
    Since ever that there was twa.

O, if it wasna lawfu'
    Lawyers wadna allow it;
If it wasna holy,
    Ministers wadna do it.

If it wasna modest,
    Maidens wadna tak' it;
If it wasna plenty,
    Puir folk wadna get it.

ANONYMOUS.

SONG OF THE MILKMAID.

FROM "QUEEN MARY."

SHAME upon you, Robin,
    Shame upon you now!
Kiss me would you? with my hands
    Milking the cow?
    Daisies grow again,
    Kingcups blow again,
And you came and kissed me milking the cow.

Robin came behind me,
    Kissed me well I vow;
Cuff him could I? with my hands
    Milking the cow?
    Swallows fly again,
    Cuckoos cry again,
And you came and kissed me milking the cow.

    Come, Robin, Robin,
    Come and kiss me now;
Help it can I? with my hands
    Milking the cow?
    Ringdoves coo again,
    All things woo again,
Come behind and kiss me milking the cow!

ALFRED, LORD TENNYSON.

COMIN' THROUGH THE RYE.

Gɪɴ a body meet a body
    Comin' through the rye,
Gin a body kiss a body,
    Need a body cry?
Every lassie has her laddie,—
    Ne'er a ane hae I;
Yet a' the lads they smile at me
    When comin' through the rye.
Amang the train there is a swain
    I dearly lo'e mysel';
But whaur his hame, or what his name,
    I dinna care to tell.

Gin a body meet a body
    Comin' frae the town,

Gin a body greet a body,
  Need a body frown?
Every lassie has her laddie,—
  Ne'er a ane hae I;
Yet a' the lads they smile at me
  When comin' through the rye.
Amang the train there is a swain
  I dearly lo'e mysel';
But whaur his hame, or what his name,
  I dinna care to tell.

ADAPTED FROM ROBERT BURNS.

WHISTLE, AND I'LL COME TO YOU, MY LAD.

O WHISTLE, and I'll come to you, my lad,
O whistle, and I'll come to you, my lad,
Tho' father and mither and a' should gae mad,
O whistle, and I'll come to you, my lad.

But warily tent, when ye come to court me,
And come na unless the back-yett be a-jee;
Syne up the back stile, and let naebody see,
And come as ye were na comin' to me.
And come, etc.
    O whistle, etc.

At kirk, or at market, whene'er ye meet me,
Gang by me as tho' that ye cared nae a flie;
But steal me a blink o' your bonnie black ee,
Yet look as ye were na lookin' at me.
Yet look, etc.
    O whistle, etc.

Aye vow and protest that ye care na for me,
And whiles ye may lightly my beauty a wee;
But court nae anither, tho' jokin' ye be,
For fear that she wile your fancy frae me.
For fear, etc.

    O whistle, and I'll come to you, my lad.

ROBERT BURNS.

SONNET UPON A STOLEN KISS.

Now gentle sleep hath closèd up those eyes
Which, waking, kept my boldest thoughts in awe;
And free access unto that sweet lip lies,
From whence I long the rosy breath to draw.
Methinks no wrong it were, if I should steal
From those two melting rubies one poor kiss;
None sees the theft that would the theft reveal,
Nor rob I her of aught what she can miss:
Nay, should I twenty kisses take away,
There would be little sign I would do so;
Why then should I this robbery delay?
O, she may awake, and therewith angry grow!
Well, if she do, I'll back restore that one,
And twenty hundred thousand more for loan.

GEORGE WITHER.

CAPRICE.

I.

She hung the cage at the window,
  "If he goes by," she said,
"He will hear my robin singing,
  And when he lifts his head,

I shall be sitting here to sew,
And he will bow to me, I know."

The robin sang a love-sweet song,
  The young man raised his head;
The maiden turned away and blushed:
  " I 'm a fool! " she said,
And went on broidering in silk
A pink-eyed rabbit, white as milk.

II.

The young man loitered slowly
  By the house three times that day;
She took her bird from the window:
  " He need not look this way."
She sat at her piano long,
And sighed, and played a death-sad song.

But when the day was done, she said,
  " I wish that he would come!
Remember, Mary, if he calls
  To-night—I 'm not at home."
So when he rang, she went—the elf!—
She went and let him in herself.

III.

They sang full long together
  Their songs love-sweet, death-sad,
The robin woke from his slumber,
  And rang out, clear and glad.
" Now go," she coldly said, " 't is late;"
And followed him—to latch the gate.

He took the rosebud from her hair,
 While, " You shall not," she said:
He closed her hand within his own,
 And while her tongue forbade,
Her will was darkened in the eclipse
Of blinding love upon his lips.

WILLIAM DEAN HOWELLS.

SLY THOUGHTS.

" I saw him kiss your cheek ! "—" 'T is true."
 " O Modesty ! "—" 'T was strictly kept:
He thought me asleep; at least, I knew
 He thought I thought he thought I slept."

COVENTRY PATMORE.

THE WHISTLE.

" You have heard," said a youth to his sweetheart,
  who stood,
 While he sat on a corn-sheaf, at daylight's de-
  cline,—
" You have heard of the Danish boy's whistle of
  wood?
 I wish that that Danish boy's whistle were
  mine."

" And what would you do with it?—tell me," she
  said,
 While an arch smile played over her beautiful
  face.

" I would blow it," he answered; " and then my
    fair maid
  Would fly to my side, and would here take her
    place."

" Is that all you wish it for? That may be yours
  Without any magic," the fair maiden cried:
" A favor so slight one's good nature secures;"
  And she playfully seated herself by his side.
" I would blow it again," said the youth, " and
    the charm
  Would work so, that not even Modesty's check
Would be able to keep from my neck your fine
    arm :"
  She smiled,—and she laid her fine arm round
  his neck.

" Yet once more would I blow, and the music
    divine
  Would bring me the third time an exquisite
    bliss :
You would lay your fair cheek to this brown one
    of mine,
  And your lips, stealing past it, would give me
    a kiss."
The maiden laughed out in her innocent glee,—
  " What a fool of yourself with your whistle
    you 'd make!
For only consider, how silly 't would be
  To sit there and whistle for—what you might
    take!"

ROBERT STORY.

8

BEHAVE YOURSEL' BEFORE FOLK.

BEHAVE yoursel' before folk,
　Behave yoursel' before folk,
And dinna be sae rude to me,
　As kiss me sae before folk.
It wouldna give me meikle pain,
Gin we were seen and heard by nane,
To tak' a kiss, or grant you ane;
　But gudesake! no before folk.
　Behave yoursel' before folk,
　Behave yoursel' before folk,—
Whate'er you do when out o' view,
　Be cautious aye before folk!

Consider, lad, how folks will crack,
And what a great affair they 'll mak'
O' naething but a simple smack,
　That 's gi'en or ta'en before folk.
　Behave yoursel' before folk,
　Behave yoursel' before folk,—
Nor gi'e the tongue o' old and young
　Occasion to come o'er folk.

I 'm sure wi' you I 've been as free
As ony modest lass should be;
But yet it doesna do to see
　Sic freedom used before folk.
　Behave yoursel' before folk,
　Behave yoursel' before folk,—
I 'll ne'er submit again to it;
　So mind you that—before folk!

Ye tell me that my face is fair:
It may be sae—I dinna care—
But ne'er again gar't blush so sair
    As ye hae done before folk.
    Behave yoursel' before folk,
    Behave yoursel' before folk,
Nor heat my cheeks wi' your mad freaks,
    But aye be douce before folk!

Ye tell me that my lips are sweet:
Sic tales, I doubt, are a' deceit;—
At ony rate, it's hardly meet
    To prie their sweets before folk.
    Behave yoursel' before folk,
    Behave yoursel' before folk,—
Gin that's the case, there's time and place,
    But surely no before folk!

But gin ye really do insist
That I should suffer to be kissed,
Gae get a license frae the priest,
    And mak' me yours before folk!
    Behave yoursel' before folk,
    Behave yoursel' before folk,—
And when we're ane, baith flesh and bane,
    Ye may tak' ten—before folk!

                ALEXANDER RODGER.

SMILE AND NEVER HEED ME.

THOUGH, when other maids stand by,
I may deign thee no reply,
Turn not then away, and sigh,—
    Smile, and never heed me!

If our love, indeed, be such
As must thrill at every touch,
Why should others learn as much?—
    Smile, and never heed me!

Even if, with maiden pride,
I should bid thee quit my side,
Take this lesson for thy guide,—
    Smile, and never heed me!
But when stars and twilight meet,
And the dew is falling sweet,
And thou hear'st my coming feet,—
    Then—thou then—mayst heed me!

                        CHARLES SWAIN.

THE DULE'S I' THIS BONNET O' MINE.

LANCASHIRE DIALECT.

THE dule's i' this bonnet o' mine:
    My ribbins 'll never be reet;
Here, Mally, aw 'm like to be fine,
    For Jamie 'll be comin' to-neet;
He met me i' th' lone t' other day
    (Aw wur gooin' for wayter to th' well),
An' he begged that aw 'd wed him i' May,
    Bi th' mass, if he 'll let me, aw will!

When he took my two honds into his,
    Good Lord, heaw they trembled between!
An' aw durstn't look up in his face,
    Becose on him seein' my een.
My cheek went as red as a rose;
    There 's never a mortal con tell

Heaw happy aw felt,—for, thae knows,
    One couldn't ha' axed him theirsel'.

But th' tale wur at th' end o' my tung:
    To let it eawt wouldn't be reet,
For aw thought to seem forrud wur wrung;
    So aw towd him aw 'd tell him to-neet.
But, Mally, thae knows very weel,
    Though it isn't a thing one should own,
Iv aw 'd th' pikein' o' the world to mysel',
    Aw 'd oather ha Jamie or noan.

Neaw, Mally, aw 've towd thae my mind;
    What would to do iv it wur thee?
" Aw 'd tak him just while he 'se inclined,
    An' a farrantly bargain he 'll be;
For Jamie's as greadly a lad
    As ever stept eawt into th' sun.
Go, jump at thy chance, an' get wed;
    An' mak th' best o' th' job when it 's done!"

Eh, dear! but it 's time to be gwon:
    Aw shouldn't like Jamie to wait;
Aw connut for shame be too soon,
    An' aw wouldn't for th' wuld be too late.
Aw 'm o' ov a tremble to th' heel:
    Dost think 'at my bonnet 'll do?
" Be off, lass,—thae looks very weel;
    He wants noan o' th' bonnet, thae foo!"
EDWIN WAUGH.

A SPINSTER'S STINT.

Six skeins and three, six skeins and three!
Good mother, so you stinted me,
And here they be,—ay, six and three!

Stop, busy wheel! stop, noisy wheel!
Long shadows down my chamber steal,
An' warn me to make haste and reel.

'T is done,—the spinning work complete,
O heart of mine, what makes you beat
So fast and sweet, so fast and sweet?

I must have wheat and pinks, to stick
My hat from brim to ribbon, thick,—
Slow hands of mine, be quick, be quick!

One, two, three stars along the skies
Begin to wink their golden eyes,—
I 'll leave my thread all knots and ties.

O moon, so red! O moon, so red!
Sweetheart of night, go straight to bed;
Love's light will answer in your stead.

A-tiptoe, beckoning me, he stands,—
Stop trembling, little foolish hands,
And stop the bands, and stop the bands!

ALICE CARY.

THE TELLTALE.

ONCE, on a golden afternoon,
With radiant faces and hearts in tune,
    Two fond lovers in dreaming mood
    Threaded a rural solitude.
Wholly happy, they only knew
That the earth was bright and the sky was blue,
    That light and beauty and joy and song
    Charmed the way as they passed along:
The air was fragrant with woodland scents;
The squirrel frisked on the roadside fence;
    And hovering near them, "Chee, chee,
        chink?"
    Queried the curious bobolink,
Pausing and peering with sidelong head,
As saucily questioning all they said;
    While the ox-eye danced on its slender stem,
    And all glad nature rejoiced with them.
Over the odorous fields were strown
Wilting windrows of grass new-mown,
    And rosy billows of clover bloom
    Surged in the sunshine and breathed perfume.
Swinging low on a slender limb,
The sparrow warbled his wedding hymn,
    And, balancing on a blackberry-brier,
    The bobolink sung with his heart on fire,—
"Chink? If you wish to kiss her, do!
Do it, do it! You coward, you!
    Kiss her! Kiss, kiss her! Who will see?
    Only we three! we three! we three!"
Under garlands of drooping vines,
Through dim vistas of sweet-breathed pines,

Past wide meadow-fields, lately mowed,
Wandered the indolent country road.
The lovers followed it, listening still,
And, loitering slowly, as lovers will,
Entered a low-roofed bridge that lay,
Dusky and cool, in their pleasant way.
Under its arch a smooth, brown stream
Silently glided, with glint and gleam,
Shaded by graceful elms that spread
Their verdurous canopy overhead,—
The stream so narrow, the boughs so wide,
They met and mingled across the tide.
Alders loved it, and seemed to keep
Patient watch as it lay asleep,
Mirroring clearly the trees and sky
And the flitting form of the dragon-fly,
Save where the swift-winged swallow played
In and out in the sun and shade,
And darting and circling in merry chase,
Dipped and dimpled its clear dark face.

Fluttering lightly from brink to brink
Followed the garrulous bobolink,
Rallying loudly, with mirthful din,
The pair who lingered unseen within.
And when from the friendly bridge at last
Into the road beyond they passed,
Again beside them the tempter went,
Keeping the thread of his argument:—
" Kiss her! kiss her! chink-a-chee-chee!
I 'll not mention it! Don't mind me!
I 'll be sentinel—I can see
All around from this tall birch-tree! "

But ah! they noted—nor deemed it strange—
In his rollicking chorus a trifling change:
   " Do it! do it! " with might and main
   Warbled the telltale—" Do it *again!* "
                 ELIZABETH AKERS.

LOVE IN THE VALLEY.

UNDER yonder beech-tree standing on the green
   sward,
Couched with her arms behind her little head,
Her knees folded up, and her tresses on her bosom,
Lies my young love sleeping in the shade.
Had I the heart to slide one arm beneath her!
Press her dreaming lips as her waist I folded slow,
Waking on the instant she could not but embrace
   me—
Ah! would she hold me, and never let me go?

Shy as the squirrel, and wayward as the swallow;
Swift as the swallow when, athwart the western
   flood,
Circleting the surface, he meets his mirrored wing-
   lets,
Is that dear one in her maiden bud.
Shy as the squirrel whose nest is in the pine-tops;
Gentle—ah! that she were jealous—as the dove!
Full of all the wildness of the woodland creatures,
Happy in herself is the maiden that I love!

What can have taught her distrust of all I tell
   her?
Can she truly doubt me when looking on my
   brows?

Nature never teaches distrust of tender love-tales;
What can have taught her distrust of all my
  vows?
No, she does not doubt me! on a dewy eve-tide,
Whispering together beneath the listening moon,
I prayed till her cheek flushed, implored till she
  faltered—
Fluttered to my bosom—ah! to fly away so soon!

When her mother tends her before the laughing
  mirror,
Tying up her laces, looping up her hair,
Often she thinks—were this wild thing wedded,
I should have more love, and much less care.
When her mother tends her before the bashful
  mirror,
Loosening her laces, combing down her curls,
Often she thinks—were this wild thing wedded,
I should lose but one for so many boys and girls.

Clambering roses peep into her chamber,
Jasmine and woodbine breathe sweet, sweet;
White-necked swallows, twittering of summer,
Fill her with balm and nested peace from head to
  feet.
Ah! will the rose-bough see her lying lonely,
When the petals fall and fierce bloom is on the
  leaves?
Will the autumn garners see her still ungathered,
When the fickle swallows forsake the weeping
  eaves?

Comes a sudden question—should a strange hand
  pluck her!

Oh! what an anguish smites me at the thought!
Should some idle lordling bribe her mind with
    jewels!
Can such beauty ever thus be bought?
Sometimes the huntsmen, prancing down the val-
    ley,
Eye the village lasses, full of sprightly mirth;
They see, as I see, mine is the fairest!
Would she were older and could read my worth!

Are there not sweet maidens, if she still deny me?
Show the bridal heavens but one bright star?
Wherefore thus then do I chase a shadow,
Clattering one note like a brown eve-jar?
So I rhyme and reason till she darts before me—
Through the milky meadows from flower to
    flower she flies,
Sunning her sweet palms to shade her dazzled eye-
    lids
From the golden love that looks too eager in her
    eyes.

When at dawn she wakens, and her fair face
    gazes
Out on the weather through the window panes,
Beauteous she looks! like a white water-lily
Bursting out of bud on the rippled river plains.
When from bed she rises, clothed from neck to
    ankle
In her long night gown, sweet as boughs of
    May,
Beauteous she looks! like a tall garden lily,
Pure from the night and perfect for the day!

Happy, happy time, when the gray star twinkles
Over the fields all fresh with bloomy dew;
When the cold-cheeked dawn grows ruddy up the
    twilight,
And the gold sun wakes and weds her in the blue.
Then when my darling tempts the early breezes,
She the only star that dies not with the dark!
Powerless to speak all the ardor of my passion,
I catch her little hand as we listen to the lark.

Shall the birds in vain then valentine their sweet-
    hearts?
Season after season tell a fruitless tale?
Will not the virgin listen to their voices?
Take the honeyed meaning, wear the bridal veil?
Fears she frosts of winter, fears she the bare
    branches?
Waits she the garlands of spring for her dower?
Is she a nightingale that will not be nested
Till the April woodland has built her bridal
    bower?

Then come, merry April, with all thy birds and
    beauties!
With thy crescent brows and thy flowery, showery
    glee;
With thy budding leafage and fresh green pas-
    tures;
And may thy lustrous crescent grow a honeymoon
    for me!
Come, merry month of the cuckoo and the violet!
Come, weeping loveliness in all thy blue delight!
Lo! the nest is ready, let me not languish longer!
Bring her to my arms on the first May night.

                        GEORGE MEREDITH.

THOUGHTS ON THE COMMANDMENTS.

" Love your neighbor as yourself,"—
　So the parson preaches:
That 's one half the Decalogue,—
　So the prayer-book teaches.
Half my duty I can do
　With but little labor,
For with all my heart and soul
　I do love my neighbor.

Mighty little credit, that,
　To my self-denial;
Not to love her, though, might be
　Something of a trial.
Why, the rosy light, that peeps
　Through the glass above her,
Lingers round her lips,—you see
　E'en the sunbeams love her.

So to make my merit more,
　I 'll go beyond the letter:—
Love my neighbor as myself?
　Yes, and ten times better.
For she 's sweeter than the breath
　Of the Spring, that passes
Through the fragrant, budding woods,
　O'er the meadow-grasses.

And I 've preached the word I know,
　For it was my duty

To convert the stubborn heart
  Of the little beauty.
Once again success has crowned
  Missionary labor,
For her sweet eyes own that she
  Also loves her neighbor.

                    GEORGE AUGUSTUS BAKER.

THE LOVE-KNOT.

TYING her bonnet under her chin,
She tied her raven ringlets in.
But not alone in the silken snare
Did she catch her lovely floating hair,
For, tying her bonnet under her chin,
She tied a young man's heart within.

They were strolling together up the hill,
Where the wind came blowing merry and chill;
And it blew the curls a frolicsome race,
All over the happy peach-colored face.
Till scolding and laughing, she tied them in,
Under her beautiful, dimpled chin.

And it blew a color, bright as the bloom
Of the pinkest fuchsia's tossing plume,
All over the cheeks of the prettiest girl
That ever imprisoned a romping curl,
Or, in tying her bonnet under her chin,
Tied a young man's heart within.

Steeper and steeper grew the hill,
Madder, merrier, chiller still,

The western wind blew down, and played
The wildest tricks with the little maid,
As, tying her bonnet under her chin,
She tied a young man's heart within.

O western wind, do you think it was fair
To play such tricks with her floating hair?
To gladly, gleefully, do your best
To blow her against the young man's breast,
Where he has gladly folded her in,
And kissed her mouth and dimpled chin?

O Ellery Vane, you little thought,
An hour ago, when you besought
This country lass to walk with you,
After the sun had dried the dew,
What terrible danger you'd be in,
As she tied her bonnet under her chin.

NORA PERRY.

THE CHESS-BOARD.

My little love, do you remember,
  Ere we were grown so sadly wise,
Those evenings in the bleak December,
Curtained warm from the snowy weather,
When you and I played chess together,
  Checkmated by each other's eyes?

Ah! still I see your soft white hand
Hovering warm o'er Queen and Knight;
  Brave Pawns in valiant battle stand;

The double Castles guard the wings;
The bishop, bent on distant things,
Moves, sidling, through the fight.

Our fingers touch; our glances meet,
And falter; falls your golden hair
Against my cheek; your bosom sweet
Is heaving. Down the field, your Queen
Rides slow, her soldiery all between,
And checks me unaware.

Ah me! the little battle's done:
Disperst is all its chivalry.
Full many a move since then have we
Mid life's perplexing checkers made,
And many a game with fortune played;
What is it we have won?
This, this at least,—if this alone:

That never, never, nevermore,
As in those old still nights of yore,
(Ere we were grown so sadly wise,)
Can you and I shut out the skies,
Shut out the world and wintry weather,
And, eyes exchanging warmth with eyes,
Play chess, as then we played together.

ROBERT BULWER, LORD LYTTON.
(Owen Meredith.)

HER LETTER.

I'm sitting alone by the fire,
Dressed just as I came from the dance,
In a robe even *you* would admire,—
It cost a cool thousand in France;

I 'm bediamonded out of all reason,
My hair is done up in a cue:
In short, sir, " the belle of the season "
Is wasting an hour on you.

A dozen engagements I 've broken;
I left in the midst of a set;
Likewise a proposal, half spoken,
That waits—on the stairs—for me yet.
They say he' ll be rich,—when he grows up,—
And then he adores me indeed.
And you, sir, are turning your nose up,
Three thousand miles off, as you read.

" And how do I like my position? "
" And what do I think of New York? "
" And now, in my higher ambition,
With whom do I waltz, flirt, or talk? "
" And isn't it nice to have riches
And diamonds and silks and all that? "
" And aren't it a change to the ditches
And tunnels of Poverty Flat? "

Well, yes,—if you saw us out driving
Each day in the park, four-in-hand;
If you saw poor dear mamma contriving
To look supernaturally grand,—
If you saw papa's picture, as taken
By Brady, and tinted at that,
You 'd never suspect he sold bacon
And flour at Poverty Flat.

And yet, just this moment, when sitting
In the glare of the grand chandelier,
9

In the bustle and glitter befitting
The " finest soirée of the year,"
In the mists of a *gaze de chambéry*
And the hum of the smallest of talk,—
Somehow, Joe, I thought of " The Ferry,"
And the dance that we had on " The Fork ;"

Of Harrison's barn, with its muster
Of flags festooned over the wall;
Of the candles that shed their soft lustre
And tallow on head-dress and shawl;
Of the steps that we took to one fiddle;
Of the dress of my queer *vis-à-vis;*
And how I once went down the middle
With the man that shot Sandy McGee;

Of the moon that was quietly sleeping
On the hill, when the time came to go;
Of the few baby peaks that were peeping
From under their bedclothes of snow;
Of that ride,—that to me was the rarest;
Of—the something you said at the gate:
Ah, Joe, then I wasn't an heiress
To " the best-paying lead in the State."

Well, well, it 's all past; yet it 's funny
To think, as I stood in the glare
Of fashion and beauty and money,
That I should be thinking, right there,
Of some one who breasted high water,
And swam the North Fork, and all that,
Just to dance with old Folinsbee's daughter,
The Lily of Poverty Flat.

But goodness! what nonsense I'm writing!
(Mamma says my taste still is low,)
Instead of my triumphs reciting,
I'm spooning on Joseph,—heigh-ho!
And I'm to be "finished" by travel,
Whatever's the meaning of that,—
O, why did papa strike pay gravel
In drifting on Poverty Flat?

Good-night,—here's the end of my paper;
Good-night,—if the longitude please,—
For maybe, while wasting my taper,
Your sun's climbing over the trees.
But know, if you haven't got riches,
And are poor, dearest Joe, and all that,
That my heart's somewhere there in the ditches,
And you've struck it,—on Poverty Flat.

BRET HARTE.

THE PLAIDIE.

Upon ane stormy Sunday,
    Coming adoon the lane,
Were a score of bonnie lassies—
    And the sweetest I maintain
        Was Caddie,
That I took unneath my plaidie,
    To shield her from the rain.

She said that the daisies blushed
    For the kiss that I had ta'en;
I wadna hae thought the lassie
    Wad sae of a kiss complain:
        "Now, laddie!

I winna stay under your plaidie,
   If I gang hame in the rain!"

But, on an after Sunday,
   When cloud there was not ane,.
This selfsame winsome lassie
   (We chanced to meet in the lane)
      Said, "Laddie,
Why dinna ye wear your plaidie?
   Wha kens but it may rain?"

CHARLES SIBLEY.

KITTY OF COLERAINE.

As beautiful Kitty one morning was tripping
   With a pitcher of milk, from the fair of Cole-
      raine,
When she saw me she stumbled, the pitcher it
      tumbled,
   And all the sweet buttermilk watered the plain.

"O, what shall I do now—'t was looking at you
      now!
   Sure, sure, such a pitcher I'll ne'er meet again!
'T was the pride of my dairy: O Barney M'Cleary!
   You're sent as a plague to the girls of Cole-
      raine."

I sat down beside her, and gently did chide her,
   That such a misfortune should give her such
      pain.
A kiss then I gave her; and ere I did leave her,
   She vowed for such pleasure she'd break it
      again.

'T was hay-making season—I can't tell the rea-
    son—
Misfortunes will never come single, 't is plain;
For very soon after poor Kitty's disaster
    The devil a pitcher was whole in Coleraine.

CHARLES DAWSON SHANLY.

KITTY NEIL.

" Ah! sweet Kitty Neil, rise up from that wheel,—
    Your neat little foot will be weary with spin-
        ning!
Come trip down with me to the sycamore-tree:
    Half the parish is there, and the dance is be-
        ginning.
The sun is gone down, but the full harvest moon
    Shines sweetly and cool on the dew-whitened
        valley;
While all the air rings with the soft, loving things
    Each little bird sings in the green shaded alley."

With a blush and a smile Kitty rose up the while,
    Her eye in the glass, as she bound her hair,
        glancing;
'T is hard to refuse when a young lover sues,
    So she couldn't but choose to go off to the
        dancing.
And now on the green the glad groups are seen,—
    Each gay-hearted lad with the lass of his
        choosing;
And Pat, without fail, leads out sweet Kitty
    Neil,—
    Somehow, when he asked, she ne'er thought of
    refusing.

Now Felix Magee put his pipes to his knee,
    And with flourish so free sets each couple in
        motion:
With a cheer and a bound the lads patter the
        ground;
    The maids move around just like swans on
        the ocean.
Cheeks bright as the rose, feet light as the doe's,
    Now coyly retiring, now boldly advancing:
Search the world all around, from the sky to the
        ground,
    No such sight can be found as an Irish lass
        dancing!

Sweet Kate! who could view your bright eyes of
        deep blue,
    Beaming humidly through their dark lashes so
        mildly,
Your fair-turnèd arm, heaving breast, rounded
        form,
    Nor feel his heart warm, and his pulses throb
        wildly?
Young Pat feels his heart, as he gazes, depart,
    Subdued by the smart of such painful yet sweet
        love:
The sight leaves his eye as he cries with a sigh,
    *Dance light, for my heart it lies under your
        feet, love!*

              JOHN FRANCIS WALLER.

THE LITTLE MILLINER.

My girl hath violet eyes and yellow hair,
A soft hand, like a lady's, small and fair,
A sweet face pouting in a white straw bonnet,
A tiny foot, and little boot upon it;
And all her finery to charm beholders
Is the gray shawl drawn tight around her
    shoulders,
The plain stuff-gown and collar white as snow,
And sweet red petticoat that peeps below.
But gladly in the busy town goes she,
Summer and winter, fearing nobodie;
She pats the pavement with her fairy feet,
With fearless eyes she charms the crowded street;
And in her pocket lie, in lieu of gold,
A lucky sixpence and a thimble old.

We lodged in the same house a year ago:
She on the topmost floor, I just below,—
She, a poor milliner, content and wise,
I, a poor city clerk, with hopes to rise;
And, long ere we were friends, I learnt to love
The little angel on the floor above.
For, every morn, ere from my bed I stirred,
Her chamber door would open, and I heard,—
And listened, blushing, to her coming down,
And palpitated with her rustling gown,
And tingled while her foot went downward slow,
Creaked like a cricket, passed, and died below;
Then peeping from the window, pleased and sly,
I saw the pretty shining face go by,

Healthy and rosy, fresh from slumber sweet,—
A sunbeam in the quiet morning street.

And every night, when in from work she tript,
Red to the ears I from my chamber slipt,
That I might hear upon the narrow stair
Her low " Good evening," as she passed me there.
And when her door was closed, below sat I,
And hearkened stilly as she stirred on high,—
Watched the red firelight shadows in the room,
Fashioned her face before me in the gloom,
And heard her close the window, lock the door,
Moving about more lightly than before,
And thought, " She is undressing now ! " and, oh !
My cheeks were hot, my heart was in a glow !
And I made pictures of her,—standing bright
Before the looking-glass in bed-gown white.
Unbinding in a knot her yellow hair,
Then kneeling timidly to say a prayer;
Till, last, the floor creaked softly overhead,
'Neath bare feet tripping to the little bed,—
And all was hushed. Yet still I hearkened on,
Till the faint sounds about the streets were gone;
And saw her slumbering with lips apart,
One little hand upon her little heart,
The other pillowing a face that smiled
In slumber like the slumber of a child,
The bright hair shining round the small white ear,
The soft breath stealing visible and clear,
And mixing with the moon's whose frosty gleam
Made round her rest a vaporous light of dream.

How free she wandered in the wicked place,
Protected only by her gentle face!

She saw bad things—how could she choose but
    see?—
She heard of wantonness and misery;
The city closed around her night and day,
But lightly, happily, she went her way.
Nothing of evil that she saw or heard
Could touch a heart so innocently stirred,—
By simple hopes that cheered it through the storm,
And little flutterings that kept it warm.
No power had she to reason out her needs,
To give the whence and wherefore of her deeds;
But she was good and pure amid the strife,
By virtue of the joy that was her life.
Here, where a thousand spirits daily fall,
Where heart and soul and senses turn to gall,
She floated, pure as innocent could be,
Like a small sea-bird on a stormy sea,
Which breasts the billows, wafted to and fro,
Fearless, uninjured, while the strong winds blow,
While the clouds gather, and the waters roar,
And mighty ships are broken on the shore.
All winter long, witless who peeped the while,
She sweetened the chill mornings with her smile;
When the soft snow was falling dimly white,
Shining among it with a child's delight,
Bright as a rose, though nipping winds might
    blow,
And leaving fairy footprints in the snow!

   'T was when the spring was coming, when the
    snow
Had melted, and fresh winds began to blow,
And girls were selling violets in the town,

That suddenly a fever struck me down.
The world was changed, the sense of life was
          pained,
And nothing but a shadow-land remained;
Death came in a dark mist and looked at me,
I felt his breathing, though I could not see,
But heavily I lay and did not stir,
And had strange images and dreams of her.
Then came a vacancy: with feeble breath,
I shivered under the cold touch of Death,
And swooned among strange visions of the dead,
When a voice called from heaven, and he fled;
And suddenly I wakened, as it seemed,
From a deep sleep wherein I had not dreamed.

And it was night, and I could see and hear,
And I was in the room I held so dear,
And unaware, stretched out upon my bed,
I hearkened for a footstep overhead.

But all was hushed. I looked around the room,
And slowly made out shapes amid the gloom.
The wall was reddened by a rosy light,
A faint fire flickered, and I knew 't was night,
Because below there was a sound of feet
Dying away along the quiet street,—
When, turning my pale face and sighing low,
I saw a vision in the quiet glow:
A little figure, in a cotton gown,
Looking upon the fire and stooping down,
Her side to me, her face illumed, she eyed
Two chestnuts burning slowly side by side,—
Her lips apart, her clear eyes strained to see,
Her little hands clasped tight around her knee,

The firelight gleaming on her golden head,
And tinting her white neck to rosy red,
Her features bright and beautiful, and pure,
With childish fear and yearning half demure.

O sweet, sweet dream! I thought, and strained
      mine eyes,
Fearing to break the spell with words and sighs.

Softly she stooped, her dear face sweetly fair,
And sweeter since a light like love was there,
Brightening, watching, more and more elate,
As the nuts glowed together in the grate,
Crackling with little jets of fiery light,
Till side by side they turned to ashes white,—
Then up she leapt, her face cast off its fear
For rapture that itself was radiance clear,
And would have clapped her little hands in glee,
But, pausing, bit her lips and peeped at me,
And met the face that yearned on her so whitely,
And gave a cry and trembled, blushing brightly,
While raised on elbow, as she turned to flee,
" *Polly!* " I cried,—and grew as red as she!

It was no dream! for soon my thoughts were
      clear,
And she could tell me all, and I could hear:
How in my sickness friendless I had lain,
How the hard people pitied not my pain;
How, in despite of what bad people said,
She left her labors, stopped beside my bed,
And nursed me, thinking sadly I would die;
How, in the end, the danger passed me by;

How she had sought to steal away before
The sickness passed, and I was strong once more.
By fits she told the story in mine ear,
And troubled all the telling with a fear
Lest by my cold man's heart she should be chid,
Lest I should think her bold in what she did;
But, lying on my bed, I dared to say,
How I had watched and loved her many a day,
How dear she was to me, and dearer still
For that strange kindness done while I was ill,
And how I could but think that Heaven above
Had done it all to bind our lives in love.
And Polly cried, turning her face away,
And seemed afraid, and answered " yea " nor
    " nay ; "
Then stealing close with little pants and sighs,
Looked on my pale thin face and earnest eyes,
And seemed in act to fling her arms about
My neck; then, blushing, paused, in fluttering
    doubt;
Last, sprang upon my heart, sighing and sob-
    bing,—
That I might feel how gladly hers was throbbing!

   Ah! ne'er shall I forget until I die,
How happy the dreamy days went by,
While I grew well, and lay with soft heart-beats,
Hearkening the pleasant murmur from the streets,
And Polly by me like a sunny beam,
And life all changed, and love a drowsy dream!
'T was happiness enough to lie and see
The little golden head bent droopingly
Over its sewing, while the still time flew,

And my fond eyes were dim with happy dew!
And then, when I was nearly well and strong,
And she went back to labor all day long,
How sweet to lie alone with half-shut eyes,
And hear the distant murmurs and the cries,
And think how pure she was from pain and sin,—
And how the summer days were coming in!
Then, as the sunset faded from the room,
To listen for her footstep in the gloom,
To pant as it came stealing up the stair,
To feel my whole life brighten unaware
When the soft tap came to the door, and when
The door was opened for her smile again!
Best, the long evenings!—when, till late at night,
She sat beside me in the quiet light,
And happy things were said and kisses won,
And serious gladness found its vent in fun.
Sometimes I would draw close her shining head,
And pour her bright hair out upon the bed,
And she would laugh, and blush, and try to scold,
While " Here," I cried, " I count my wealth in
    gold!

Once, like a little sinner for transgression,
She blushed upon my breast, and made confession:
How, when that night I woke and looked around,
I found her busy with a charm profound,—
One chestnut was herself, my girl confessed,
The other was the person she loved best,
And if they burned together side by side,
He loved her, and she would become his bride;
And burn indeed they did, to her delight,—
And had the pretty charm not proved right?

Thus much, and more, with timorous joy, she
  said,
While her confessor, too, grew rosy red,—
And close together pressed two blissful faces,
As I absolved the sinner, with embraces.

  And here is winter come again, winds blow,
The houses and the streets are white with snow;
And in the long and pleasant eventide,
Why, what is Polly making at my side?
What but a silk gown, beautiful and grand,
We bought together lately in the Strand!
What but a dress to go to church in soon,
And wear right queenly 'neath a honeymoon!
And who shall match her with her new straw
  bonnet,
Her tiny foot and little boot upon it;
Embroidered petticoat and silk gown new,
And shawl she wears as few fine ladies do?
And she will keep, to charm away all ill,
The lucky sixpence in her pocket still;
And we will turn, come fair or cloudy weather,
To ashes, like the chestnuts, close together!

                              ROBERT BUCHANAN.

ATALANTA'S RACE.

FROM "THE EARTHLY PARADISE."

ATALANTA VICTORIOUS.

AND there two runners did the sign abide
Foot set to foot,—a young man slim and fair,
Crisp-haired, well knit, with firm limbs often
  tried

In places where no man his strength may spare;
Dainty his thin coat was, and on his hair
A golden circlet of renown he wore,
And in his hand an olive garland bore.

But on this day with whom shall he contend?
A maid stood by him like Diana clad
When in the woods she lists her bow to bend,
Too fair for one to look on and be glad,
Who scarcely yet has thirty summers had,
If he must still behold her from afar;
Too fair to let the world live free from war.

She seemed all earthly matters to forget;
Of all tormenting lines her face was clear,
Her wide gray eyes upon the goal were set
Calm and unmoved as though no soul were near;
But her foe trembled as a man in fear,
Nor from her loveliness one moment turned
His anxious face with fierce desire that burned.

Now through the hush there broke the trumpet's
    clang
Just as the setting sun made eventide.
Then from light feet a spurt of dust there sprang,
And swiftly were they running side by side;
But silent did the thronging folk abide
Until the turning-post was reached at last,
And round about it still abreast they passed.

But when the people saw how close they ran,
When half-way to the starting-point they were,
A cry of joy broke forth, whereat the man

Headed the white-foot runner, and drew near
Unto the very end of all his fear;
And scarce his straining feet the ground could
        feel,
And bliss unhoped for o'er his heart 'gan steal.

But midst the loud victorious shouts he heard
Her footsteps drawing nearer, and the sound
Of fluttering raiment, and thereat afeard
His flushed and eager face he turned around,
And even then he felt her past him bound
Fleet as the wind, but scarcely saw her there
Till on the goal she laid her fingers fair.

There stood she breathing like a little child
Amid some warlike clamor laid asleep,
For no victorious joy her red lips smiled,
Her cheek its wonted freshness did but keep;
No glance lit up her clear gray eyes and deep,
Though some divine thought softened all her face
As once more rang the trumpet through the place.

But her late foe stopped short amidst his course,
One moment gazed upon her piteously,
Then with a groan his lingering feet did force
To leave the spot whence he her eyes could see;
And, changed like one who knows his time must be
But short and bitter, without any word
He knelt before the bearer of the sword;

Then high rose up the gleaming deadly blade,
Bared of its flowers, and through the crowded
        place

Was silence now, and midst of it the maid
Went by the poor wretch at a gentle pace,
And he to hers upturned his sad white face;
Nor did his eyes behold another sight
Ere on his soul there fell eternal night.

ATALANTA CONQUERED.

Now has the lingering month at last gone by,
Again are all folk round the running place,
Nor other seems the dismal pageantry
Than heretofore, but that another face
Looks o'er the smooth course ready for the race;
For now, beheld of all, Milanion
Stands on the spot he twice has looked upon.

But yet—what change is this that holds the
    maid?
Does she indeed see in his glittering eye
More than disdain of the sharp shearing blade,
Some happy hope of help and victory?
The others seemed to say, " We come to die,
Look down upon us for a little while,
That dead, we may bethink us of thy smile."

But he—what look of mastery was this
He cast on her? why were his lips so red?
Why was his face so flushed with happiness?
So looks not one who deems himself but dead,
E'en if to death he bows a willing head;
So rather looks a god well pleased to find
Some earthly damsel fashioned to his mind.

Why must she drop her lids before his gaze,
And even as she casts adown her eyes
10

Redden to note his eager glance of praise,
And wish that she were clad in other guise?
Why must the memory to her heart arise
Of things unnoticed when they first were heard,
Some lover's song, some answering maiden's
      word?

  What makes these longings, vague, without a
      name,
And this vain pity never felt before,
This sudden languor, this contempt of fame,
This tender sorrow for the time past o'er,
These doubts that grow each minute more and
      more?
Why does she tremble as the time grows near,
And weak defeat and woful victory fear?

  But while she seemed to hear her beating heart,
Above their heads the trumpet blast rang out,
And forth they sprang; and she must play her
      part;
Then flew her white feet, knowing not a doubt,
Though slackening once, she turned her head
      about,
But then she cried aloud and faster fled
Than e'er before, and all men deemed him dead.

  But with no sound he raised aloft his hand,
And thence what seemed a ray of light there flew
And past the maid rolled on along the sand;
Then trembling she her feet together drew,
And in her heart a strong desire there grew
To have the toy; some god she thought had given
That gift to her, to make of earth a heaven.

Then from the course with eager steps she ran
And in her odorous bosom laid the gold.
But when she turned again, the great-limbed man
Now well ahead she failed not to behold,
And, mindful of her glory waxing cold,
Sprang up and followed him in hot pursuit,
Though with one hand she touched the golden
    fruit.

Note, too, the bow that she was wont to bear
She laid aside to grasp the glittering prize,
And o'er her shoulder from the quiver fair
Three arrows fell and lay before her eyes
Unnoticed, as amidst the people's cries
She sprang to head the strong Milanion,
Who now the turning-post had wellnigh won.

But as he set his mighty hand on it,
White fingers underneath his own were laid,
And white limbs from his dazzled eyes did flit.
Then he the second fruit cast by the maid;
But she ran on awhile, then as afraid
Wavered and stopped, and turned and made no
    stay
Until the globe with its bright fellow lay.

Then, as a troubled glance she cast around,
Now far ahead the Argive could she see,
And in her garment's hem one hand she wound
To keep the double prize, and strenuously
Sped o'er the course, and little doubt had she
To win the day, though now but scanty space
Was left betwixt him and the winning place.

Short was the way unto such wingèd feet,
Quickly she gained upon him till at last
He turned about her eager eyes to meet,
And from his hand the third fair apple cast.
She wavered not, but turned and ran so fast
After the prize that should her bliss fulfil,
That in her hand it lay ere it was still.

Nor did she rest, but turned about to win
Once more an unblest, woful victory—
And yet—and yet—why does her breath begin
To fail her, and her feet drag heavily?
Why fails she now to see if far or nigh
The goal is? Why do her gray eyes grow dim?
Why do these tremors run through every limb?

She spreads her arms abroad some stay to find
Else must she fall, indeed, and findeth this,
A strong man's arms about her body twined.
Nor may she shudder now to feel his kiss,
So wrapped she is in new, unbroken bliss:
Made happy that the foe the prize hath won,
She weeps glad tears for all her glory done.

WILLIAM MORRIS.

IV.

WOOING AND WINNING.

THE PASSIONATE SHEPHERD TO HIS LOVE.

COME live with me and be my love,
And we will all the pleasures prove,
That hills and valleys, dales and fields,
Woods or craggy mountains yield.

And we will sit upon the rocks,
Seeing the shepherds feed their flocks
By shallow rivers, to whose falls
Melodious birds sing madrigals.

And will I make thee beds of roses,
And a thousand fragrant posies;
A cap of flowers and a kirtle
Embroidered all with leaves of myrtle;

A gown made of the finest wool
Which from our pretty lambs we pull;
Fair-linèd slippers for the cold,
With buckles of the purest gold;

A belt of straw, and ivy buds,
With coral clasps and amber studs.
And if these pleasures thee may move,
Come live with me, and be my love.

The shepherd-swains shall dance and sing
For thy delight each May morning;
If these delights thy mind may move,
Then live with me, and be my love.

CHRISTOPHER MARLOWE.

THE NYMPH'S REPLY.

If all the world and love were young,
And truth in every shepherd's tongue,
These pretty pleasures might me move
To live with thee, and be thy love.

Time drives the flocks from field to fold,
When rivers rage and rocks grow cold;
And Philomel becometh dumb,
The rest complain of cares to come.

The flowers do fade, and wanton fields
To wayward winter reckoning yields;
A honey tongue, a heart of gall,
Is fancy's spring, but sorrow's fall.

Thy gown, thy shoes, thy beds of roses,
Thy cap, the kirtle, and thy posies,

Soon break, soon wither, soon forgotten,
In folly ripe, in reason rotten.

Thy belt of straw and ivy buds,
Thy coral clasps and amber studs;
All these in me no means can move
To come to thee and be thy love.

But could youth last, and love still breed,
Had joys no date, nor age no need,
Then these delights my mind might move
To live with thee and be thy love.

SIR WALTER RALEIGH.

GOLDEN EYES.

Ah, Golden Eyes, to win you yet,
I bring mine April coronet,
The lovely blossoms of the spring,
For you I weave, to you I bring:
These roses with the lilies wet,
The dewy dark-eyed violet,
Narcissus, and the wind-flower wet.
Wilt thou disdain mine offering,
    Ah, Golden Eyes?
Crowned with thy lover's flowers, forget
The pride wherein thy heart is set,
For thou, like these or anything,
Hast but thine hour of blossoming,
Thy spring, and then—the long regret,
    Ah, Golden Eyes!

From the Greek of RUFINUS.
Translation of ANDREW LANG.

PHILLIDA AND CORYDON.

In the merry month of May,
In a morn by break of day,
With a troop of damsels playing
Forth I rode, forsooth, a-maying,

When anon by a woodside,
Where as May was in his pride,
I espièd, all alone,
Phillida and Corydon.

Much ado there was, God wot!
He would love and she would not:
She said, "Never man was true:"
He says, "None was false to you."
He said he had loved her long:
She says, "Love should have no wrong."

Corydon he would kiss her then.
She says, "Maids must kiss no men
Till they do for good and all."
Then she made the shepherd call
All the heavens to witness, truth
Never loved a truer youth.

Thus, with many a pretty oath,
Yea and nay, and faith and troth,—
Such as silly shepherds use
When they will not love abuse,—
Love, which had been long deluded,
Was with kisses sweet concluded;
And Phillida, with garlands gay,
Was made the lady of the May.

NICHOLAS BRETON.

THE BAILIFF'S DAUGHTER OF
ISLINGTON.

THERE was a youthe, and a well-beloved youthe,
  And he was a squire's son;
He loved the bayliffes daughter deare,
  That lived in Islington.

Yet she was coye, and would not believe
  That he did love her soe,
Noe nor at any time would she
  Any countenance to him showe.

But when his friendes did understand
  His fond and foolish minde,
They sent him up to faire London,
  An apprentice for to binde.

And when he had been seven long yeares,
  And never his love could see,—
" Many a teare have I shed for her sake,
  When she little thought of mee."

Then all the maids of Islington
  Went forth to sport and playe,
All but the bayliffes daughter deare;
  She secretly stole awaye.

She pulled off her gowne of greene,
  And put on ragged attire,
And to faire London she would go
  Her true love to enquire.

And as she went along the high road,
  The weather being hot and drye,
She sat her downe upon a green bank,
  And her true love came riding bye.

She started up, with colour soe redd,
  Catching hold of his bridle-reine;
" One penny, one penny, kind sir," she sayd,
  " Will ease me of much paine."

" Before I give you one penny, sweet-heart,
  Praye tell me where you were borne."
" At Islington, kind sir," sayd shee,
  " Where I have had many a scorne."

" I prythee, sweet-heart, then tell to mee,
  O tell me whether you knowe
The bayliffes daughter of Islington."
  " She is dead, sir, long agoe."

" If she be dead, then take my horse,
  My saddle and bridle also;
For I will into some farr countrye,
  Where noe man shall me knowe."

" O staye, O staye, thou goodlye youthe,
  She standeth by thy side;
She is here alive, she is not dead,
  And readye to be thy bride."

" O farewell griefe, and welcome joye,
  Ten thousand times therefore;
For nowe I have founde mine owne true love,
  Whom I thought I should never see more."

ANONYMOUS.

WHERE ARE YOU GOING, MY PRETTY MAID?

" WHERE are you going, my pretty maid? "
" I am going a-milking, sir," she said.
" May I go with you, my pretty maid? "
" You 're kindly welcome, sir," she said.
" What is your father, my pretty maid? "
" My father 's a farmer, sir," she said.
" What is your fortune, my pretty maid? "
" My face is my fortune, sir," she said.
" Then I won't marry you, my pretty maid."
" Nobody asked you, sir," she said.

ANONYMOUS.

MY EYES! HOW I LOVE YOU.

My eyes! how I love you,
You sweet little dove you!
There 's no one above you,
    Most beautiful Kitty.

So glossy your hair is,
Like a sylph's or a fairy's;
And your neck, I declare, is
    Exquisitely pretty.

Quite Grecian your nose is,
And your cheeks are like roses,
So delicious—O Moses!
    Surpassingly sweet!

Not the beauty of tulips,
Nor the taste of mint-juleps,
Can compare with your two lips,
    Most beautiful Kate!

Not the black eyes of Juno,
Nor Minerva's of blue, no,
Nor Venus's, you know,
    Can equal your own!

O, how my heart prances,
And frolics and dances,
When their radiant glances
    Upon me are thrown!

And now, dearest Kitty,
It's not very pretty,
Indeed it's a pity,
    To keep me in sorrow!

So, if you'll but chime in,
We'll have done with our rhymin',
Swap Cupid for Hymen,
    And be married to-morrow.

           JOHN GODFREY SAXE.

THE BROOKSIDE.

I wandered by the brookside,
I wandered by the mill;
I could not hear the brook flow,—
The noisy wheel was still;

There was no burr of grasshopper,
No chirp of any bird,
But the beating of my own heart
Was all the sound I heard.

I sat beneath the elm-tree;
I watched the long, long shade,
And, as it grew still longer,
I did not feel afraid;
For I listened for a footfall,
I listened for a word,—
But the beating of my own heart
Was all the sound I heard.

He came not,—no, he came not,—
The night came on alone,—
The little stars sat, one by one,
Each on his golden throne;
The evening wind passed by my cheek,
The leaves above were stirred,—
But the beating of my own heart
Was all the sound I heard.

Fast silent tears were flowing,
When something stood behind;
A hand was on my shoulder,—
I knew its touch was kind:
It drew me nearer,—nearer,—
We did not speak one word,
For the beating of our own hearts
Was all the sound we heard.

RICHARD MONCKTON MILNES,
LORD HOUGHTON.

THE LITTLE RED LARK.

O SWAN of slenderness,
Dove of tenderness,
  Jewel of joys, arise!
The little red lark,
Like a soaring spark
  Of song, to his sunburst flies;
But till thou art arisen,
Earth is a prison,
  Full of my lonesome sighs:
Then awake and discover,
To thy fond lover,
  The morn of thy matchless eyes.

The dawn is dark to me,
Hark! oh, hark to me,
  Pulse of my heart, I pray!
And out of thy hiding
With blushes gliding,
  Dazzle me with thy day.
Ah, then once more to thee
Flying I 'll pour to thee
  Passion so sweet and gay,
The larks shall listen,
And dew-drops glisten,
  Laughing on every spray.

                    ALFRED PERCEVAL GRAVES.

LOVE.

ALL thoughts, all passions, all delights,
Whatever stirs this mortal frame,
All are but ministers of Love,
 And feed his sacred flame.

Oft in my waking dreams do I
Live o'er again that happy hour,
When midway on the mount I lay
 Beside the ruined tower.

The moonshine stealing o'er the scene
Had blended with the lights of eve;
And she was there, my hope, my joy,
 My own dear Genevieve!

She leaned against the armèd man,
The statue of the armèd knight;
She stood and listened to my lay,
 Amid the lingering light.

Few sorrows hath she of her own,
My hope! my joy! my Genevieve!
She loves me best whene'er I sing
 The songs that make her grieve.

I played a soft and doleful air,
I sang an old and moving story,—
An old rude song, that suited well
 That ruin wild and hoary.

She listened with a flitting blush,
With downcast eyes and modest grace;
For well she knew, I could not choose
    But gaze upon her face.

I told her of the Knight that wore
Upon his shield a burning brand;
And that for ten long years he wooed
    The Lady of the Land.

I told her how he pined: and ah!
The deep, the low, the pleading tone
With which I sang another's love
    Interpreted my own.

She listened with a flitting blush,
With downcast eyes and modest grace;
And she forgave me that I gazed
    Too fondly on her face.

But when I told the cruel scorn
That crazed that bold and lovely Knight,
And that he crossed the mountain-woods,
    Nor rested day nor night;

That sometimes from the savage den,
And sometimes from the darksome shade,
And sometimes starting up at once
    In green and sunny glade,

There came and looked him in the face
An angel beautiful and bright;
And that he knew it was a Fiend,
    This miserable Knight!

And that unknowing what he did,
He leaped amid a murderous band,
And saved from outrage worse than death
    The Lady of the Land;

And how she wept, and clasped his knees;
And how she tended him in vain;
And ever strove to expiate
    The scorn that crazed his brain;

And that she nursed him in a cave,
And how his madness went away,
When on the yellow forest-leaves
    A dying-man he lay;

—His dying words—but when I reached
That tenderest strain of all the ditty,
My faltering voice and pausing harp
    Disturbed her soul with pity!

All impulses of soul and sense
Had thrilled my guileless Genevieve;
The music and the doleful tale,
    The rich and balmy eve;

And hopes, and fears that kindle hope,
An undistinguishable throng,
And gentle wishes long subdued,
    Subdued and cherished long.

She wept with pity and delight,
She blushed with love, and virgin shame;
And like the murmur of a dream,
    I heard her breathe my name.

11

Her bosom heaved,—she stepped aside,
As conscious of my look she stept,—
Then suddenly, with timorous eye
    She fled to me and wept.

She half enclosed me with her arms,
She pressed me with a meek embrace;
And bending back her head, looked up,
    And gazed upon my face.

'T was partly love, and partly fear,
And partly 't was a bashful art
That I might rather feel than see
    The swelling of her heart.

I calmed her fears, and she was calm,
And told her love with virgin pride;
And so I won my Genevieve,
    My bright and beauteous Bride.
               SAMUEL TAYLOR COLERIDGE.

SOMEBODY.

SOMEBODY 's courting somebody,
    Somewhere or other to-night;
Somebody 's whispering to somebody,
Somebody 's listening to somebody,
    Under this clear moonlight.

Near the bright river's flow,
Running so still and slow,
Talking so soft and low,
    She sits with Somebody.

Pacing the ocean's shore,
Edged by the foaming roar,
Words never used before
  Sound sweet to Somebody.

Under the maple-tree
Deep though the shadow be,
Plain enough they can see,
  Bright eyes has Somebody.

No one sits up to wait,
Though she is out so late,
All know she's at the gate,
  Talking with Somebody.

Tiptoe to parlor door;
Two shadows on the floor!
Moonlight, reveal no more,—
  Susy and Somebody.

Two, sitting side by side
Float with the ebbing tide,
" Thus, dearest, may we glide
  Through life," says Somebody.

Somewhere, Somebody
Makes love to Somebody,
  To-night.

                              ANONYMOUS.

THE EXCHANGE.

We pledged our hearts, my love and I,—
　　I in my arms the maiden clasping;
I could not tell the reason why,
　　But, O, I trembled like an aspen!

Her father's love she bade me gain;
　　I went, and shook like any reed!
I strove to act the man,—in vain!
　　We had exchanged our hearts indeed.

SAMUEL TAYLOR COLERIDGE.

LOVE'S LOGIC.

I. HER RESPECTABLE PAPA'S.

" My dear, be sensible! Upon my word
This—for a woman even—is absurd;
His income 's not a hundred pounds, I know.
He 's not worth loving."—" But I love him so! "

II. HER MOTHER'S.

" You silly child, he is well made and tall;
But looks are far from being all in all.
His social standing 's low, his family 's low.
He 's not worth loving."—" And I love him so! "

III. HER ETERNAL FRIEND'S.

" Is that he picking up the fallen fan?
My dear! he 's such an awkward, ugly man!
You must be certain, pet, to answer ' No.'
He 's not worth loving."—" And I love him so! "

IV. HER BROTHER'S.

" By Jove! were I a girl—through horrid hap—
I wouldn't have a milk-and-water chap.
The man has not a single spark of ' go.'
He 's not worth loving."—" Yet I love him so!"

V. HER OWN.

" And were he everything to which I 've listened:
Though he were ugly, awkward (and he isn't),
Poor, low-born, and destitute of ' go,'
He is worth loving, for I love him so."

ANONYMOUS.

THE NIGHT-PIECE.

TO JULIA.

HER eyes the glow-worme lend thee,
The shooting-starres attend thee,
  And the elves also,
  Whose little eyes glow
Like the sparks of fire, befriend thee.

No Will-o'-th'-wispe mislight thee,
Nor snake nor slow-worm bite thee;
  But on thy way,
  Not making stay,
Since ghost there 's none t' affright thee!

Let not the darke thee cumber;
What though the moon does slumber?
  The stars of the night
  Will lend thee their light,
Like tapers cleare, without number.

Then, Julia, let me woo thee,
Thus, thus to come unto me;
And when I shall meet
Thy silvery feet,
My soule I'le pour into thee!

ROBERT HERRICK.

SWEET MEETING OF DESIRES.

FROM " THE ANGEL IN THE HOUSE."

I GREW assured, before I asked,
That she'd be mine without reserve,
And in her unclaimed graces basked
At leisure, till the time should serve,—
With just enough of dread to thrill
The hope, and make it trebly dear:
Thus loath to speak the word, to kill
Either the hope or happy fear.

Till once, through lanes returning late,
Her laughing sisters lagged behind;
And ere we reached her father's gate,
We paused with one presentient mind;
And, in the dim and perfumed mist
Their coming stayed, who, blithe and free,
And very women, loved to assist
A lover's opportunity.

Twice rose, twice died, my trembling word;
To faint and frail cathedral chimes
Spake time in music, and we heard
The chafers rustling in the limes.

Her dress, that touched me where I stood;
   The warmth of her confided arm;
Her bosom's gentle neighborhood;
   Her pleasure in her power to charm;

Her look, her love, her form, her touch!
   The least seemed most by blissful turn,—
Blissful but that it pleased too much,
   And taught the wayward soul to yearn.
It was as if a harp with wires
   Was traversed by the breath I drew;
And O, sweet meeting of desires!
   She, answering, owned that she loved too.
              COVENTRY PATMORE.

STORY OF THE GATE.

Across the pathway, myrtle-fringed,
     Under the maple, it was hinged—
     The little wooden gate;
'T was there within the quiet gloam,
When I had strolled with Nelly home,
     I used to pause and wait

Before I said to her good-night,
Yet loath to leave the winsome sprite
     Within the garden's pale;
And there, the gate between us two,
We 'd linger as all lovers do,
     And lean upon the rail.

And face to face, eyes close to eyes,
Hands meeting hands in feigned surprise,
     After a stealthy quest,—

So close I 'd bend, ere she 'd retreat,
That I 'd grow drunken from the sweet
    Tuberose upon her breast.

We 'd talk—in fitful style, I ween—
With many a meaning glance between
    The tender words and low;
We 'd whisper some dear, sweet conceit,
Some idle gossip we 'd repeat,
    And then I 'd move to go.

" Good - night," I 'd say; " good - night — good-
    bye ! "
" Good-night "—from her with half a sigh—
    " Good-night ! " " *Good*-night ! "   And then—
And then I do *not* go, but stand,
Again lean on the railing, and—
    Begin it all again.

Ah ! that was many a day ago—
That pleasant summer-time—although
    The gate is standing yet;
A little cranky, it may be,
A little weather-worn—like me—
    Who never can forget

The happy— " End "? My cynic friend,
Pray save your sneers—there was no " end."
    Watch yonder chubby thing !
That is our youngest, hers and mine;
See how he climbs, his legs to twine
    About the gate and swing.

                                T. H. ROBERTSON.

DORIS: A PASTORAL.

I sat with Doris, the shepherd-maiden;
  Her crook was laden with wreathèd flowers:
I sat and wooed her, through sunlight wheeling
  And shadows stealing, for hours and hours.

And she, my Doris, whose lap encloses
  Wild summer-roses of sweet perfume,
The while I sued her, kept hushed and hearkened,
  Till shades had darkened from gloss to gloom.

She touched my shoulder with fearful finger;
  She said, " We linger, we must not stay:
My flock 's in danger, my sheep will wander;
  Behold them yonder, how far they stray!"

I answered bolder, " Nay, let me hear you,
  And still be near you, and still adore!
No wolf nor stranger will touch one yearling:
  Ah! stay my darling, a moment more!"

She whispered, sighing, " There will be sorrow
  Beyond to-morrow, if I lose to-day;
My fold unguarded, my flock unfolded,
  I shall be scolded and sent away."

Said I, denying, " If they do miss you,
  They ought to kiss you when you get home;
And well rewarded by friend and neighbor
  Should be the labor from which you come."

" They might remember," she answered meekly,
　" That lambs are weakly, and sheep are wild;
But if they love me, it 's none so fervent:
　I am a servant, and not a child."

Then each hot ember glowed within me,
　And love did win me to swift reply:
" Ah! do but prove me; and none shall bind you,
　Nor fray nor find you, until I die."

She blushed and started, and stood awaiting,
　As if debating in dreams divine;
But I did brave them; I told her plainly
　She doubted vainly, she must be mine.

So we twin-hearted, from all the valley
　Did rouse and rally her nibbling ewes;
And homeward drave them, we two together,
　Through blooming heather and gleaming dews.

That simple duty fresh grace did lend her,
　My Doris tender, my Doris true;
That I, her warder, did always bless her,
　And often press her to take her due.

And now in beauty she fills my dwelling,
　With love excelling, and undefiled;
And love doth guard her, both fast and fervent,
　No more a servant, nor yet a child.

ARTHUR JOSEPH MUNBY.

AMONG THE HEATHER.

ONE evening walking out, I o'ertook a modest col-
leen,
When the wind was blowing cool, and the harvest
leaves were falling:
" Is our way by chance the same? might we travel
on together? "
" Oh, I keep the mountain side," she replied,
" among the heather."

" Your mountain air is sweet when the days are
long and sunny,
When the grass grows round the rocks, and the
whin-bloom smells like honey;
But the winter's coming fast with its foggy,
snowy weather,
And you'll find it bleak and chill on your hill,
among the heather."

She praised her mountain home, and I'll praise
it too, with reason,
For where Molly is there's sunshine and flow'rs
at every season.
Be the moorland black or white, does it signify a
feather,
Now I know the way by heart, every part, among
the heather?

The sun goes down in haste, and the night falls
thick and stormy;
Yet I'd travel twenty miles to the welcome that's
before me;

Singing hi! for Eskydun, in the teeth of wind and
weather!
Love 'll warm me as I go through the snow,
among the heather.

WILLIAM ALLINGHAM.

RORY O'MORE;

OR, ALL FOR GOOD LUCK.

Young Rory O'More courted Kathleen bawn,—
He was bold as a hawk, she as soft as the dawn;
He wished in his heart pretty Kathleen to please,
And he thought the best way to do that was to
tease.
"Now, Rory, be aisy!" sweet Kathleen would
cry,
Reproof on her lip, but a smile in her eye,—
"With your tricks, I don't know, in troth, what
I'm about;
Faith! you've tazed till I've put on my cloak in-
side out."
"Och! jewel," says Rory, "that same is the way
Ye've thrated my heart for this many a day;
And 't is plazed that I am, and why not, to be
sure?
For 't is all for good luck," says bold Rory O'More.

"Indeed, then," says Kathleen, "don't think of
the like,
For I half gave a promise to soothering Mike:
The ground that I walk on he loves, I'll be
bound—"

" Faith ! " says Rory, " I 'd rather love you than
the ground."

" Now, Rory, I 'll cry if you don't let me go ;
Sure I dream every night that I 'm hating you
so ! "

" Och ! " says Rory, " that same I 'm delighted to
hear,
For dhrames always go by conthraries, my dear.
So, jewel, kape dhraming that same till ye die,
And bright morning will give diity night the
black lie !
And 't is plazed that I am, and why not, to be
sure ?
Since 't is all for good luck," says bold Rory
O'More.

" Arrah, Kathleen, my darlint, you 've tazed me
enough ;
Sure I 've thrashed, for your sake, Dinny Grimes
and Jim Duff ;
And I 've made myself, drinking your health, quite
a baste,—
So I think after that, I may talk to the praste."
Then Rory, the rogue, stole his arm round her
neck,
So soft and so white, without freckle or speck ;
And he looked in her eyes, that were beaming with
light,
And he kissed her sweet lips,—don't you think
he was right ?
" Now, Rory, leave off, sir,—you 'll hug me no
more,—
That 's eight times to-day that you 've kissed me
before."

" Then here goes another," says he, " to make sure!
For there's luck in odd numbers," says Rory
    O'More.

SAMUEL LOVER.

COOKING AND COURTING.

FROM TOM TO NED.

DEAR Ned, no doubt you'll be surprised
    When you receive and read this letter.
I've railed against the marriage state;
    But then, you see, I knew no better.
I've met a lovely girl out here;
    Her manner is—well—very winning:
We're soon to be—well, Ned, my dear,
    I'll tell you all, from the beginning.

I went to ask her out to ride
    Last Wednesday—it was perfect weather.
She said she couldn't possibly:
    The servants had gone off together
(Hibernians always rush away,
    At cousins' funerals to be looking);
Pies must be made, and she must stay,
    She said, to do that branch of cooking.

" O, let me help you," then I cried:
    " I'll be a cooker too—how jolly!"
She laughed, and answered, with a smile,
    " All right! but you'll repent your folly;
For I shall be a tyrant, sir,
    And good hard work you'll have to grapple;

So sit down there, and don't you stir,
  But take this knife, and pare that apple."

She rolled her sleeve above her arm,—
  That lovely arm, so plump and rounded;
Outside, the morning sun shone bright;
  Inside, the dough she deftly pounded.
Her little fingers sprinkled flour,
  And rolled the pie-crust up in masses:
I passed the most delightful hour
  Mid butter, sugar, and molasses.

With deep reflection her sweet eyes
  Gazed on each pot and pan and kettle.
She sliced the apples, filled her pies,
  And then the upper crust did settle.
Her rippling waves of golden hair
  In one great coil were tightly twisted;
But locks would break it, here and there,
  And curl about where'er they listed.

And then her sleeve came down, and I
  Fastened it up—her hands were doughy;
O, it did take the longest time!—
  Her arm, Ned, was so round and snowy.
She blushed, and trembled, and looked shy;
  Somehow that made me all the bolder;
Her arch lips looked so red that I—
  Well—found her head upon my shoulder.

We're to be married, Ned, next month;
  Come and attend the wedding revels.
I really think that bachelors
  Are the most miserable devils!

You 'd better go for some girl's hand;
And if you are uncertain whether
You dare to make a due demand,
Why, just try cooking pies together.

ANONYMOUS.

CA' THE YOWES.

Ca' the yowes to the knowes,*
Ca' them whare the heather grows,
Ca' them whare the burnie rows †
My bonnie dearie.

As I gaed down the water side,
There I met my shepherd lad,
He rowed me sweetly in his plaid,
And he ca'd me his dearie.

Will ye gang down the water side,
And see the waves sae sweetly glide
Beneath the hazels spreading wide?
The moon it shines fu' clearly.

I was bred up at nae sic school,
My shepherd lad, to play the fool;
And a' the day to sit in dool,
And naebody to see me.

Ye shall get gowns and ribbons meet,
Cauf-leather shoon upon your feet,
And in my arms ye'se lie and sleep,
And ye shall be my dearie.

* Knolls.   † Rolls.

If ye 'll but stand to what ye 've said,
I 'se gang wi' you, my shepherd lad;
And ye may row me in your plaid,
    And I shall be your dearie.

While waters wimple to the sea,
While day blinks in the lift sae hie;
Till clay-cauld death shall blin' my ee,
    Ye aye shall be my dearie.
                 ISABEL PAGAN.

THE SILLER CROUN.

" AND ye sall walk in silk attire,
    And siller hae to spare,
Gin ye 'll consent to be his bride,
    Nor think o' Donald mair."

O, wha wad buy a silken goun
    Wi' a puir broken heart?
Or what 's to me a siller croun
    Gin frae my love I part?

The mind whose meanest wish is pure
    Far dearest is to me,
And ere I 'm forced to break my faith,
    I 'll lay me doun an' dee.

For I hae vowed a virgin's vow
    My lover's fate to share,
An' he has gi'en to me his heart,
    And what can man do mair?

12

His mind and manners won my heart:
  He gratefu' took the gift;
And did I wish to seek it back,
  It wad be waur than theft.

The langest life can ne'er repay
  The love he bears to me,
And ere I 'm forced to break my faith,
  I 'll lay me doun an' dee.

SUSANNA BLAMIRE.

DUNCAN GRAY CAM' HERE TO WOO.

DUNCAN GRAY cam' here to woo—
    Ha, ha! the wooing o't!
On blythe Yule night when we were fou—
    Ha, ha! the wooing o't!
Maggie coost her head fu' high,
Looked asklent and unco skeigh,
Gart poor Duncan stand abeigh—
    Ha, ha! the wooing o't!

Duncan fleeched and Duncan prayed—
    Ha, ha! the wooing o't!
Meg was deaf as Ailsa craig—
    Ha, ha! the wooing o't!
Duncan sighed baith out and in,
Grat his een baith bleer't and blin',
Spak o' lowpin' o'er a linn—
    Ha, ha! the wooing o't!

Time and chance are but a tide—
    Ha, ha! the wooing o't!

Slighted love is sair to bide—
      Ha, ha! the wooing o't!
Shall I, like a fool, quoth he,
For a haughty hizzie dee?
She may gae to—France, for me!
      Ha, ha! the wooing o't!

How it comes let doctors tell—
      Ha, ha! the wooing o't!
Meg grew sick as he grew heal—
      Ha, ha! the wooing o't!
Something in her bosom wrings,—
For relief a sigh she brings;
And O, her een they speak sic things!
      Ha, ha! the wooing o't!

Duncan was a lad o' grace—
      Ha, ha! the wooing o't!
Maggie's was a piteous case—
      Ha, ha! the wooing o't!
Duncan could na be her death:
Swelling pity smoored his wrath.
Now they 're crouse and canty baith,
      Ha, ha! the wooing o't!

                    ROBERT BURNS.

HOW TO ASK AND HAVE.

" Oh, 't is time I should talk to your mother,
    Sweet Mary," says I.
"Oh, don't talk to my mother," says Mary,
    Beginning to cry:

" For my mother says men are deceivers,
    And never, I know, will consent;
She says girls in a hurry who marry
    At leisure repent."

" Then suppose I would talk to your father,
    Sweet Mary," says I.
" Oh, don't talk to my father," says Mary,
    Beginning to cry:
" For my father, he loves me so dearly,
    He 'll never consent I should go—
If you talk to my father," says Mary,
    " He 'll surely say ' No.' "

" Then how shall I get you, my jewel?
    Sweet Mary," says I.
" If your father and mother 's so cruel,
    Most surely I 'll die!"
" Oh, never say die, dear," says Mary:
    " A way now to save you I see:
Since my parents are both so contrary—
    You 'd better ask *me*."

SAMUEL LOVER.

LIVE IN MY HEART AND PAY NO RENT.

'VOURNEEN, when your days were bright,
Never an eye did I dare to lift to you,
But now, in your fortune's blight,
False ones are flying in sunshine that knew you;
    But still on one welcome true rely,
    Tho' the crops may fail, and the cow go dry,

And your cabin be burned, and all be spent,
Come, live in my heart and pay no rent;
　Come, come, live in my heart,
Live in my heart and pay no rent;
　Come, come, live in my heart,
Live in my heart, mavourneen!

'Vourneen, dry up those tears,
The sensible people will tell you to wait, dear,
But ah! in the wasting of Love's young years,
On our innocent hearts we 're committing a chate,
　　dear.
　For hearts when they 're young should make
　　the vow,
　For when they are old they don't know how;
So marry at once and you 'll not repent,
When you live in my heart and pay no rent,
　Come, come, live in my heart,
Live in my heart and pay no rent,
　Come, come, live in my heart,
Live in my heart, mavourneen!

SAMUEL LOVER.

WIDOW MACHREE.

Widow Machree, it 's no wonder you frown,—
　　Och hone! Widow Machree;
Faith, it ruins your looks, that same dirty black
　　gown,—
　　Och hone! Widow Machree;
　How altered your air,
　With that close cap you wear,—

'T is destroying your hair,
That should be flowing free:
Be no longer a churl
Of its black silken curl,—
    Och hone! Widow Machree.

Widow Machree, now the summer is come,—
        Och hone! Widow Machree;
When everything smiles, should a beauty look
        glum?
        Och hone! Widow Machree!
    See, the birds go in pairs,
    And the rabbits and hares;
    Why, even the bears
    Now in couples agree;
    And the mute little fish,
    Though they can't spake, they wish,—
        Och hone! Widow Machree!

Widow Machree, and when winter comes in,—
        Och hone! Widow Machree,—
To be poking the fire all alone is a sin,
        Och hone! Widow Machree!
    Sure the shovel and tongs
    To each other belongs,
    And the kettle sings songs
    Full of family glee;
    While alone with your cup
    Like a hermit you sup,
        Och hone! Widow Machree!

And how do you know, with the comforts I 've
        towld,—
        Och hone! Widow Machree!

But you 're keeping some poor fellow out in the
    cowld?
    Och hone! Widow Machree!
  With such sins on your head,
  Sure your peace would be fled;
  Could you sleep in your bed
  Without thinking to see
  Some ghost or some sprite,
  That would wake you at night,
    Crying " Och hone! Widow Machree! "

Then take my advice, darling Widow Machree,—
    Och hone! Widow Machree!—
And with my advice, faith, I wish you 'd take me,
    Och hone! Widow Machree!
  You 'd have me to desire
  Then to stir up the fire;
  And sure Hope is no liar
  In whispering to me
  That the ghosts would depart
  When you 'd me near your heart,—
    Och hone! Widow Machree!

               SAMUEL LOVER.

WIDOW MALONE.

Did you hear of the Widow Malone,
          Ohone!
Who lived in the town of Athlone,
          Alone!
  O, she melted the hearts
  Of the swains in them parts:

So lovely the Widow Malone.
>> Ohone!
So lovely the Widow Malone.

Of lovers she had a full score,
>> Or more,
And fortunes they all had galore,
>> In store;
From the minister down
To the clerk of the Crown
All were courting the Widow Malone,
>> Ohone!
All were courting the Widow Malone.

But so modest was Mistress Malone,
>> 'T was known
That no one could see her alone,
>> Ohone!
Let them ogle and sigh,
They could ne'er catch her eye,
So bashful the Widow Malone,
>> Ohone!
So bashful the Widow Malone.

Till one Misther O'Brien, from Clare
>> (How quare!
It 's little for blushing they care
>> Down there),
Put his arm round her waist,—
Gave ten kisses at laste,—
" O," says he, " you 're my Molly Malone,
>> My own!
O," says he, " you 're my Molly Malone!"

And the widow they all thought so shy,
          My eye!
Ne'er thought of a simper or sigh,—
          For why?
  But, " Lucius," says she,
  " Since you 've now made so free,
You may marry your Mary Malone.
          Ohone!
You may marry your Mary Malone."

There 's a moral contained in my song,
          Not wrong;
And one comfort, it 's not very long,
          But strong,—
  If for widows you die,
  Learn to kiss, not sigh;
For they 're all like sweet Mistress Malone,
          Ohone!
O, they 're all like sweet Mistress Malone!
               CHARLES LEVER.

I 'M NOT MYSELF AT ALL.

Oh, I 'm not myself at all,
  Molly dear, Molly dear!
I 'm not myself at all.
  Nothing caring, nothing knowing,
  'T is after you I 'm going,
  Faith, your shadow 't is I 'm growing,
    Molly dear, Molly dear!
And I 'm not myself at all.
  Th' other day I went confessin',
  And I asked the father's blessin',

" But," says I, " don't give me one intirely:
    For I fretted so last year,
      But the half of me is here,
So give the other half to Molly Brierly."
      Oh, I 'm not myself at all!
    Oh, I 'm not myself at all,
        Molly dear, Molly dear!
  My appetite 's so small:
      I once could pick a goose;
      But my buttons is no use,
      Faith, my tightest coat is loose,
        Molly dear.
    And I 'm not myself at all!
      If thus it is I waste,
      You 'd betther, dear, make haste,
Before your lover 's gone away intirely;
      If you don't soon change your mind,
      Not a bit of me you 'll find,
And what 'ud you think o' that, Molly Brierly?
      Oh, I 'm not myself at all!

    Oh, my shadow on the wall,
        Molly dear, Molly dear,
  Isn't like myself at all,
      For I 've got so very thin,
      Myself says 't isn't him,
      But that purty girl so slim,
        Molly dear.
    And I 'm not myself at all!
      If thus I smaller grew,
      All fretting, dear, for you,
'T is you should make up the deficiency,
      So just let Father Taaff

Make you my betther half,
And you will not the worse for the addition
    be—
  Oh, I 'm not myself at all!
I 'll be not myself at all,
    Molly dear, Molly dear,
  Till you my own I call!
    Since a change o'er me there came
    Sure you might change your name,
    And 't would just come to the same,
      Molly dear,
  'T would just come to the same:
    For if you and I were one,
    All confusion would be gone,
And 't would simplify the matther intirely;
    And 't would save us so much bother,
    When we 'd both be one another—
So listen now to rayson, Molly Brierly;
    Oh, I 'm not myself at all!
              SAMUEL LOVER.

I PRITHEE SEND ME BACK MY HEART.

I PRITHEE send me back my heart,
  Since I cannot have thine;
For if from yours you will not part,
  Why then shouldst thou have mine?

Yet, now I think on 't, let it lie;
  To find it were in vain;
For thou 'st a thief in either eye
  Would steal it back again.

Why should two hearts in one breast lie,
  And yet not lodge together?
O Love! where is thy sympathy
  If thus our breasts thou sever?

But love is such a mystery,
  I cannot find it out;
For when I think I 'm best resolved
  I then am most in doubt.

Then farewell care, and farewell woe;
  I will no longer pine;
For I 'll believe I have her heart
  As much as she has mine.

                    SIR JOHN SUCKLING.

LOVE ME LITTLE, LOVE ME LONG.

ORIGINALLY PRINTED IN 1569.

LOVE me little, love me long!
Is the burden of my song:
Love that is too hot and strong
        Burneth soon to waste.
Still I would not have thee cold,—
Not too backward, nor too bold;
Love that lasteth till 't is old
        Fadeth not in haste.
Love me little, love me long!
Is the burden of my song.

If thou lovest me too much,
'T will not prove as true a touch;

Love me little more than such,—
    For I fear the end.
I'm with little well content,
And a little from thee sent
Is enough, with true intent
    To be steadfast, friend.

Say thou lovest me, while thou live
I to thee my love will give,
Never dreaming to deceive
    While that life endures;
Nay, and after death, in sooth,
I to thee will keep my truth,
As now when in my May of youth:
    This my love assures.

Constant love is moderate ever,
And it will through life persever;
Give me that with true endeavor,—
    I will it restore.
A suit of durance let it be,
For all weathers,—that for me,—
For the land or for the sea:
    Lasting evermore.

Winter's cold or summer's heat,
Autumn's tempests on it beat;
It can never know defeat,
    Never can rebel.
Such the love that I would gain,
Such the love, I tell thee plain,
Thou must give, or woo in vain:
    So to thee—farewell!

                ANONYMOUS.

THE COURTIN'.

God makes sech nights, all white an' still
    Fur 'z you can look or listen;
Moonshine an' snow on field an' hill,
    All silence an' all glisten.

Zekle crep' up quite unbeknown
    An' peeked in thru' the winder,
An' there sot Huldy all alone,
    'Ith no one nigh to hender.

A fireplace filled the room's one side,
    With half a cord o' wood in—
There warn't no stoves (tell comfort died)
    To bake ye to a puddin'.

The wa'nut logs shot sparkles out
    Towards the pootiest, bless her!
An' leetle flames danced all about
    The chiny on the dresser.

Agin the chimbley crook-necks hung,
    An' in amongst 'em rusted
The ole queen's arm thet gran'ther Young
    Fetched back from Concord busted.

The very room, coz she was in,
    Seemed warm from floor to ceilin',
An' she looked full ez rosy agin
    Ez the apples she was peelin'.

'T was kin o' kingdom-come to look
   On sech a blessèd cretur,
A dogrose blushin' to a brook
   Ain't modester nor sweeter.

He was six foot o' man, A 1,
   Clean grit an' human natur';
None couldn't quicker pitch a ton,
   Nor dror a furrer straighter.

He 'd sparked it with full twenty gals,
   Hed squired 'em, danced 'em, druv 'em,
Fust this one, an' then thet, by spells—
   All is, he couldn't love 'em.

But long o' her his veins 'ould run
   All crinkly like curled maple,
The side she breshed felt full o' sun
   Ez a south slope in Ap'il.

She thought no v'ice hed such a swing
   Ez hisn in the choir;
My! when he made Ole Hundred ring,
   She *knowed* the Lord was nigher.

An' she 'd blush scarlit, right in prayer,
   When her new meetin'-bunnet
Felt somehow thru' its crown a pair
   O' blue eyes sot upon it.

Thet night, I tell ye, she looked *some!*
   She seemed to 've gut a new soul,

For she felt sartin-sure he 'd come,
Down to her very shoe-sole.

She heered a foot, an' knowed it tu,
A-raspin' on the scraper,—
All ways to once her feelin's flew
Like sparks in burnt-up paper.

He kin' o' l'itered on the mat,
Some doubtfle o' the sekle,
His heart kep' goin' pitty-pat,
But hern went pity Zekle.

An' yit she gin her cheer a jerk
Ez though she wished him furder,
An' on her apples kep' to work,
Parin' away like murder.

"You want to see my Pa, I s'pose?"
"Wall no . . . I come dasignin'"—
"To see my Ma? She 's sprinklin' clo'es
Agin to-morrer's i'nin'."

To say why gals act so or so,
Or don't, 'ould be presumin';
Mebby to mean *yes* an' say *no*
Comes nateral to women.

He stood a spell on one foot fust,
Then stood a spell on t' other,
An' on which one he felt the wust
He couldn't ha' told ye nuther.

Says he, " I 'd better call agin; "
  Says she, " Think likely, Mister; "
Thet last word pricked him like a pin,
  An' . . . Wal, he up an' kist her.

When Ma bimeby upon 'em slips,
  Huldy sot pale ez ashes,
All kin' o' smily roun' the lips
  An' teary roun' the lashes.

For she was jes' the quiet kind
  Whose naters never vary,
Like streams that keep a summer mind
  Snow-hid in Jenooary.

The blood clost roun' her heart felt glued
  Too tight for all expressin',
Tell mother see how metters stood,
  And gin 'em both her blessin'.

Then her red come back like the tide
  Down to the Bay o' Fundy,
An' all I know is they was cried
  In meetin' come nex' Sunday.

                    JAMES RUSSELL LOWELL.

———

POPPING CORN.*

AND there they sat, a-popping corn,
  John Styles and Susan Cutter—
John Styles as fat as any ox,
  And Susan fat as butter.

* From " Famous Single and Fugitive Poems."—ROSSITER
JOHNSON, Editor.   Henry Holt & Co., Publishers.
  13

And there they sat and shelled the corn,
    And raked and stirred the fire,
And talked of different kinds of corn,
    And hitched their chairs up nigher.

Then Susan she the popper shook,
    Then John he shook the popper,
Till both their faces grew as red
    As saucepans made of copper.

And then they shelled, and popped, and ate,
    All kinds of fun a-poking,
While he haw-hawed at her remarks,
    And she laughed at his joking.

And still they popped, and still they ate—
    John's mouth was like a hopper—
And stirred the fire, and sprinkled salt,
    And shook and shook the popper.

The clock struck nine—the clock struck ten,
    And still the corn kept popping;
It struck eleven, and then struck twelve,
    And still no signs of stopping.

And John he ate, and Sue she thought—
    The corn did pop and patter—
Till John cried out, " The corn 's a-fire!
    Why, Susan, what 's the matter? "

Said she, " John Styles, it 's one o'clock;
    You 'll die of indigestion;
I 'm sick of all this popping corn—
    Why don't you pop the question? "

ANONYMOUS.

THE FRIAR OF ORDERS GRAY.

It was a friar of orders gray
  Walked forth to tell his beads;
And he met with a lady fair
  Clad in a pilgrim's weeds.

" Now Christ thee save, thou reverend friar;
  I pray thee tell to me,
If ever at yon holy shrine
  My true-love thou didst see."

" And how should I know your true-love
  From many another one? "
" O, by his cockle hat, and staff,
  And by his sandal shoon.

" But chiefly by his face and mien,
  That were so fair to view;
His flaxen locks that sweetly curled,
  And eyes of lovely blue."

" O lady, he is dead and gone!
  Lady, he's dead and gone!
And at his head a green grass turf,
  And at his heels a stone.

" Within these holy cloisters long
  He languished, and he died,
Lamenting of a lady's love,
  And 'plaining of her pride.

" Here bore him barefaced on his bier
  Six proper youths and tall,
And many a tear bedewed his grave
  Within yon kirkyard wall."

" And art thou dead, thou gentle youth?
  And art thou dead and gone?
And didst thou die for love of me?
  Break, cruel heart of stone!"

" O, weep not, lady, weep not so;
  Some ghostly comfort seek;
Let not vain sorrow rive thy heart,
  Nor tears bedew thy cheek."

" O, do not, do not, holy friar,
  My sorrow now reprove;
For I have lost the sweetest youth
  That e'er won lady's love.

" And now, alas! for thy sad loss
  I'll evermore weep and sigh;
For thee I only wished to live,
  For thee I wish to die."

" Weep no more, lady, weep no more,
  Thy sorrow is in vain;
For violets plucked, the sweetest showers
  Will ne'er make grow again.

" Our joys as wingèd dreams do fly;
  Why then should sorrow last?

Since grief but aggravates thy loss,
   Grieve not for what is past."

" O, say not so, thou holy friar;
   I pray thee, say not so;
For since my true-love died for me,
   'T is meet my tears should flow.

" And will he never come again?
   Will he ne'er come again?
Ah, no! he is dead, and laid in his grave,
   Forever to remain.

" His cheek was redder than the rose;
   The comeliest youth was he!
But he is dead and laid in his grave:
   Alas, and woe is me!"

" Sigh no more, lady, sigh no more,
   Men were deceivers ever:
One foot on sea and one on land,
   To one thing constant never.

" Hadst thou been fond, he had been false,
   And left thee sad and heavy;
For young men ever were fickle found,
   Since summer trees were leafy."

" Now say not so, thou holy friar,
   I pray thee say not so;
My love he had the truest heart,
   O, he was ever true!

" And art thou dead, thou much-loved youth,
    And didst thou die for me?
Then farewell home; for evermore
    A pilgrim I will be.

" But first upon my true-love's grave
    My weary limbs I 'll lay,
And thrice I 'll kiss the green-grass turf
    That wraps his breathless clay."

" Yet stay, fair lady; rest awhile
    Beneath this cloister wall;
The cold wind through the hawthorn blows,
    And drizzly rain doth fall."

" O, stay me not, thou holy friar,
    O, stay me not, I pray,
No drizzly rain that falls on me
    Can wash my fault away."

" Yet stay, fair lady, turn again,
    And dry those pearly tears;
For see, beneath this gown of gray
    Thy own true-love appears.

" Here forced by grief and hopeless love,
    These holy weeds I sought;
And here, amid these lonely walls,
    To end my days I thought.

" But haply, for my year of grace
    Is not yet passed away,

Might I still hope to win thy love,
  No longer would I stay."

" Now farewell grief, and welcome joy
  Once more unto my heart;
For since I have found thee, lovely youth,
  We nevermore will part."

Adapted from old ballads by THOMAS PERCY.

THE HERMIT.

FROM " THE VICAR OF WAKEFIELD."

" TURN, gentle Hermit of the dale,
  And guide my lonely way
To where yon taper cheers the vale
  With hospitable ray.

" For here forlorn and lost I tread,
  With fainting steps and slow;
Where wilds, immeasurably spread,
  Seem lengthening as I go."

" Forbear, my son," the Hermit cries,
  " To tempt the dangerous gloom;
For yonder faithless phantom flies
  To lure thee to thy doom.

" Here to the houseless child of want
  My door is open still;
And though my portion is but scant,
  I give it with good will.

" Then turn to-night, and freely share
   Whate'er my cell bestows;
My rushy couch and frugal fare,
   My blessing and repose.

" No flocks that range the valley free
   To slaughter I condemn;
Taught by that Power that pities me,
   I learn to pity them:

" But from the mountain's grassy side
   A guiltless feast I bring;
A scrip with herbs and fruits supplied,
   And water from the spring.

" Then, pilgrim, turn, thy cares forego;
   All earth-born cares are wrong:
Man wants but little here below,
   Nor wants that little long."

Soft as the dew from heaven descends,
   His gentle accents fell:
The modest stranger lowly bends,
   And follows to the cell.

Far in a wilderness obscure
   The lonely mansion lay;
A refuge to the neighboring poor,
   And strangers led astray.

No stores beneath its humble thatch
   Required a master's care:

The wicket, opening with a latch,
  Received the harmless pair.

And now, when busy crowds retire
  To take their evening rest,
The Hermit trimmed his little fire,
  And cheered his pensive guest;

And spread his vegetable store,
  And gayly pressed and smiled;
And, skilled in legendary lore,
  The lingering hours beguiled.

Around, in sympathetic mirth,
  Its tricks the kitten tries;
The cricket chirrups on the hearth;
  The crackling fagot flies.

But nothing could a charm impart
  To soothe the stranger's woe;
For grief was heavy at his heart,
  And tears began to flow.

His rising cares the Hermit spied,
  With answering care opprest:
" And whence, unhappy youth," he cried,
  " The sorrows of thy breast?

" From better habitations spurned,
  Reluctant dost thou rove?
Or grieve for friendship unreturned,
  Or unregarded love?

" Alas! the joys that fortune brings
   Are trifling, and decay;
And those who prize the paltry things
   More trifling still than they.

" And what is friendship but a name,
   A charm that lulls to sleep;
A shade that follows wealth or fame,
   And leaves the wretch to weep?

" And love is still an emptier sound,
   The modern fair one's jest;
On earth unseen, or only found
   To warm the turtle's nest.

" For shame, fond youth! thy sorrows hush,
   And spurn the sex," he said;
But while he spoke, a rising blush
   His lovelorn guest betrayed.

Surprised, he sees new beauties rise,
   Swift mantling to the view;
Like colors o'er the morning skies,
   As bright, as transient too.

The bashful look, the rising breast,
   Alternate spread alarms:
The lovely stranger stands confest
   A maid in all her charms.

" And, ah! forgive a stranger rude,
   A wretch forlorn," she cried;

" Whose feet unhallowed thus intrude
   Where heaven and you reside.

" But let a maid thy pity share,
   Whom love has taught to stray;
Who seeks for rest, but finds despair
   Companion of her way.

" My father lived beside the Tyne,
   A wealthy lord was he;
And all his wealth was marked as mine,—
   He had but only me.

" To win me from his tender arms,
   Unnumbered suitors came;
Who praised me for imputed charms,
   And felt, or feigned, a flame.

" Each hour a mercenary crowd
   With richest proffers strove:
Among the rest young Edwin bowed,
   But never talked of love.

" In humble, simplest habit clad,
   No wealth or power had he;
Wisdom and worth were all he had,
   But these were all to me.

" And when beside me in the dale
   He carolled lays of love,
His breath lent fragrance to the gale
   And music to the grove.

" The blossom opening to the day,
    The dews of heaven refined,
Could naught of purity display
    To emulate his mind.

" The dew, the blossoms of the tree,
    With charms inconstant shine;
Their charms were his, but, woe to me!
    Their constancy was mine.

" For still I tried each fickle art,
    Importunate and vain;
And while his passion touched my heart,
    I triumphed in his pain:

" Till, quite dejected with my scorn,
    He left me to my pride;
And sought a solitude forlorn,
    In secret, where he died.

" But mine the sorrow, mine the fault,
    And well my life shall pay;
I 'll seek the solitude he sought,
    And stretch me where he lay.

" And there forlorn, despairing, hid,
    I 'll lay me down and die;
'T was so for me that Edwin did,
    And so for him will I."

" Forbid it, Heaven!" the Hermit cried,
    And clasped her to his breast:

The wondering fair one turned to chide,—
    'T was Edwin's self that pressed.

" Turn, Angelina, ever dear,
    My charmer, turn to see
Thy own, thy long-lost Edwin here,
    Restored to love and thee.

" Thus let me hold thee to my heart,
    And every care resign:
And shall we never, never part,
    My life,—my all that 's mine?

" No, never from this hour to part,
    We 'll live and love so true:
The sigh that rends thy constant heart
    Shall break thy Edwin's too."

                    OLIVER GOLDSMITH.

THE LAIRD O' COCKPEN.

THE Laird o' Cockpen he 's proud and he 's great,
His mind is ta'en up with the things o' the state;
He wanted a wife his braw house to keep,
But favor wi' wooin' was fashious to seek.

Doun by the dyke-side a lady did dwell,
At his table-head he thought she 'd look well;
M'Clish's ae daughter o' Claverse-ha' Lee,
A penniless lass wi' a lang pedigree.

His wig was weel pouthered, and guid as when
    new;
His waistcoat was white, his coat it was blue;

He put on a ring, a sword, and cocked hat,—
And wha could refuse the Laird wi' a' that?

He took the gray mare, and rade cannilie,—
And rapped at the yett o' Claverse-ha' Lee;
"Gae tell Mistress Jean to come speedily ben:
She's wanted to speak wi' the Laird o' Cockpen."

Mistress Jean she was makin' the elder-flower
    wine;
"And what brings the Laird at sic a like time?"
She put aff her apron, and on her silk gown,
Her mutch wi' red ribbons, and gaed awa' down.

And when she cam' ben, he boued fu' low,
And what was his errand he soon let her know.
Amazed was the Laird when the lady said, Na,
And wi' a laigh curtsie she turnèd awa'.

Dumfoundered he was, but nae sigh did he gi'e;
He mounted his mare, and rade cannilie,
And aften he thought, as he gaed through the
    glen,
"She's daft to refuse the Laird o' Cockpen."

And now that the Laird his exit had made,
Mistress Jean she reflected on what she had said;
"O, for ane I'll get better, it's waur I'll get ten;
I was daft to refuse the Laird o' Cockpen."

Neist time that the Laird and the lady were seen,
They were gaun arm and arm to the kirk on the
    green;

Now she sits in the ha' like a weel-tappit hen,
But as yet there 's nae chickens appeared at Cockpen.

CAROLINA OLIPHANT, BARONESS NAIRNE.

OTHELLO'S DEFENCE.

FROM " OTHELLO," ACT I. SC. 3.

OTHELLO.—Most potent, grave, and reverend
 signiors,
My very noble and approved good masters,—
That I have ta'en away this old man's daughter,
It is most true; true, I have married her:
The very head and front of my offending
Hath this extent, no more. Rude am I in my
 speech,
And little blessed with the soft phrase of peace;
For since these arms of mine had seven years'
 pith,
Till now some nine moons wasted, they have
 used
Their dearest action in the tented field;
And little of this great world can I speak,
More than pertains to feats of broil and battle;
And therefore little shall I grace my cause
In speaking for myself. Yet, by your gracious
 patience,
I will a round unvarnished tale deliver
Of my whole course of love; what drugs, what
 charms,
What conjuration, and what mighty magic,—
For such proceeding I am charged withal,—

I won his daughter.

. . . . .

I 'll present
How I did thrive in this fair lady's love,
And she in mine.

. . . . .

Her father loved me; oft invited me;
Still questioned me the story of my life,
From year to year;—the battles, sieges, fortunes,
That I have passed.
I ran it through, even from my boyish days,
To the very moment that he bade me tell it:
Wherein I spake of most disastrous chances,
Of moving accidents by flood and field;
Of hair-breadth 'scapes i' the imminent deadly
         breach;
Of being taken by the insolent foe,
And sold to slavery; of my redemption thence,
And portance in my travel's history:
Wherein of antres vast, and deserts idle,
Rough quarries, rocks, and hills whose heads
         touch heaven,
It was my hint to speak,—such was the process;
And of the Cannibals that each other eat,
The Anthropophagi, and men whose heads
Do grow beneath their shoulders. This to hear,
Would Desdemona seriously incline:
But still the house affairs would draw her thence;
Which ever as she could with haste despatch,
She 'd come again, and with a greedy ear
Devour up my discourse. Which I observing,
Took once a pliant hour; and found good means
To draw from her a prayer of earnest heart,

That I would all my pilgrimage dilate,
Whereof by parcels she had something heard,
But not intentively: I did consent;
And often did beguile her of her tears,
When I did speak of some distressful stroke,
That my youth suffered. My story being done,
She gave me for my pains a world of sighs:
She swore,—in faith 't was strange, 't was pass-
    ing strange;
'T was pitiful, 't was wondrous pitiful:
She wished she had not heard it; yet she wished
That Heaven had made her such a man: she
    thanked me;
And bade me, if I had a friend that loved her,
I should teach him how to tell my story,
And that would woo her. Upon this hint, I spake:
She loved me for the dangers I had passed,
And I loved her that she did pity them.
This only is the witchcraft I have used:
Here comes the lady, let her witness it.

SHAKESPEARE.

THE EARL O' QUARTERDECK.

A NEW OLD BALLAD.

THE wind it blew, and the ship it flew;
  And it was " Hey for hame!
And ho for hame!" But the skipper cried,
  " Haud her oot o'er the saut sea faem."

Then up and spoke the King himsel':
  " Haud on for Dumferline!"
14

Quo the skipper, " Ye 're king upo' the land—
    I'm king upo' the brine."

And he took the helm intil his hand,
    And he steered the ship sae free;
Wi' the wind astarn, he crowded sail,
    And stood right out to sea.

Quo the king, " There 's treason in this I vow;
    This is something underhand!
'Bout ship!" Quo the skipper, " Yer grace for-
        gets
    Ye are king but o' the land!"

And still he held to the open sea;
    And the east-wind sank behind;
And the west had a bitter word to say,
    Wi' a white-sea roarin' wind.

And he turned her head into the north.
    Said the king: " Gar fling him o'er."
Quo the fearless skipper: " It 's a' ye 're worth!
    Ye 'll ne'er see Scotland more."

The king crept down the cabin-stair,
    To drink the gude French wine.
And up she came, his daughter fair,
    And luikit ower the brine.

She turned her face to the drivin' hail,
    To the hail but and the weet;
Her snood it brak, and, as lang 's hersel',
    Her hair drave out i' the sleet.

She turned her face frae the drivin' win'—
  " What 's that ahead? " quo she.
The skipper he threw himsel' frae the win',
  And he drove the helm a-lee.

" Put to yer hand, my lady fair!
  Put to yer hand," quo he;
" Gin she dinna face the win' the mair,
  It 's the waur for you and me."

For the skipper kenned that strength is strength,
  Whether woman's or man's at last.
To the tiller the lady she laid her han',
  And the ship laid her cheek to the blast.

For that slender body was full o' soul,
  And the will is mair than shape;
As the skipper saw when they cleared the berg,
  And he heard her quarter scrape.

Quo the skipper: " Ye are a lady fair,
  And a princess grand to see;
But ye are a woman, and a man wad sail
  To hell in yer company."

She liftit a pale and queenly face;
  Her een flashed, and syne they swim.
" And what for no to heaven? " she says,
  And she turned awa' frae him.

But she took na her han' frae the good ship's helm,
  Until the day did daw;

And the skipper he spak, but what he said
  It was said atween them twa.

And then the good ship she lay to,
  With the land far on the lee;
And up came the king upo' the deck,
  Wi' wan face and bluidshot ee.

The skipper he louted to the king:
  " Gae wa', gae wa'," said the king.
Said the king, like a prince, " I was a' wrang,
  Put on this ruby ring."

And the wind blew lowne, and the stars cam' oot,
  And the ship turned to the shore;
And, afore the sun was up again,
  They saw Scotland ance more.

That day the ship hung at the pier-heid,
  And the king he stept on the land.
" Skipper, kneel down," the king he said,
  " Hoo daur ye afore me stand? "

The skipper he louted on his knee,
  The king his blade he drew:
Said the king, " How daured ye contre me?
  I 'm aboard my ain ship noo.

" I canna mak ye a king," said he,
  " For the Lord alone can do that;
And besides ye took it intil yer ain han'
  And crooned yersel' sae pat!

" But wi' what ye will I redeem my ring;
  For ance I am at your beck.
And first, as ye loutit Skipper o' Doon,
  Rise up Yerl o' Quarterdeck."

The skipper he rose and looked at the king
  In his een for all his croon;
Said the skipper, " Here is yer grace's ring,
  And yer daughter is my boon."

The reid blude sprang into the king's face,—
  A wrathful man to see:
" The rascal loon abuses our grace;
  Gae hang him upon yon tree."

But the skipper he sprang aboard his ship,
  And he drew his biting blade;
And he struck the chain that held her fast,
  But the iron was ower weel made.

And the king he blew a whistle loud;
  And tramp, tramp, down the pier,
Cam' twenty riders on twenty steeds,
  Clankin' wi' spur and spear.

" He saved your life!" cried the lady fair;
  " His life ye daurna spill!"
" Will ye come atween me and my hate?"
  Quo the lady, " And that I will!"

And on cam' the knights wi' spur and spear,
  For they heard the iron ring.

"Gin ye care na for yer father's grace,
  Mind ye that I am the king."

" I kneel to my father for his grace,
  Right lowly on my knee;
But I stand and look the king in the face,
  For the skipper is king o' me."

She turned and she sprang upo' the deck,
  And the cable splashed in the sea.
The good ship spread her wings sae white,
  And away with the skipper goes she.

Now was not this a king's daughter,
  And a brave lady beside?
And a woman with whom a man might sail
  Into the heaven wi' pride?

GEORGE MACDONALD.

AUX ITALIENS.

At Paris it was, at the opera there;
  And she looked like a queen in a book that
      night,
With the wreath of pearl in her raven hair,
  And the brooch on her breast so bright.

Of all the operas that Verdi wrote,
  The best, to my taste, is the Trovatore;
And Mario can soothe, with a tenor note,
  The souls in purgatory.

The moon on the tower slept soft as snow;
  And who was not thrilled in the strangest way,

As we heard him sing, while the gas burned low,
 "*Non ti scordar di me*"?

The emperor there, in his box of state,
 Looked grave, as if he had just then seen
The red flag wave from the city gate,
 Where his eagles in bronze had been.

The empress, too, had a tear in her eye:
 You 'd have said that her fancy had gone back
 again,
For one moment, under the old blue sky,
 To the old glad life in Spain.

Well! there in our front-row box we sat
 Together, my bride betrothed and I;
My gaze was fixed on my opera hat,
 And hers on the stage hard by.

And both were silent, and both were sad;—
 Like a queen she leaned on her full white arm,
With that regal, indolent air she had;
 So confident of her charm!

I have not a doubt she was thinking then
 Of her former lord, good soul that he was,
Who died the richest and roundest of men,
 The Marquis of Carabas.

I hope that, to get to the kingdom of heaven,
 Through a needle's eye he had not to pass;
I wish him well for the jointure given
 To my lady of Carabas.

Meanwhile, I was thinking of my first love
  As I had not been thinking of aught for years;
Till over my eyes there began to move
  Something that felt like tears.

I thought of the dress that she wore last time,
  When we stood 'neath the cypress-trees to-
      gether,
In that lost land, in that soft clime,
  In the crimson evening weather;

Of that muslin dress (for the eve was hot);
  And her warm white neck in its golden chain;
And her full soft hair, just tied in a knot,
  And falling loose again;

And the jasmine flower in her fair young breast;
  (O the faint, sweet smell of that jasmine
      flower!)
And the one bird sings alone to his nest;
  And the one star over the tower.

I thought of our little quarrels and strife,
  And the letter that brought me back my ring;
And it all seemed then, in the waste of life,
  Such a very little thing!

For I thought of her grave below the hill,
  Which the sentinel cypress-tree stands over:
And I thought, "Were she only living still,
  How I could forgive her and love her!"

And I swear, as I thought of her thus, in that
      hour,
  And of how, after all, old things are best,

That I smelt the smell of that jasmine flower
  Which she used to wear in her breast.

It smelt so faint, and it smelt so sweet,
  It made me creep, and it made me cold!
Like the scent that steals from the crumbling
      sheet
  Where a mummy is half unrolled.

And I turned and looked: she was sitting there,
  In a dim box over the stage; and drest
In that muslin dress, with that full soft hair,
  And that jasmine in her breast!

I was here, and she was there;
  And the glittering horseshoe curved between!—
From my bride betrothed, with her raven hair
  And her sumptuous scornful mien,

To my early love with her eyes downcast,
  And over her primrose face the shade,
(In short, from the future back to the past,)
  There was but a step to be made.

To my early love from my future bride
  One moment I looked. Then I stole to the door,
I traversed the passage; and down at her side
  I was sitting, a moment more.

My thinking of her, or the music's strain,
  Or something which never will be exprest,
Had brought her back from the grave again,
  With the jasmine in her breast.

She is not dead, and she is not wed!
  But she loves me now, and she loved me then!
And the very first word that her sweet lips said,
  My heart grew youthful again.

The marchioness there, of Carabas,
  She is wealthy, and young, and handsome still;
And but for her—well, we 'll let that pass;
  She may marry whomever she will.

But I will marry my own first love,
  With her primrose face, for old things are best;
And the flower in her bosom, I prize it above
  The brooch in my lady's breast.

The world is filled with folly and sin,
  And love must cling where it can, I say:
For beauty is easy enough to win;
  But one isn't loved every day.

And I think, in the lives of most women and men,
    There 's a moment when all would go smooth
        and even,
If only the dead could find out when
  To come back and be forgiven.

But O, the smell of that jasmine flower!
  And O, that music! and O, the way
That voice rang out from the donjon tower,
  Non ti scordar di me,
    Non ti scordar di me!

                    ROBERT BULWER LYTTON (*Owen Meredith*).

V.

CAUTIONS AND COMPLAINTS.

———

LET NOT WOMAN E'ER COMPLAIN.

Let not woman e'er complain
  Of inconstancy in love;
Let not woman e'er complain
  Fickle man is apt to rove;
Look abroad through Nature's range,
Nature's mighty law is change;
Ladies, would it not be strange
  Man should then a monster prove?

Mark the winds, and mark the skies;
  Ocean's ebb and ocean's flow;
Sun and moon but set to rise,
  Round and round the seasons go.
Why then ask of silly man,
To oppose great Nature's plan?
We'll be constant while we can,—
  You can be no more, you know.

ROBERT BURNS.

TO CHLOE.

AN APOLOGY FOR GOING INTO THE COUNTRY.

CHLOE, we must not always be in heaven,
  Forever toying, ogling, kissing, billing;
The joys for which I thousands would have
    given,
  Will presently be scarcely worth a shilling.

Thy neck is fairer than the Alpine snows,
  And, sweetly swelling, beats the down of doves;
Thy cheek of health, a rival to the rose;
  Thy pouting lips, the throne of all the loves;
Yet, though thus beautiful beyond expression,
That beauty fadeth by too much possession.

Economy in love is peace to nature,
Much like economy in worldly matter;
We should be prudent, never live too fast;
Profusion will not, cannot always last.

Lovers are really spendthrifts,—'t is a shame,—
Nothing their thoughtless, wild career can tame,
  Till penury stares them in the face;
And when they find an empty purse,

Grown calmer, wiser, how the fault they curse,
  And, limping, look with such a sneaking grace!
Job's war-horse fierce, his neck with thunder
    hung,
Sunk to an humble hack that carries dung.

Smell to the queen of flowers, the fragrant rose—
Smell twenty times—and then, my dear, thy nose
Will tell thee (not so much for scent athirst)
The twentieth drank less flavor than the first.

Love, doubtless, is the sweetest of all fellows;
   Yet often should the little god retire.
Absence, dear Chloe, is a pair of bellows,
   That keeps alive the sacred fire.
                DR. JOHN WOLCOTT (*Peter Pindar*).

A WOMAN'S ANSWER.

I WILL not let you say a woman's part
   Must be to give exclusive love alone;
Dearest, although I love you so, my heart
   Answers a thousand claims besides your own.

I love,—what do I not love? Earth and air
   Find space within my heart, and myriad things
You would not deign to heed are cherished there,
   And vibrate on its very inmost strings.

I love the summer, with her ebb and flow
   Of light and warmth and music, that have
      nursed
Her tender buds to blossoms . . . and you know
   It was in the summer that I saw you first.

I love the winter dearly too, . . . but then
   I owe it so much; on a winter's day,
Bleak, cold, and stormy, you returned again
   When you had been those weary months away.

I love the stars like friends; so many nights
　　I gazed at them, when you were far from me,
Till I grew blind with tears . . . those far-off
　　　lights
　　Could watch you, whom I longed in vain to see.

I love the flowers; happy hours lie
　　Shut up within their petals close and fast:
You have forgotten, dear; but they and I
　　Keep every fragment of the golden Past.

I love, too, to be loved; all loving praise
　　Seems like a crown upon my life,—to make
It better worth the giving, and to raise
　　Still nearer to your own the heart you take.

I love all good and noble souls;—I heard
　　One speak of you but lately, and for days,
Only to think of it, my soul was stirred
　　In tender memory of such generous praise.

I love all those who love you, all who owe
　　Comfort to you; and I can find regret
Even for those poorer hearts who once could
　　　know,
　　And once could love you, and can now forget.

Well, is my heart so narrow,—I, who spare
　　Love for all these? Do I not even hold
My favorite books in special tender care,
　　And prize them as a miser does his gold?

The poets that you used to read to me
　　While summer twilights faded in the sky;

But most of all I think Aurora Leigh,
  Because—because—do you remember why?

Will you be jealous? Did you guess before
  I loved so many things?—Still you the best:—
Dearest, remember that I love you more,
  O, more a thousand times, than all the rest!

ADELAIDE ANNE PROCTER.

LOVE'S BLINDNESS.

SONNET CXLVIII.

O ME! what eyes hath Love put in my head
Which have no correspondence with true sight!
Or, if they have, where is my judgment fled
That censures falsely what they see aright?
If that be fair whereon my false eyes dote,
What means the world to say it is not so?
If it be not, then love doth well denote
Love's eye is not so true as all men's: No,
How can it? O how can Love's eye be true,
That is so vexed with watching and with tears?
No marvel then, though I mistake my view:
The sun itself sees not till heaven clears.
    O cunning Love! with tears thou keep'st me
        blind,
    Lest eyes well-seeing thy foul faults should
        find!

SHAKESPEARE.

"FULL MANY A GLORIOUS MORNING."

SONNET XXXIII.

FULL many a glorious morning have I seen
Flatter the mountain-tops with sovereign eye,
Kissing with golden face the meadows green,
Gilding pale streams with heavenly alchemy;
Anon permit the basest clouds to ride,
With ugly rack on his celestial face,
And from the forlorn world his visage hide,
Stealing unseen to west with this disgrace:
Even so my sun one early morn did shine
With all-triumphant splendor on my brow;
But out, alack! he was but one hour mine,
The region cloud hath masked him from me now.
   Yet him for this my love no whit disdaineth;
    Suns of the world may stain when heaven's sun
      staineth.

SHAKESPEARE.

ALEXIS, HERE SHE STAYED.

ALEXIS, here she stayed; among these pines,
Sweet hermitress, she did alone repair;
Here did she spread the treasure of her hair,
More rich than that brought from the Colchian
    mines.
She sate her by these muskèd eglantines,
The happy place the print seems yet to bear;
Her voice did sweeten here thy sugared lines,

To which winds, trees, beasts, birds, did lend
     their ear.
Me here she first perceived, and here a morn
Of bright carnations did o'erspread her face;
Here did she sigh, here first my hopes were born,
And I first got a pledge of promised grace:
  But, ah! what served it to be happy so,
  Sith passèd pleasures double but new woe?
            WILLIAM DRUMMOND.

RIVALRY IN LOVE.

  OF all the torments, all the cares,
    With which our lives are curst;
  Of all the plagues a lover bears,
    Sure rivals are the worst!
  By partners in each other kind,
    Afflictions easier grow;
  In love alone we hate to find
    Companions of our woe.

  Sylvia, for all the pangs you see
    Are laboring in my breast,
  I beg not you would favor me;—
    Would you but slight the rest!
  How great soe'er your rigors are,
    With them alone I'll cope;
  I can endure my own despair,
    But not another's hope.
            WILLIAM WALSH.

15

MY DEAR AND ONLY LOVE.

PART FIRST.

My dear and only love, I pray,
   This noble world of thee
Be governed by no other sway
   But purest monarchie.
For if confusion have a part,
   Which virtuous souls abhore,
And hold a synod in thy heart,
   I 'll never love thee more.

Like Alexander I will reign,
   And I will reign alone,
My thoughts shall evermore disdain
   A rival on my throne.
He either fears his fate too much,
   Or his deserts are small,
That puts it not unto the touch,
   To win or lose it all.

But I must rule and govern still
   And always give the law,
And have each subject at my will,
   And all to stand in awe.
But 'gainst my battery if I find
   Thou shun'st the prize so sore
As that thou set'st me up a blind,
   I 'll never love thee more.

If in the empire of thy heart,
   Where I should solely be,

Another do pretend a part,
  And dares to vie with me;
Or if committees thou erect,
  And go on such a score,
I 'll sing and laugh at thy neglect,
  And never love thee more.

But if thou wilt be constant then,
  And faithful of thy word,
I 'll make thee glorious by my pen,
  And famous by my sword.
I 'll serve thee in such noble ways
  Was never heard before;
I 'll crown and deck thee all with bays,
  And love thee ever more.

PART SECOND.

My dear and only love, take heed,
  Lest thou thyself expose,
And let all longing lovers feed
  Upon such looks as those.
A marble wall then build about,
  Beset without a door;
But if thou let thy heart fly out,
  I 'll never love thee more.

Let not their oaths, like volleys shot,
  Make any breach at all;
Nor smoothness of their language plot
  Which way to scale the wall;
Nor balls of wild-fire love consume
  The shrine which I adore;
For if such smoke about thee fume,
  I 'll never love thee more.

I think thy virtues be too strong
  To suffer by surprise;
Those victualled by my love so long,
  The siege at length must rise,
And leave thee rulèd in that health
  And state thou wast before;
But if thou turn a commonwealth,
  I 'll never love thee more.

Or if by fraud, or by consent,
  Thy heart to ruine come,
I 'll sound no trumpet as I wont,
  Nor march by tuck of drum;
But hold my arms, like ensigns, up,
  Thy falsehood to deplore,
And bitterly will sigh and weep,
  And never love thee more.

I 'll do with thee as Nero did
  When Rome was set on fire,
Not only all relief forbid,
  But to a hill retire,
And scorn to shed a tear to see
  Thy spirit grown so poor;
But smiling sing, until I die,
  I 'll never love thee more.

Yet, for the love I bare thee once,
  Lest that thy name should die,
A monument of marble-stone
  The truth shall testifie;
That every pilgrim passing by
  May pity and deplore

My case, and read the reason why
    I can love thee no more.

The golden laws of love shall be
    Upon this pillar hung,—
A simple heart, a single eye,
    A true and constant tongue;
Let no man for more love pretend
    Than he has hearts in store;
True love begun shall never end;
    Love one and love no more.

Then shall thy heart be set by mine,
    But in far different case;
For mine was true, so was not thine,
    But lookt like Janus' face.
For as the waves with every wind,
    So sail'st thou every shore,
And leav'st my constant heart behind,—
    How can I love thee more?

My heart shall with the sun be fixed
    For constancy most strange,
And thine shall with the moon be mixed,
    Delighting ay in change.
Thy beauty shined at first more bright,
    And woe is me therefore,
That ever I found thy love so light
    I could love thee no more!

The misty mountains, smoking lakes,
    The rocks' resounding echo,
The whistling wind that murmur makes,

Shall with me sing hey ho!
The tossing seas, the tumbling boats,
  Tears dropping from each shore,
Shall tune with me their turtle notes—
  I 'll never love thee more.

As doth the turtle, chaste and true,
  Her fellow's death regrete,
And daily mourns for his adieu,
  And ne'er renews her mate;
So, though thy faith was never fast,
  Which grieves me wondrous sore,
Yet I shall live in love so chaste,
  That I shall love no more.

And when all gallants ride about
  These monuments to view,
Whereon is written, in and out,
  Thou traitorous and untrue;
Then in a passion they shall pause,
  And thus say, sighing sore,
" Alas! he had too just a cause
  Never to love thee more."

And when that tracing goddess Fame
  From east to west shall flee,
She shall record it, to thy shame,
  How thou hast lovèd me;
And how in odds our love was such
  As few have been before;
Thou loved too many, and I too much,
  So I can love no more.

JAMES GRAHAM, MARQUIS OF MONTROSE.

THE FAITHFUL LOVERS.

I 'd been away from her three years,—about that,
 And I returned to find my Mary true;
And though I 'd question her, I did not doubt that
 It was unnecessary so to do.

'T was by the chimney-corner we were sitting:
 " Mary," said I, " have you been always true? "
" Frankly," says she, just pausing in her knit-
 ting,
 " I don't think I 've unfaithful been to you:
But for the three years past I 'll tell you what
I 've done; then say if I 've been true or not.

" When first you left my grief was uncontrollable;
 Alone I mourned my miserable lot;
And all who saw me thought me inconsolable,
 Till Captain Clifford came from Aldershot.
To flirt with him amused me while 't was new:
I don't count that unfaithfulness—do you?

" The next—oh! let me see—was Frankie Phipps;
 I met him at my uncle's, Christmas-tide,
And 'neath the mistletoe, where lips meet lips,
 He gave me his first kiss—" And here she
 sighed.
" We stayed six weeks at uncle's—how time flew!
I don't count that unfaithfulness—do you?

" Lord Cecil Fossmore—only twenty-one—
 Lent me his horse. O, how we rode and raced!

We scoured the downs—we rode to hounds—such
        fun!
    And often was his arm about my waist,—
That was to lift me up and down. But who
Would call just that unfaithfulness?   Would
        you?

"Do you know Reggy Vere? Ah, how he sings!
    We met,—'t was at a picnic. O such weather!
He gave me, look, the first of these two rings
    When we were lost in Cliefden woods together.
Ah, what a happy time we spent,—we two!
I don't count that unfaithfulness to you.

"I've yet another ring from him; d'ye see
    The plain gold circlet that is shining here?"
I took her hand: "O Mary! can it be
    That you—" Quoth she, "that I am Mrs. Vere.
I don't call that unfaithfulness—do you?"
"No," I replied, "for I am married too."

ANONYMOUS.

THE CHRONICLE.

MARGARITA first possessed,
If I remember well, my breast,
    Margarita first of all;
But when awhile the wanton maid
With my restless heart had played,
    Martha took the flying ball.

Martha soon did it resign
To the beauteous Catharine.
    Beauteous Catharine gave place

(Though loath and angry she to part
With the possession of my heart)
   To Eliza's conquering face.

Eliza till this hour might reign,
Had she not evil counsels ta'en;
   Fundamental laws she broke,
And still new favorites she chose,
Till up in arms my passions rose,
   And cast away her yoke.

Mary then, and gentle Anne,
Both to reign at once began;
   Alternately they swayed;
And sometimes Mary was the fair,
And sometimes Anne the crown did wear,
   And sometimes both I obeyed.

Another Mary then arose,
And did rigorous laws impose;
   A mighty tyrant she!
Long, alas! should I have been
Under that iron-sceptred queen,
   Had not Rebecca set me free.

When fair Rebecca set me free,
'T was then a golden time with me:
   But soon those pleasures fled;
For the gracious princess died
In her youth and beauty's pride,
   And Judith reignèd in her stead.

One month, three days and half an hour
Judith held the sovereign power:
   Wondrous beautiful her face!

But so weak and small her wit,
That she to govern was unfit,
   And so Susanna took her place.

But when Isabella came,
Armed with a resistless flame,
   And the artillery of her eye;
Whilst she proudly marched about,
Greater conquests to find out,
   She beat out Susan, by the by.

But in her place I then obeyed
Blackeyed Bess, her viceroy maid,
   To whom ensued a vacancy:
Thousand worse passions then possessed
The interregnum of my breast;
   Bless me from such anarchy!

Gentle Henrietta then,
And a third Mary, next began;
   Then Joan, and Jane, and Audria;
And then a pretty Thomasine,
And then another Catharine,
   And then a long *et cætera.*

But I will briefer with them be,
Since few of them were long with me.
   An higher and a nobler strain
My present emperess does claim.
Heleonora, first o' th' name,
   Whom God grant long to reign!

ABRAHAM COWLEY.

CONSTANCY.

ONE eve of beauty, when the sun
   Was on the streams of Guadalquiver,
To gold converting, one by one,
   The ripples of the mighty river,
Beside me on the bank was seated
   A Seville girl, with auburn hair,
And eyes that might the world have cheated,—
   A wild, bright, wicked, diamond pair!

She stooped, and wrote upon the sand,
   Just as the loving sun was going,
With such a soft, small, shining hand,
   I could have sworn 't was silver flowing.
Her words were three, and not one more,
   What could Diana's motto be?
The siren wrote upon the shore,—
   " *Death, not inconstancy!* "

And then her two large languid eyes
   So turned on mine, that, devil take me!
I set the air on fire with sighs,
   And was the fool she chose to make me!
Saint Francis would have been deceived
   With such an eye and such a hand;
But one week more, and I believed
   As much the woman as the sand.

                  ANONYMOUS.

THE AGE OF WISDOM.

Ho! pretty page, with the dimpled chin,
　That never has known the barber's shear,
All your wish is woman to win;
This is the way that boys begin,—
　Wait till you come to forty year.

Curly gold locks cover foolish brains;
　Billing and cooing is all your cheer,—
Sighing, and singing of midnight strains,
Under Bonnybell's window-panes,—
　Wait till you come to forty year.

Forty times over let Michaelmas pass;
　Grizzling hair the brain doth clear;
Then you know a boy is an ass,
Then you know the worth of a lass,—
　Once you have come to forty year.

Pledge me round; I bid ye declare,
　All good fellows whose beards are gray,—
Did not the fairest of the fair
Common grow and wearisome ere
　Ever a month was past away?

The reddest lips that ever have kissed,
　The brightest eyes that ever have shone,
May pray and whisper and we not list,
Or look away and never be missed,—
　Ere yet ever a month is gone.

Gillian's dead! God rest her bier,—
  How I loved her twenty years syne!
Marian's married; but I sit here,
Alone and merry at forty year,
  Dipping my nose in the Gascon wine.

                WILLIAM MAKEPEACE THACKERAY.

THE COMMON DOOM.

VICTORIOUS men of earth, no more
  Proclaim how wide your empires are:
Though you bind in every shore,
  And your triumphs reach as far
        As night or day,
  Yet you proud monarchs must obey,
And mingle with forgotten ashes, when
Death calls ye to the crowd of common men.

  Devouring famine, plague, and war,
    Each able to undo mankind,
  Death's servile emissaries are;
    Nor to these alone confined—
        He hath at will
  More quaint and subtle ways to kill.
A smile or kiss, as he will use the art,
Shall have the cunning skill to break a heart.

                JAMES SHIRLEY.

THE AUTHOR'S RESOLUTION, IN A SONNET.

FROM " FAIR VIRTUE."

SHALL I, wasting in despair,
Die, because a woman 's Fair?
Or make pale my cheeks with care,
'Cause another's rosy are?
Be She fairer than the Day,
Or the flowery meads in May!
  If She be not so to me,
    What care I, how Fair She be?

Should my heart be grieved or pined,
'Cause I see a woman Kind?
Or a well disposèd nature
Joinèd with a lovely feature?
Be She meeker, kinder than
Turtle dove, or pelican!
  If She be not so to me,
    What care I, how Kind She be?

Shall a woman's virtues move
Me to perish for her love?
Or her well deserving known
Make me quite forget mine own?
Be She with that Goodness blest
Which may gain her, name of Best!
  If She be not such to me,
    What care I, how Good She be?

'Cause her fortune seems too high,
Shall I play the fool, and die?
Those that bear a noble mind,
Where they want of riches find,
Think " What with them they would do!"
That, without them, dare to woo!
   And unless that mind I see,
   What care I, though Great She be?

Great, or Good, or Kind, or Fair,
I will ne'er the more despair!
If She love me (this believe!)
I will die ere She shall grieve!
If She slight me, when I woo;
I can scorn, and let her go!
   For if She be not for me!
   What care I, for whom She be?

GEORGE WITHER.

ANSWER TO MASTER WITHER'S SONG, "SHALL I, WASTING IN DESPAIR."

[Wither's Song, or "Sonnet," appeared first in his "Fidelia" in 1615, and later with some changes (as printed above) in "Fair Virtue," 1622. Jonson's parody, here given, came out in a Collection of Verses, in 1620.]

SHALL I mine affections slack,
'Cause I see a woman's Black?
Or myself, with care cast down,
'Cause I see a woman Brown?
Be She blacker than the night,
Or the blackest jet in sight!

If She be not so to me,
    What care I, how Black She be?

Shall my foolish heart be burst,
'Cause I see a woman's curst?
Or a thwarting hoggish nature
Joinèd in as bad a feature?
Be She curst, or fiercer than
Brutish beast, or savage man!
    If she be not so to me,
        What care I, how Curst She be?

Shall a woman's vices make
Me her vices quite forsake?
Or her faults to me make known,
Make me think that I have none?
Be She of the most accurst,
And deserve the name of worst!
    If She be not so to me,
        What care I, how Bad She be?

'Cause her fortunes seem too low,
Shall I therefore let her go?
He that bears an humble mind
And with riches can be kind.
Think how kind a heart he'd have,
If he were some servile slave!
    And if that same mind I see,
        What care I, how Poor She be?

Poor, or Bad, or Curst, or Black,
I will ne'er the more be slack!
If she hate me (then believe!)
She shall die, ere I will grieve!

If She like me, when I woo;
I can like and love her too!
    If that She be fit for me!
    What care I, what others be?

BEN JONSON.

FOREVER UNCONFESSED.

THEY seemed to those who saw them meet
The worldly friends of every day,
Her smile was undisturbed and sweet,
His courtesy was free and gay.

But yet if one the other's name
In some unguarded moment heard,
The heart you thought so calm and tame,
Would struggle like a captured bird:

And letters of mere formal phrase
Were blistered with repeated tears,—
And this was not the work of days,
But had gone on for years and years!

Alas, that Love was not too strong
For maiden shame and manly pride!
Alas, that they delayed too long
The goal of mutual bliss beside.

Yet what chance could then reveal,
And neither would be first to own,
Let fate and courage now conceal,
When truth could bring remorse alone.

RICHARD MONCKTON MILNES,
LORD HOUGHTON.

16

ADVICE TO A GIRL.

NEVER love unless you can
Bear with all the faults of man!
Men sometimes will jealous be
Though but little cause they see,
And hang the head as discontent,
And speak what straight they will repent.

Men, that but one Saint adore,
Make a show of love to more;
Beauty must be scorned in none,
Though but truly served in one:
For what is courtship but disguise?
True hearts may have dissembling eyes.

Men, when their affairs require,
Must awhile themselves retire;
Sometimes hunt, and sometimes hawk,
And not ever sit and talk:—
If these and such-like you can bear,
Then like, and love, and never fear!

THOMAS CAMPION.

SI JEUNESSE SAVAIT!

WHEN the veil from the eyes is lifted
    The seer's head is gray;
When the sailor to shore has drifted
    The sirens are far away.
Why must the clearer vision,
    The wisdom of Life's late hour,

Come, as in Fate's derision,
    When the hand has lost its power?
Is there a rarer being,
    Is there a fairer sphere
Where the strong are not unseeing,
    And the harvests are not sere;
Where, ere the seasons dwindle,
    They yield their due return;
Where the lamps of knowledge kindle
    While the flames of youth still burn?
O, for the young man's chances!
    O, for the old man's will!
Those flee while this advances,
    And the strong years cheat us still.

                    EDMUND CLARENCE STEDMAN.

WAITING FOR THE GRAPES.

That I love thee, charming maid, I a thousand
        times have said,
    And a thousand times more I have sworn it,
But 't is easy to be seen in the coldness of your
        mien
    That you doubt my affection—or scorn it.
                                        Ah me!

Not a single grain of sense is in the whole of
        these pretences
    For rejecting your lover's petitions;
Had I windows in my bosom, O, how gladly I' d
        expose 'em,
    To undo your fantastic suspicions!
                                        Ah me!

You repeat I 've known you long, and you hint I
      do you wrong,
  In beginning so late to pursue ye;
But 't is folly to look glum because people did not
      come
  Up the stairs of your nursery to woo ye.
                            Ah me!

In a grapery one walks without looking at the
      stalks,
  While the bunches are green that they 're bear-
      ing:
All the pretty little leaves that are dangling at
      the eaves
  Scarce attract e'en a moment of staring.
                            Ah me!

But when time has swelled the grapes to a richer
      style of shapes,
  And the sun has lent warmth to their blushes,
Then to cheer us and to gladden, to chant us
      and to madden,
  Is the ripe ruddy glory that rushes.
                            Ah me!

O, 't is then that mortals pant while they gaze on
      Bacchus' plant,—
  O, 't is then,—will my simile serve ye?
Should a damsel fair repine, though neglected
      like a vine?
  Both erelong shall turn heads topsy-turvy.
                            Ah me!
                  WILLIAM MAGINN.

GIVE ME MORE LOVE OR MORE DISDAIN.

GIVE me more love or more disdain;
　The torrid or the frozen zone
Brings equal ease unto my pain;
　The temperate affords me none;
Either extreme, of love or hate,
Is sweeter than a calm estate.

Give me a storm; If it be love,
　Like Danaë in a golden shower,
I swim in pleasure; if it prove
　Disdain, that torrent will devour
My vulture hopes; and he's possessed
Of heaven that's but from hell released;
Then crown my joys, or cure my pain;
Give me more love or more disdain.

THOMAS CAREW.

AFFAIRE D'AMOUR.

FOR E. W. W.

ONE pale November day
　Flying Summer paused,
　　They say:
　And growing bolder,
　O'er rosy shoulder
Threw her lover such a glance
That Autumn's heart began to dance.
　(O happy lover!)

A leafless peach-tree bold
  Thought for him she smiled,
      I 'm told;
  And, stirred by love,
  His sleeping sap did move,
Decking each naked branch with green
To show her that her look was seen!
     (Alas, poor lover!)

But Summer, laughing, fled,
  Nor knew he loved her!
      'T is said
  The peach-tree sighed,
  And soon he gladly died:
And Autumn, weary of the chase
Came on at Winter's sober pace
     (O careless lover!)

MARGARET DELAND.

A RENUNCIATION.

IF women could be fair, and yet not fond,
Or that their love were firm, not fickle still,
I would not marvel that they make men bond
By service long to purchase their good-will;
But when I see how frail those creatures are,
I muse that men forget themselves so far.

To mark the choice they make, and how they
    change,
How oft from Phœbus they do flee to Pan;
Unsettled still, like haggards wild they range,

These gentle birds that fly from man to man;
Who would not scorn and shake them from the
    fist,
And let them fly, fair fools, which way they list?

Yet for disport we fawn and flatter both,
To pass the time when nothing else can please,
And train them to our lure with subtle oath,
Till, weary of their wiles, ourselves we ease;
And then we say when we their fancy try,
To play with fools, O, what a fool was I!
EDWARD VERE, EARL OF OXFORD.

———

WHY SO PALE AND WAN?

W<small>HY</small> so pale and wan, fond lover?
    Pr'y thee, why so pale?
Will, when looking well can't move her,
    Looking ill prevail?
    Pr'y thee, why so pale?

Why so dull and mute, young sinner?
    Pr'y thee, why so mute?
Will, when speaking well can't win her,
    Saying nothing do 't?
    Pr'y thee, why so mute?

Quit, quit, for shame! this will not move,
    This cannot take her:
If of herself she will not love,
    Nothing can make her:
    The devil take her!
SIR JOHN SUCKLING.

A WOMAN'S QUESTION.

BEFORE I trust my fate to thee,
  Or place my hand in thine,
Before I let thy future give
  Color and form to mine,
Before I peril all for thee, question thy soul to-
    night for me.

I break all slighter bonds, nor feel
  A shadow of regret:
Is there one link within the past
  That holds thy spirit yet?
Or is thy faith as clear and free as that which I
    can pledge to thee?

Does there within thy dimmest dreams
  A possible future shine,
Wherein thy life could henceforth breathe,
  Untouched, unshared by mine?
If so, at any pain or cost, O, tell me before all is
    lost!

Look deeper still. If thou canst feel,
  Within thy inmost soul,
That thou hast kept a portion back,
  While I have staked the whole,
Let no false pity spare the blow, but in true
    mercy tell me so.

Is there within thy heart a need
  That mine cannot fulfil?

One cord that any other hand
  Could better wake or still?
Speak now, lest at some future day my whole life
    wither and decay.

Lives there within thy nature hid
  The demon-spirit, Change,
Shedding a passing glory still
  On all things new and strange?
It may not be thy fault alone—but shield my heart
    against thine own.

Couldst thou withdraw thy hand one day
  And answer to my claim,
That Fate, and that to-day's mistake—
  Not thou—had been to blame?
Some soothe their conscience thus; but thou wilt
    surely warn and save me now.

Nay, answer *not*,—I dare not hear,
  The words would come too late;
Yet I would spare thee all remorse,
  So, comfort thee, my fate—
Whatever on my heart may fall — remember, I
    would risk it all!

ADELAIDE ANNE PROCTER.

VI.

LOVERS.

NOT AT ALL, OR ALL IN ALL.

FROM " MERLIN AND VIVIEN."

IN Love, if Love be Love, if Love be ours,
Faith and unfaith can ne'er be equal powers;
Unfaith in aught is want of faith in all.

It is the little rift within the lute,
That by and by will make the music mute,
And ever widening slowly silence all.

The little rift within the lover's lute
Or little pitted speck in garnered fruit,
That rotting inward, slowly molders all.

It is not worth the keeping: let it go:
But shall it? answer, darling, answer, no.
And trust me not at all or all in all.

ALFRED, LORD TENNYSON.

WHEN DO I SEE THEE MOST?

FROM "THE HOUSE OF LIFE."

WHEN do I see thee most, belovèd one?
When in the light the spirits of mine eyes
Before thy face, their altar, solemnize
The worship of that Love through thee made
    known?
Or when, in the dusk hours (we two alone),
Close-kissed, and eloquent of still replies
Thy twilight-hidden glimmering visage lies,
And my soul only sees thy soul its own?
O love, my love! if I no more should see
Thyself, nor on the earth the shadow of thee,
Nor image of thine eyes in any spring,—
How then should sound upon Life's darkening
    slope
The ground-whirl of the perished leaves of Hope,
The wind of Death's imperishable wing!

DANTE GABRIEL ROSSETTI.

BEAUTY.

'T IS much immortal beauty to admire,
But more immortal beauty to withstand;
The perfect soul can overcome desire,
If beauty with divine delight be scanned.
For what is beauty but the blooming child
Of fair Olympus, that in night must end,
And be forever from that bliss exiled,
If admiration stand too much its friend?

The wind may be enamored of a flower,
The ocean of the green and laughing shore,
The silver lightning of a lofty tower,—
But must not with too near a love adore;
Or flower and margin and cloud-cappèd tower
Love and delight shall with delight devour!

LORD EDWARD THURLOW.

LOVE IN THE WINDS.

WHEN I am standing on a mountain crest,
Or hold the tiller in the dashing spray,
My love of you leaps foaming in my breast,
Shouts with the winds and sweeps to their foray;
My heart bounds with the horses of the sea,
And plunges in the wild ride of the night,
Flaunts in the teeth of tempest the large glee
That rides out Fate and welcomes gods to fight.
Ho, love, I laugh aloud for love of you,
Glad that our love is fellow to rough weather,—
No fretful orchid hothoused from the dew,
But hale and hardy as the highland heather,
Rejoicing in the wind that stings and thrills,
Comrade of ocean, playmate of the hills.

RICHARD HOVEY.

KISSING HER HAIR.

KISSING her hair, I sat against her feet:
Wove and unwove it,—wound, and found it sweet;
Made fast therewith her hands, drew down her
eyes,
Deep as deep flowers, and dreamy like dim skies;

With her own tresses bound, and found her fair,—
    Kissing her hair.

Sleep were no sweeter than her face to me,—
Sleep of cold sea-bloom under the cold sea:
What pain could get between my face and hers?
What new sweet thing would Love not relish
    worse?
Unless, perhaps, white Death had kissed me
    there,—
    Kissing her hair.

               ALGERNON CHARLES SWINBURNE.

MY SWEET SWEETING.

FROM A MS. TEMP. HENRY VIII.

    AH, my sweet sweeting;
    My little pretty sweeting,
My sweeting will I love wherever I go;
    She is so proper and pure,
Full, steadfast, stable, and demure,
    There is none such, you may be sure,
      As my sweet sweeting.

In all this world, as thinketh me,
Is none so pleasant to my ee,
That I am glad so oft to see,
    As my sweet sweeting.
When I behold my sweeting sweet,
Her face, her hands, her minion feet,
They seem to me there is none so mete,
    As my sweet sweeting.

Above all other praise must I,
And love my pretty pygsnye,
For none I find so womanly
    As my sweet sweeting.

ANONYMOUS.

LINES TO AN INDIAN AIR.

SERENADE.

I ARISE from dreams of thee
    In the first sweet sleep of night,
When the winds are breathing low,
    And the stars are shining bright.
I arise from dreams of thee,
    And a spirit in my feet
Has led me—who knows how?—
    To thy chamber-window, sweet!

The wandering airs they faint
    On the dark, the silent stream,—
The champak odors fail
    Like sweet thoughts in a dream;
The nightingale's complaint,
    It dies upon her heart,
As I must die on thine,
    O, belovèd as thou art!

O, lift me from the grass!
    I die, I faint, I fail!
Let thy love in kisses rain
    On my lips and eyelids pale.
My cheek is cold and white, alas!
    My heart beats loud and fast:

O, press it close to thine again,
  Where it will break at last!
PERCY BYSSHE SHELLEY.

SERENADE.

FROM "THE SPANISH STUDENT."

STARS of the summer night!
  Far in yon azure deeps,
Hide, hide your golden light!
  She sleeps!
My lady sleeps!
    Sleeps!

Moon of the summer night!
  Far down yon western steeps,
Sink, sink in silver light!
  She sleeps!
My lady sleeps!
    Sleeps!

Wind of the summer night!
  Where yonder woodbine creeps,
Fold, fold thy pinions light!
  She sleeps!
My lady sleeps!
    Sleeps!

Dreams of the summer night!
  Tell her, her lover keeps
Watch, while in slumbers light
  She sleeps!
My lady sleeps!
    Sleeps!
HENRY WADSWORTH LONGFELLOW.

FIRST LOVE.

FROM " DON JUAN," CANTO I.

'T is sweet to hear,
At midnight on the blue and moonlit deep,
The song and oar of Adria's gondolier,
   By distance mellowed, o'er the waters sweep;
'T is sweet to see the evening star appear;
   'T is sweet to listen as the night-winds creep
From leaf to leaf; 't is sweet to view on high
The rainbow, based on ocean, span the sky.

'T is sweet to hear the watch-dog's honest bark
   Bay deep-mouthed welcome as we draw near
      home;
'T is sweet to know there is an eye will mark
   Our coming, and look brighter when we come;
'T is sweet to be awakened by the lark,
   Or lulled by falling waters; sweet the hum
Of bees, the voice of girls, the song of birds,
The lisp of children, and their earliest words.

Sweet is the vintage, when the showering grapes
   In Bacchanal profusion reel to earth,
Purple and gushing: sweet are our escapes
   From civic revelry to rural mirth;
Sweet to the miser are his glittering heaps;
   Sweet to the father is his first-born's birth;
Sweet is revenge,—especially to women,
Pillage to soldiers, prize-money to seamen.

.   .   .   .   .   .

'T is sweet to win, no matter how, one's laurels,
　By blood or ink; 't is sweet to put an end
To strife; 't is sometimes sweet to have our quar-
　　rels,
　Particularly with a tiresome friend;
Sweet is old wine in bottles, ale in barrels;
　Dear is the helpless creature we defend
Against the world; and dear the school-boy spot
We ne'er forget, though there we are forgot.

But sweeter still than this, than these, than all,
　Is first and passionate love,—it stands alone,
Like Adam's recollection of his fall;
　The tree of knowledge has been plucked,—all 's
　　known,—
And life yields nothing further to recall
　Worthy of this ambrosial sin, so shown,
No doubt in fable, as the unforgiven
Fire which Prometheus filched for us from heaven.
　　　　　　　　　　　　　　LORD BYRON.

SIR LAUNCELOT AND QUEEN GUINE-
VERE.

　LIKE souls that balance joy and pain,
　With tears and smiles from heaven again
　The maiden Spring upon the plain
　Came in a sun-lit fall of rain.
　　　In crystal vapor everywhere
　Blue isles of heaven laughed between,
　And far, in forest-deeps unseen,
　The topmost elm-tree gathered green
　　　From draughts of balmy air.

17

Sometimes the linnet piped his song;
Sometimes the throstle whistled strong;
Sometimes the sparhawk, wheeled along,
Hushed all the groves from fear of wrong:
　　By grassy capes with fuller sound
In curves the yellowing river ran,
And drooping chestnut-buds began
To spread into the perfect fan,
　　Above the teeming ground.

Then, in the boyhood of the year,
Sir Launcelot and Queen Guinevere
Rode thro' the coverts of the deer,
With blissful treble ringing clear.
　　She seemed a part of joyous Spring;
A gown of grass-green silk she wore,
Buckled with golden clasps before;
A light-green tuft of plumes she bore
　　Closed in a golden ring.

Now on some twisted ivy-net,
Now by some tinkling rivulet,
In mosses mixed with violet
Her cream-white mule his pastern set:
　　And fleeter now she skimmed the plains
Than she whose elfin prancer springs
By night to eery warblings,
When all the glimmering moorland rings
　　With jingling bridle-reins.

As fast she fled thro' sun and shade,
The happy winds upon her played,
Blowing the ringlet from the braid:

She looked so lovely, as she swayed
  The rein with dainty finger-tips,
A man had given all other bliss,
And all his worldly worth for this,
To waste his whole heart in one kiss
  Upon her perfect lips.

ALFRED, LORD TENNYSON.

I SAW TWO CLOUDS AT MORNING.

I saw two clouds at morning,
  Tinged by the rising sun,
And in the dawn they floated on,
  And mingled into one;
I thought that morning cloud was blest,
It moved so sweetly to the west.

I saw two summer currents
  Flow smoothly to their meeting,
And join their course, with silent force,
  In peace each other greeting;
Calm was their course through banks of green,
While dimpling eddies played between.

Such be your gentle motion,
  Till life's last pulse shall beat;
Like summer's beam, and summer's stream,
  Float on, in joy, to meet
A calmer sea, where storms shall cease,
A purer sky, where all is peace.

JOHN GARDINER CALKINS BRAINARD.

MY BEAUTIFUL LADY.

I LOVE my Lady; she is very fair;
Her brow is wan, and bound by simple hair;
  Her spirit sits aloof, and high,
  But glances from her tender eye
    In sweetness droopingly.

As a young forest while the wind drives through,
My life is stirred when she breaks on my view;
  Her beauty grants my will no choice
  But silent awe, till she rejoice
    My longing with her voice.

Her warbling voice, though ever low and mild,
Oft makes me feel as strong wine would a child;
  And though her hand be airy light
  Of touch, it moves me with its might,
    As would a sudden fright.

A hawk high poised in air, whose nerved wing-
    tips
Tremble with might suppressed, before he dips,
  In vigilance, scarce more intense
  Than I, when her voice holds my sense
    Contented in suspense.

Her mention of a thing, august or poor,
Makes it far nobler than it was before:
  As where the sun strikes life will gush,
  And what is pale receive a flush,
    Rich hues, a richer blush.

My Lady's name, when I hear strangers use,
Not meaning her, to me sounds lax misuse;
 I love none but my Lady's name;
 Maud, Grace, Rose, Marian, all the same
  Are harsh, or blank and tame.

My Lady walks as I have watched a swan
Swim where a glory on the water shone:
 There ends of willow branches ride,
 Quivering in the flowing tide,
  By the deep river's side.

Fresh beauties, howsoe'er she moves, are stirred:
As the sunned bosom of a humming bird
 At each pant lifts some fiery hue,
 Fierce gold, bewildering green or blue;
  The same, yet ever new.

THOMAS WOOLNER.

MY LOVE.

(HER PORTRAIT.)

My love is beautiful and sweet.
All good and gentle graces meet
In her, in loveliness complete.

My love is precious. Nor for me
In all this world on land or sea
Can other worthy treasure be.

My love is constant. In her eyes
True, pure, and steadfast, beauty lies
Serene and noble as the skies.

RUSSELL POWELL JACOBY.

A CHRISTMAS SCENE.

OR, LOVE IN THE COUNTRY.

I.

THE hill blast comes howling through leaf-rifted
    trees
That late were as harp-strings to each gentle
    breeze;
The strangers and cousins and every one flown,
While we sit happy-hearted—together—alone.

II.

Some are off to the mountain, and some to the
    fair,
The snow is on their cheek, on mine your black
    hair;
Papa with his farming is busy to-day,
And mamma's too good-natured to ramble this
    way.

III.

The girls are gone—are they not?—into town,
To fetch bows and bonnets, perchance a *beau*,
    down;
Ah! tell them, dear Kate, 't is not fair to co-
    quette—
Though you, you bold lassie, are fond of it yet!

IV.

You 're not—do you say?—just remember last
    night,
You gave Harry a rose, and you dubbed him your
    knight;

Poor lad! if he loved you—but no, darling! no,
You 're too thoughtful and good to fret any one so.

V.

The painters are raving of light and of shade,
And Harry, the poet, of lake, hill, and glade;
While the light of your eye and your soft wavy
    form
Suit a proser like me, by the hearth bright and
    warm.

VI.

The snow on those hills is uncommonly grand,
But you know, Kate, it 's not half so white as
    your hand,
And say what you will of the gray Christmas sky,
Still I *slightly* prefer my dark girl's gray eye.

VII.

Be quiet, and sing me " The Bonny Cuckoo,"
For it bids us the summer and winter love
    through;
And then I 'll read out an old ballad that shows
How Tyranny perished, and Liberty rose.

VIII.

My Kate! I 'm so happy, your voice whispers soft,
And your cheek flushes wilder from kissing so oft,
For town or for country, for mountains or farms,
What care I?—My darling's entwined in my arms.

THOMAS OSBORNE DAVIS.

BEDOUIN LOVE-SONG.

FROM the Desert I come to thee,
　On a stallion shod with fire;
And the winds are left behind
　In the speed of my desire.
Under thy window I stand,
　And the midnight hears my cry:
I love thee, I love but thee!
　With a love that shall not die
　　Till the sun grows cold,
　　And the stars are old,
　　And the leaves of the Judgment
　　Book unfold!

Look from thy window, and see
　My passion and my pain!
I lie on the sands below,
　And I faint in thy disdain.
Let the night-winds touch thy brow
　With the heat of my burning sigh,
And melt thee to hear the vow
　Of a love that shall not die
　　Till the sun grows cold,
　　And the stars are old,
　　And the leaves of the Judgment
　　Book unfold!

My steps are nightly driven,
　By the fever in my breast,
To hear from thy lattice breathed
　The word that shall give me rest.

Open the door of thy heart,
And open thy chamber door,
And my kisses shall teach thy lips
The love that shall fade no more
Till the sun grows cold,
And the stars are old,
And the leaves of the Judgment
Book unfold!

BAYARD TAYLOR.

ZARA'S EAR-RINGS.

FROM THE SPANISH.

" My ear-rings! my ear-rings! they 've dropt into
the well,
And what to say to Muça, I cannot, cannot tell."
'T was thus, Granada's fountain by, spoke Albu-
harez' daughter,—
" The well is deep, far down they lie, beneath the
cold blue water.
To me did Muça give them, when he spake his sad
farewell,
And what to say when he comes back, alas! I cannot tell.

" My ear-rings! my ear-rings! they were pearls in
silver set,
That when my Moor was far away, I ne'er should
him forget,
That I ne'er to other tongue should list, nor smile
on other's tale,
But remember he my lips had kissed, pure as those
ear-rings pale.

When he comes back and hears that I have
    dropped them in the well,
O, what will Muça think of me, I cannot, cannot
    tell.

" My ear-rings! my ear-rings! he 'll say they should
    have been,
Not of pearl and of silver, but of gold and glitter-
    ing sheen,
Of jasper and of onyx, and of diamond shining
    clear,
Changing to the changing light, with radiance in-
    sincere;
That changeful mind unchanging gems are not
    befitting well,—
Thus will he think,—and what to say, alas! I can-
    not tell.

" He 'll think when I to market went I loitered by
    the way;
He 'll think a willing ear I lent to all the lads
    might say;
He 'll think some other lover's hand among my
    tresses noosed,
From the ears where he had placed them my rings
    of pearl unloosed;
He 'll think when I was sporting so beside this
    marble well,
My pearls fell in,—and what to say, alas! I cannot
    tell.

" He 'll say I am a woman, and we are all the
    same;
He 'll say I loved when he was here to whisper
    of his flame—

But when he went to Tunis my virgin troth had
      broken,
And thought no more of Muça, and cared not for
      his token.
My ear-rings! my ear-rings! O, luckless, luckless
      well!
For what to say to Muça, alas! I cannot tell.

" I 'll tell the truth to Muça, and I hope he will
      believe,
That I have thought of him at morn, and thought
      of him at eve;
That musing on my lover, when down the sun was
      gone,
His ear-rings in my hand I held, by the fountain
      all alone,
And that my mind was o'er the sea, when from
      my hand they fell,
And that deep his love lies in my heart, as they
      lie in the well."

JOHN GIBSON LOCKHART.

HESPERIA.

OUT of the golden remote wild west where the sea
      without shore is,
  Full of the sunset, and sad, if at all, with the
      fulness of joy,
As a wind sets in with the autumn that blows
      from the region of stories,
  Blows with a perfume of songs and of memories
      beloved from a boy,

Blows from the capes of the past oversea to the
      bays of the present,
    Filled as with shadow of sound with the pulse
      of invisible feet,
Far out to the shallows and straits of the future,
      by rough ways or pleasant,
    Is it thither the wind's wings beat? is it hither
      to me, O my sweet?
For thee, in the stream of the deep tide-wind blow-
      ing in with the water,
    Thee I behold as a bird borne in with the wind
      from the west,
Straight from the sunset, across white waves
      whence rose as a daughter
    Venus thy mother, in years when the world was
      a water at rest.
Out of the distance of dreams, as a dream that
      abides after slumber,
    Strayed from the fugitive flock of the night,
      when the moon overhead
Wanes in the wan waste heights of the heaven,
      and stars without number
    Die without sound, and are spent like lamps
      that are burnt by the dead,
Comes back to me, stays by me, lulls me with
      touch of forgotten caresses,
    One warm dream clad about with a fire as of
      life that endures;
The delight of thy face, and the sound of thy feet,
      and the wind of thy tresses,
    And all of a man that regrets, and all of a maid
      that allures.
But thy bosom is warm for my face and profound
      as a manifold flower,

Thy silence as music, thy voice as an odor that
    fades in a flame;
Not a dream, not a dream is the kiss of thy mouth,
    and the bountiful hour
    That makes n   forget what was sin, and would
        make me forget were it shame.
Thine eyes that are quiet, thy hands that are
    tender, thy lips that are loving,
    Comfort and cool me as dew in the dawn of a
        moon like a dream;
And my heart yearns baffled and blind, moved
    vainly toward thee, and moving
    As the refluent seaweed moves in the languid
        exuberant stream,
Fair as a rose is on earth, as a rose under water
    in prison,
    That stretches and swings to the slow passionate
        pulse of the sea,
Closed up from the air and the sun, but alive, as
    a ghost re-arisen,
    Pale as the love that revives as a ghost re-arisen
        in me.
From the bountiful infinite west, from the happy
    memorial places
    Full of the stately repose and the lordly de-
        light of the dead,
Where the fortunate islands are lit with the light
    of ineffable faces,
    And the sound of a sea without wind is about
        them, and sunset is red,
Come back to redeem and release me from love
    that recalls and represses,
    That cleaves to my flesh as a flame, till the ser-
        pent has eaten his fill;

From the bitter delights of the dark, and the fever-
ish, furtive caresses
  That murder the youth in a man or ever his
heart have its will.
Thy lips cannot laugh and thine eyes cannot weep;
thou art pale as a rose is,
  Paler and sweeter than leaves that cover the
blush of the bud;
And the heart of the flower is compassion, and pity
the core it encloses,
  Pity, not love, that is born of the breath and
decays with the blood.
As the cross that a wild nun clasps till the edge
of it bruises her bosom,
  So love wounds as we grasp it, and blackens and
burns as a flame;
I have loved overmuch in my life: when the live
bud bursts with the blossom,
  Bitter as ashes or tears is the fruit, and the wine
thereof shame.
As a heart that its anguish divides is the green bud
cloven asunder;
  As the blood of a man self-slain is the flush of
the leaves that allure;
And the perfume as poison and wine to the brain,
a delight and a wonder;
  And the thorns are too sharp for a boy, too
slight for a man, to endure.
Too soon did I love it, and lost love's rose; and I
cared not for glory's:
  Only the blossoms of sleep and of pleasure were
mixed in my hair.

Was it myrtle or poppy thy garland was woven
    with, O my Dolores?
  Was it pallor or slumber, or blush as of blood,
    that I found in thee fair?
For desire is a respite from love, and the flesh, not
    the heart, is her fuel;
  She was sweet to me once, who am fled and
    escaped from the rage of her reign;
Who behold as of old time at hand as I turn, with
    her mouth growing cruel,
  And flushed as with wine with the blood of her
    lovers, Our Lady of Pain.
Low down where the thicket is thicker with thorns
    than with leaves in the summer,
  In the brake is a gleaming of eyes and a hissing
    of tongues that I knew;
And the lithe long throats of her snakes reach
    round her, their mouths overcome her,
  And her lips grow cool with their foam, made
    moist as a desert with dew.
With the thirst and the hunger of lust though her
    beautiful lips be so bitter,
  With the cold foul foam of the snakes they
    soften and redden and smile;
And her fierce mouth sweetens, her eyes wax wide
    and her eyelashes glitter,
  And she laughs with a savor of blood in her face,
    and a savor of guile.
She laughs, and her hands reach hither, her hair
    blows hither and hisses
  As a low-lit flame in a wind, back-blown till it
    shudder and leap;

Let her lips not again lay hold on my soul, nor
 her poisonous kisses,
  To consume it alive and divide from thy bosom,
  Our Lady of Sleep.
Ah, daughter of sunset and slumber, if now it re-
 turn into prison,
  Who shall redeem it anew? but we, if thou wilt,
  let us fly;
Let us take to us, now that the white skies thrill
 with a moon unarisen,
  Swift horses of fear or of love, take flight and
  depart and not die.
They are swifter than dreams, they are stronger
 than death; there is none that hath ridden,
  None that shall ride in the dim strange ways of
  his life as we ride:
By the meadows of memory, the highlands of hope,
 and the shore that is hidden,
  Where life breaks loud and unseen, a sonorous
  invisible tide;
By the sands where sorrow has trodden, the salt
 pools bitter and sterile,
  By the thundering reef and the low sea wall
  and the channel of years,
Our wild steeds press on the night, strain hard
 through pleasure and peril,
  Labor and listen and pant not or pause for the
  peril that nears;
And the sound of them trampling the way cleaves
 night as an arrow asunder,
  And slow by the sand-hill and swift by the down
  with its glimpses of grass,

Sudden and steady the music, as eight hoofs tram-
     ple and thunder,
   Rings in the ear of the low blind wind of the
     night as we pass;
Shrill shrieks in our faces the blind bland air that
     was mute as a maiden,
   Stung into storm by the speed of our passage,
     and deaf where we past;
And our spirits too burn as we bound, thine holy
     but mine heavy-laden,
   As we burn with the fire of our flight; ah, love,
     shall we win at the last?

ALGERNON CHARLES SWINBURNE.

COME INTO THE GARDEN, MAUD.

Come into the garden, Maud,
   For the black bat, night, has flown!
Come into the garden, Maud,
   I am here at the gate alone;
And the woodbine spices are wafted abroad,
   And the musk of the roses blown.

For a breeze of morning moves,
   And the planet of Love is on high,
Beginning to faint in the light that she loves,
   On a bed of daffodil sky,—
To faint in the light of the sun that she loves,
   To faint in its light, and to die.

All night have the roses heard
   The flute, violin, bassoon;
18

All night has the casement jessamine stirred
　To the dancers dancing in tune,—
Till the silence fell with the waking bird,
　And a hush with the setting moon.

I said to the lily, " There is but one
　With whom she has heart to be gay.
When will the dancers leave her alone?
　She is weary of dance and play."
Now half to the setting moon are gone,
　And half to the rising day;
Low on the sand and loud on the stone
　The last wheel echoes away.

I said to the rose, " The brief night goes
　In babble and revel and wine.
O young lord-lover, what sighs are those
　For one that will never be thine?
But mine, but mine," so I swear to the rose,
　" For ever and ever mine!"

And the soul of the roses went into my blood,
　As the music clashed in the hall;
And long by the garden lake I stood,
　For I heard your rivulet fall
From the lake to the meadow and on to the wood,
　Our wood, that is dearer than all;

From the meadow your walks have left so sweet
　That whenever a March-wind sighs,
He sets the jewel-print of your feet
　In violets blue as your eyes,
To the woody hollows in which we meet,
　And the valleys of Paradise.

The slender acacia would not shake
　　One long milk-bloom on the tree;
The white lake-blossom fell into the lake,
　　As the pimpernel dozed on the lea;
But the rose was awake all night for your sake,
　　Knowing your promise to me;
The lilies and roses were all awake,
　　They sighed for the dawn and thee.

Queen rose of the rosebud garden of girls,
　　Come hither! the dances are done;
In gloss of satin and glimmer of pearls,
　　Queen lily and rose in one;
Shine out, little head, sunning over with curls,
　　To the flowers, and be their sun.

There has fallen a splendid tear
　　From the passion-flower at the gate.
She is coming, my dove, my dear;
　　She is coming, my life, my fate!
The red rose cries, " She is near, she is near; "
　　And the white rose weeps, " She is late; "
The larkspur listens, " I hear, I hear; "
　　And the lily whispers, " I wait."

She is coming, my own, my sweet!
　　Were it ever so airy a tread,
My heart would hear her and beat,
　　Were it earth in an earthly bed;
My dust would hear her and beat,
　　Had I lain for a century dead;
Would start and tremble under her feet,
　　And blossom in purple and red.

ALFRED, LORD TENNYSON.

LOCHINVAR.

LADY HERON'S SONG. FROM " MARMION."

CANTO V.

O, YOUNG Lochinvar is come out of the west,
Through all the wide Border his steed was the
    best;
And, save his good broadsword, he weapon had
    none,
He rode all unarmed, and he rode all alone.
So faithful in love, and so dauntless in war,
There never was knight like the young Lochinvar.

He stayed not for brake, and he stopped not for
    stone,
He swam the Eske River where ford there was
    none;
But, ere he alighted at Netherby gate,
The bride had consented, the gallant came late;
For a laggard in love, and a dastard in war,
Was to wed the fair Ellen of brave Lochinvar.

So boldly he entered the Netherby Hall,
Among bridesmen, and kinsmen, and brothers, and
    all.
Then spoke the bride's father, his hand on his
    sword
(For the poor craven bridegroom said never a
    word),
" O, come ye in peace here, or come ye in war,
Or to dance at our bridal, young Lord Lochin-
    var?"

" I long wooed your daughter, my suit you de-
    nied;—
Love swells like the Solway, but ebbs like its
    tide,—
And now I am come, with this lost love of mine,
To lead but one measure, drink one cup of wine.
There are maidens in Scotland more lovely by far,
That would gladly be bride to the young Loch-
    invar."

The bride kissed the goblet; the knight took it up,
He quaffed off the wine, and threw down the cup.
She looked down to blush, and she looked up to
    sigh,
With a smile on her lips, and a tear in her eye.
He took her soft hand, ere her mother could
    bar,—
" Now tread we a measure," said young Lochin-
    var.

So stately his form, and so lovely her face,
That never a hall such a galliard did grace;
While her mother did fret, and her father did
    fume,
And the bridegroom stood dangling his bonnet and
    plume;
And the bridemaidens whispered, " 'T were better
    by far
To have matched our fair cousin with young
    Lochinvar."

One touch to her hand, and one word in her ear,
When they reached the hall-door, and the charger
    stood near;

So light to the croupe the fair lady he swung,
So light to the saddle before her he prung;
" She is won! we are gone! over bank, bush, and
       scaur;
They 'll have fleet steeds that follow," quoth young
       Lochinvar.

There was mounting 'mong Græmes of the Neth-
       erby clan;
Forsters, Fenwicks, and Musgraves, they rode and
       they ran;
There was racing and chasing on Cannobie Lee,
But the lost bride of Netherby ne'er did they see.
So daring in love, and so dauntless in war,
Have ye e'er heard of gallant like young Loch-
       invar?

SIR WALTER SCOTT.

WHEN YOUR BEAUTY APPEARS.

" When your beauty appears,
    In its graces and airs,
All bright as an angel new dropt from the skies,
    At distance I gaze, and am awed by my fears,
So strangely you dazzle my eyes!

" But when without art
    Your kind thoughts you impart,
When your love runs in blushes through every
       vein,
    When it darts from your eyes, when it pants
       at your heart,
Then I know that you 're woman again."

" There 's a passion and pride
   In our sex," she replied;
" And thus (might I gratify both) I would do,—
   Still an angel appear to each lover beside,
But still be a woman to you."

THOMAS PARNELL.

WHAT MY LOVER SAID.

By the merest chance, in the twilight gloom,
   In the orchard path he met me;
In the tall, wet grass, with its faint perfume,
And I tried to pass, but he made no room,
   Oh, I tried, but he would not let me.
So I stood and blushed till the grass grew red,
   With my face bent down above it,
While he took my hand as he whispering said—
(How the clover lifted each pink, sweet head
To listen to all that my lover said,—
   Oh, the clover in bloom, I love it!)

In the high, wet grass went the path to hide,
   And the low, wet leaves hung over;
But I could not pass upon either side,
For I found myself, when I vainly tried,
   In the arms of my steadfast lover.
And he held me there and he raised my head,
   While he closed the path before me,
And he looked down into my eyes and said—
(How the leaves bent down from the boughs o'er-
      head,
To listen to all that my lover said,—
   Oh, the leaves hanging lowly o'er me!)

Had he moved aside but a little way,
    I could surely then have passed him;
And he knew I never could wish to stay,
And would not have heard what he had to say,
    Could I only aside have cast him.
It was almost dark, and the moments sped,
    And the searching night wind found us,
But he drew me nearer and softly said—
(How the pure sweet wind grew still, instead,
To listen to all that my lover said,—
    Oh, the whispering wind around us!)

I am sure he knew, when he held me fast,
    That I must be all unwilling;
For I tried to go, and I would have passed,
As the night was come with its dew, at last,
    And the sky with its stars was filling.
But he clasped me close when I would have fled,
    And he made me hear his story,
And his soul came out from his lips and said—
(How the stars crept out where the white moon
        led,
To listen to all that my lover said,—
    Oh, the moon and the stars in glory!)

I know that the grass and the leaves will not tell,
    And I 'm sure that the wind, precious rover,
Will carry my secret so safely and well
    That no being shall ever discover
One word of the many that rapidly fell
    From the soul-speaking lips of my lover;
And the moon and the stars that looked over
Shall never reveal what a fairy-like spell

They wove round about us that night in the dell,
  In the path through the dew-laden clover,
Nor echo the whispers that made my heart swell
  As they fell from the lips of my lover.

HOMER GREENE.

PALABRAS CARIÑOSAS.

(SPANISH AIR.)

GOOD-NIGHT! I have to say good-night
To such a host of peerless things!
Good-night unto the slender hand
All queenly with its weight of rings;
Good-night to fond, uplifted eyes,
Good-night to chestnut braids of hair,
Good-night unto the perfect mouth,
And all the sweetness nestled there—
    The snowy hand detains me, then
    I 'll have to say Good-night again!

But there will come a time, my love,
When, if I read our stars aright,
I shall not linger by this porch
With my farewells. Till then, good-night!
You wish the time were now? And I.
You do not blush to wish it so?
You would have blushed yourself to death
To own so much a year ago—
    What, both these snowy hands! ah, then
    I 'll have to say Good-night again!

THOMAS BAILEY ALDRICH.

SEVEN TIMES THREE.

LOVE.

I LEANED out of window, I smelt the white clover,
　　Dark, dark was the garden, I saw not the gate;
" Now, if there be footsteps, he comes, my one
　　　　lover—
　　Hush, nightingale, hush! O sweet nightingale,
　　　　wait
　　　　　　Till I listen and hear
　　　　　　If a step draweth near,
　　　　　　For my love he is late!

" The skies in the darkness stoop nearer and
　　　　nearer,
　　A cluster of stars hangs like fruit in the tree,
The fall of the water comes sweeter, comes clearer:
　　To what art thou listening, and what dost thou
　　　　see?
　　　　　　Let the star-clusters glow,
　　　　　　Let the sweet waters flow,
　　　　　　And cross quickly to me.

" You night-moths that hover where honey brims
　　　　over
　　From sycamore blossoms, or settle or sleep;
You glow-worms, shine out, and the pathway dis-
　　　　cover
　　To him that comes darkling along the rough
　　　　steep.
　　　　　　Ah, my sailor, make haste,
　　　　　　For the time runs to waste,
　　　　　　And my love lieth deep,—

" Too deep for swift telling; and yet, my one lover,
  I 've conned thee an answer, it waits thee to-
      night."
By the sycamore passed he, and through the white
    clover;
Then all the sweet speech I had fashioned took
    flight;
      But I 'll love him more, more
      Than e'er wife loved before,
      Be the days dark or bright.

JEAN INGELOW.

WHEN THE KYE COMES HAME.

  Come, all ye jolly shepherds
    That whistle through the glen,
  I 'll tell ye of a secret
    That courtiers dinna ken:
  What is the greatest bliss
    That the tongue o' man can name?
  'T is to woo a bonny lassie
    When the kye comes hame!
      When the kye comes hame,
      When the kye comes hame,
    'Tween the gloaming and the mirk,
      When the kye comes hame!

  'T is not beneath the coronet,
    Nor canopy of state,
  'T is not on couch of velvet,
    Nor arbor of the great,—
  'T is beneath the spreading birk,
    In the glen without the name,

Wi' a bonny, bonny lassie,
    When the kye comes hame!
        When the kye comes hame, etc.

There the blackbird bigs his nest
    For the mate he loes to see,
And on the topmost bough,
    O, a happy bird is he;
Where he pours his melting ditty,
    And love is a' the theme,
And he 'll woo his bonny lassie
    When the kye comes hame!
        When the kye comes hame, etc.

When the blewart bears a pearl,
    And the daisy turns a pea,
And the bonny lucken gowan
    Has fauldit up her ee,
Then the laverock frae the blue lift
    Doops down, an' thinks nae shame
To woo his bonny lassie
    When the kye comes hame!
        When the kye comes hame, etc.

See yonder pawkie shepherd,
    That lingers on the hill,
His ewes are in the fauld,
    An' his lambs are lying still;
Yet he downa gang to bed,
    For his heart is in a flame,
To meet his bonny lassie
    When the kye comes hame!
        When the kye comes hame, etc.

When the little wee bit heart
  Rises high in the breast,
An' the little wee bit starn
  Rises red in the east,
O there 's a joy sae dear,
  That the heart can hardly frame,
Wi' a bonny, bonny lassie,
  When the kye comes hame!
    When the kye comes hame, etc.

Then since all nature joins
  In this love without alloy,
O, wha wad prove a traitor
  To Nature's dearest joy?
O, wha wad choose a crown,
  Wi' its perils and its fame,
And *miss* his bonny lassie
  When the kye comes hame!
    When the kye comes hame,
      When the kye comes hame!
'Tween the gloaming and the mirk,
  When the kye comes hame!

JAMES HOGG.

THE MILKMAID'S SONG.

Turn, turn, for my cheeks they burn,
Turn by the dale, my Harry!
Fill pail, fill pail,
He has turned by the dale,
And there by the stile waits Harry.
Fill, fill,
Fill pail, fill,

For there by the stile waits Harry!
The world may go round, the world may stand
        still,
But I can milk and marry,
Fill pail,
I can milk and marry.

Wheugh, wheugh!
O, if we two
Stood down there now by the water,
I know who 'd carry me over the ford
As brave as a soldier, as proud as a lord,
Though I don't live over the water.
Wheugh, wheugh! he 's whistling through.
He 's whistling " The Farmer's Daughter."
Give down, give down,
 My crumpled brown!
He shall not take the road to the town,
For I 'll meet him beyond the water.
Give down, give down,
 My crumpled brown!
And send me to my Harry.
The folk o' towns
May have silken gowns,
But I can milk and marry,
Fill pail,
I can milk and marry.

Wheugh, wheugh! he has whistled through,
He has whistled through the water.
Fill, fill, with a will, a will,
For he 's whistled through the water,
And he 's whistling down
The way to the town,

And it 's not " The Farmer's Daughter ! "
Churr, churr ! goes the cockchafer,
The sun sets over the water,
Churr, churr ! goes the cockchafer,
I 'm too late for my Harry !
And, O, if he goes a-soldiering,
The cows they may low, the bells they may ring,
But I 'll neither milk nor marry,
Fill pail,
Neither milk nor marry.

My brow beats on thy flank, Fill pail,
Give down, good wench, give down !
I know the primrose bank, Fill pail,
Between him and the town.
Give down, good wench, give down, Fill pail,
And he shall not reach the town !
Strain, strain ! he 's whistling again,
He 's nearer by half a mile.
More, more ! O, never before
Were you such a weary while !
Fill, fill ! he 's crossed the hill,
I can see him down by the stile,
He 's passed the hay, he 's coming this way,
He 's coming to me, my Harry !
Give silken gowns to the folk o' towns,
He 's coming to me, my Harry !
There 's not so grand a dame in the land,
That she walks to-night with Harry !
Come late, come soon, come sun, come moon,
O, I can milk and marry,
Fill pail,
I can milk and marry.

Wheugh, wheugh! he has whistled through,
My Harry! my lad! my lover!
Set the sun and fall the dew,
Heigh-ho, merry world, what's to do
That you're smiling over and over?
Up on the hill and down in the dale,
And along the tree-tops over the vale
Shining over and over,
Low in the grass and high in the bough,
Shining over and over,
O world, have you ever a lover?
You were so dull and cold just now,
O world, have you ever a lover?
I could not see a leaf on the tree,
And now I could count them, one, two, three,
Count them over and over,
Leaf from leaf like lips apart,
Like lips apart for a lover.
And the hillside beats with my beating heart,
And the apple-tree blushes all over,
And the May bough touched me and made me
      start,
And the wind breathes warm like a lover.

Pull, pull! and the pail is full,
And milking's done and over.
Who would not sit here under the tree?
What a fair, fair thing's a green field to see!
Brim, brim, to the rim, ah me!
I have set my pail on the daisies!
It seems so light,—can the sun be set?
The dews must be heavy, my cheeks are wet,
I could cry to have hurt the daisies!

Harry is near, Harry is near,
My heart's as sick as if he were here,
My lips are burning, my cheeks are wet,
He hasn't uttered a word as yet,
But the air's astir with his praises.
My Harry!
The air's astir with your praises.

He has scaled the rock by the pixy's stone,
He's among the kingcups,—he picks me one,
I love the grass that I tread upon
When I go to my Harry!
He has jumped the brook, he has climbed the
    knowe,
There's never a faster foot I know,
But still he seems to tarry.
O Harry! O Harry! my love, my pride,
My heart is leaping, my arms are wide!
Roll up, roll up, you dull hillside,
Roll up, and bring my Harry!
They may talk of glory over the sea,
But Harry's alive, and Harry's for me,
My love, my lad, my Harry!
Come spring, come winter, come sun, come snow,
What cares Dolly, whether or no,
While I can milk and marry?
Right or wrong, and wrong or right,
Quarrel who quarrel, and fight who fight,
But I'll bring my pail home every night
To love, and home, and Harry!
We'll drink our can, we'll eat our cake,
There's beer in the barrel, there's bread in the
    bake.
19

The world may sleep, the world may wake,
But I shall milk and marry,
And marry,
I shall milk and marry.

SYDNEY DOBELL.

SALLY IN OUR ALLEY.

OF all the girls that are so smart
　There's none like pretty Sally;
She is the darling of my heart,
　And she lives in our alley.
There is no lady in the land
　Is half so sweet as Sally;
She is the darling of my heart,
　And she lives in our alley.

Her father he makes cabbage-nets,
　And through the streets does cry 'em;
Her mother she sells laces long
　To such as please to buy 'em;
But sure such folks could ne'er beget
　So sweet a girl as Sally!
She is the darling of my heart,
　And she lives in our alley.

When she is by I leave my work,
　I love her so sincerely;
My master comes like any Turk,
　And bangs me most severely.
But let him bang his bellyful,
　I'll bear it all for Sally;

For she 's the darling of my heart,
  And she lives in our alley.

Of all the days that 's in the week
  I dearly love but one day,
And that 's the day that comes betwixt
  The Saturday and Monday;
For then I 'm drest all in my best
  To walk abroad with Sally;
She is the darling of my heart,
  And she lives in our alley.

My master carries me to church,
  And often am I blamèd
Because I leave him in the lurch
  As soon as text is namèd.
I leave the church in sermon-time,
  And slink away to Sally;
She is the darling of my heart,
  And she lives in our alley.

When Christmas comes about again,
  O, then I shall have money!
I 'll hoard it up, and box it all,
  And give it to my honey;
I would it were ten thousand pound!
  I 'd give it all to Sally;
She is the darling of my heart,
  And she lives in our alley.

My master and the neighbors all
  Make game of me and Sally,
And, but for her, I 'd better be
  A slave, and row a galley;

But when my seven long years are out,
  O, then I 'll marry Sally!
O, then we 'll wed, and then we 'll bed,—
  But not in our alley!

HENRY CAREY.

ON THE ROAD.

I 's boun' to see my gal to-night—
  Oh, lone de way, my dearie!
De moon ain't out, de stars ain't bright—
  Oh, lone de way, my dearie!
Dis hoss o' mine is pow'ful slow,
But when I does git to yo' do'
Yo' kiss 'll pay me back, an' mo',
  Dough lone de way, my dearie.

De night is skeery-lak an' still—
  Oh, lone de way, my dearie!
'Cept fu' dat mou'nful whippo'will—
  Oh, lone de way, my dearie!
De way so long wif dis slow pace,
'T 'u'd seem to me lak savin' grace
Ef you was on a nearer place,
  Fu' lone de way, my dearie.

I hyeah de hootin' of de owl—
  Oh, lone de way, my dearie!
I wish dat watch-dog wouldn't howl—
  Oh, lone de way, my dearie!
An' evaht'ing bofe right an' lef',
Seem p'in'tly lak hit put itse'f

In shape to skeer me half to def—
 Oh, lone de way, my dearie!

I whistles so 's I won't be feared—
 Oh, lone de way, my dearie!
But anyhow I 's kin' o' skeered,
 Fu' lone de way, my dearie.
De sky been lookin' mighty glum,
But you kin mek hit lighten some,
Ef you 'll jes' say you 's glad I come,
 Dough lone de way, my dearie.

PAUL LAWRENCE DUNBAR.

GANGING *TO* AND GANGING *FRAE.*

Nae star was glintin' out aboon,
The cluds were dark and hid the moon;
The whistling gale was in my teeth,
And round me was the deep snaw wreath;
But on I went the dreary mile,
And sung right cantie a' the while
I gae my plaid a closer fauld;
My hand was warm, my heart was bauld,
I didna heed the storm and cauld,
  While ganging *to* my Katie.

But when I trod the same way back,
It seemed a sad and waefu' track;
The brae and glen were lone and lang;
I didna sing my cantie sang;
I felt how sharp the sleet did fa',
And couldna face the wind at a'.

Oh, sic a change! how could it be?
I ken fu' well, and sae may ye—
The sunshine had been gloom to me
  While ganging *frae* my Katie.

ELIZA COOK.

THE SPINNING-WHEEL SONG.

MELLOW the moonlight to shine is beginning;
Close by the window young Eileen is spinning;
Bent o'er the fire, her blind grandmother, sitting,
Is croaning, and moaning, and drowsily knit-
    ting,—
" Eileen, achora, I hear some one tapping."
" 'T is the ivy, dear mother, against the glass flap-
    ping."
" Eileen, I surely hear somebody sighing."
" 'T is the sound, mother dear, of the summer
    wind dying."
Merrily, cheerily, noisily whirring,
Swings the wheel, spins the reel, while the foot 's
    stirring;
Sprightly, and lightly, and airily ringing,
Thrills the sweet voice of the young maiden sing-
    ing.

" What 's that noise that I hear at the window, I
    wonder?"
" 'T is the little birds chirping the holly-bush
    under."
" What makes you be shoving and moving your
    stool on,

And singing all wrong that old song of 'The
　　Coolun' ?"
There's a form at the casement,—the form of her
　　true-love,—
And he whispers, with face bent, " I 'm waiting for
　　you, love;
Get up on the stool, through the lattice step
　　lightly,
We 'll rove in the grove while the moon's shining
　　brightly."
Merrily, cheerily, noisily whirring,
Swings the wheel, spins the reel, while the foot 's
　　stirring;
Sprightly, and lightly, and airily ringing,
Thrills the sweet voice of the young maiden sing-
　　ing.

The maid shakes her head, on her lip lays her
　　fingers,
Steals up from her seat,—longs to go, and yet
　　lingers;
A frightened glance turns to her drowsy grand-
　　mother,
Puts one foot on the stool, spins the wheel with
　　the other.
Lazily, easily, swings now the wheel round;
Slowly and lowly is heard now the reel's sound;
Noiseless and light to the lattice above her
The maid, steps,—then leaps to the arms of her
　　lover.
Slower—and　slower—and　slower　the　wheel
　　swings;
Lower—and lower—and lower the reel rings;

Ere the reel and the wheel stop their ringing and
    moving,
Through the grove the young lovers by moonlight
    are roving.

JOHN FRANCIS WALLER.

THE WELCOME.

COME in the evening, or come in the morning;
Come when you 're looked for or come without
    warning;
Kisses and welcome you 'll find here before you,
And the oftener you come here the more I 'll adore
    you!
  Light is my heart since the day we were
    plighted;
  Red is my cheek that they told me was blighted;
  The green of the trees looks far greener than
    ever,
  And the linnets are singing, " True lovers don't
    sever ! "

I 'll pull you sweet flowers, to wear if you choose
    them !
Or, after you 've kissed them, they 'll lie on my
    bosom ;
I 'll fetch from the mountain its breeze to inspire
    you ;
I 'll fetch from my fancy a tale that won't tire
    you.
  O, your step 's like the rain to the summer-
    vexed farmer,

Or sabre and shield to a knight without armor;
I 'll sing you sweet songs till the stars rise
    above me,
Then, wandering, I 'll wish you in silence to
    love me.

We 'll look through the trees at the cliff and the
    eyrie;
We-'ll tread round the rath on the track of the
    fairy;
We 'll look on the stars, and we 'll list to the river,
Till you ask of your darling what gift you can give
    her.
    O, she 'll whisper you, " Love, as unchangeably
        beaming,
    And trust, when in secret, most tunefully
        streaming;
Till the starlight of heaven above us shall
    quiver,
    As our souls flow in one down eternity's river."

So come in the evening, or come in the morning;
Come when you 're looked for, or come without
    warning;
Kisses and welcome you 'll find here before you,
And the oftener you come here the more I 'll adore
    you!
    Light is my heart since the day we were
        plighted;
    Red is my cheek that they told me was blighted;
    The green of the trees looks far greener than
        ever,
    And the linnets are singing, " True lovers don't
        sever ! "

THOMAS DAVIS.

FETCHING WATER FROM THE WELL.

Early on a sunny morning, while the lark was
singing sweet,
Came, beyond the ancient farm-house, sounds of
lightly tripping feet.
'T was a lowly cottage maiden going,—why, let
young hearts tell,—
With her homely pitcher laden, fetching water
from the well.
Shadows lay athwart the pathway, all along the
quiet lane,
And the breezes of the morning moved them to
and fro again.
O'er the sunshine, o'er the shadow, passed the
maiden of the farm,
With a charmèd heart within her, thinking of no
ill or harm.
Pleasant, surely, were her musings, for the nodding leaves in vain
Sought to press their brightening image on her
ever-busy brain.
Leaves and joyous birds went by her, like a dim,
half-waking dream;
And her soul was only conscious of life's gladdest
summer gleam.
At the old lane's shady turning lay a well of
water bright,
Singing, soft, its hallelujah to the gracious morning light.
Fern-leaves, broad and green, bent o'er it where its
silvery droplets fell,

And the fairies dwelt beside it, in the spotted fox-
glove bell.

Back she bent the shading fern-leaves, dipt the
pitcher in the tide,—

Drew it, with the dripping waters flowing o'er its
glazèd side.

But before her arm could place it on her shiny,
wavy hair,

By her side a youth was standing!—Love rejoiced
to see the pair!

Tones of tremulous emotion trailed upon the
morning breeze,

Gentle words of heart-devotion whispered 'neath
the ancient trees.

But the holy, blessèd secrets it becomes me not to
tell :

Life had met another meaning, fetching water
from the well!

Down the rural lane they sauntered. He the
burden-pitcher bore;

She, with dewy eyes down looking, grew more
beauteous than before!

When they neared the silent homestead, up he
raised the pitcher light;

Like a fitting crown he placed it on her hair of
wavelets bright:

Emblem of the coming burdens that for love of
him she 'd bear,

Calling every burden blessèd, if his love but
lighted there.

Then, still waving benedictions, further, further
off he drew,

While his shadow seemed a glory that across the
pathway grew.

Now about her household duties silently the
    maiden went,
And an ever-radiant halo o'er her daily life was
    blent.
Little knew the agèd matron as her feet like music
    fell,
What abundant treasure found she fetching water
    from the well!

ANONYMOUS.

LADY CLARE.

It was the time when lilies blow,
    And clouds are highest up in air,
Lord Ronald brought a lily-white doe
    To give his cousin, Lady Clare.

I trow they did not part in scorn:
    Lovers long-betrothed were they:
They too will wed the morrow morn:
    God's blessing on the day!

" He does not love me for my birth,
    Nor for my lands so broad and fair;
He loves me for my own true worth,
    And that is well," said Lady Clare.

In there came old Alice the nurse,
    Said, " Who was this that went from thee? "
" It was my cousin," said Lady Clare,
    " To-morrow he weds with me."

" O God be thanked! " said Alice the nurse,
    " That all comes round so just and fair:

Lord Ronald is heir of all your lands,
  And you are *not* the Lady Clare."

" Are ye out of your mind, my nurse, my nurse ? "
  Said Lady Clare, " that ye speak so wild ? "
" As God 's above," said Alice the nurse,
  " I speak the truth ! you are my child.

" The old Earl's daughter died at my breast ;
  I speak the truth, as I live by bread !
I buried her like my own sweet child,
  And put my child in her stead."

" Falsely, falsely have ye done,
  O mother," she said, " if this be true,
To keep the best man under the sun
  So many years from his due."

" Nay, now, my child," said Alice the nurse,
  " But keep the secret for your life,
And all you have will be Lord Ronald's,
  When you are man and wife."

" If I 'm a beggar born," she said,
  " I will speak out, for I dare not lie,
Pull off, pull off, the brooch of gold,
  And fling the diamond necklace by."

" Nay now, my child," said Alice the nurse,
  " But keep the secret all ye can."
She said, " Not so : but I will know
  If there be any faith in man."

" Nay now, what faith?" said Alice the nurse,
  " The man will cleave unto his right."
" And he shall have it," the lady replied,
  " Tho' I should die to-night."

" Yet give one kiss to your mother dear!
  Alas, my child, I sinned for thee."
" O mother, mother, mother," she said,
  " So strange it seems to me.

" Yet here 's a kiss for my mother dear,
  My mother dear, if this be so,
And lay your hand upon my head,
  And bless me, mother, ere I go."

She clad herself in a russet gown,
  She was no longer Lady Clare:
She went by dale and she went by down,
  With a single rose in her hair.

The lily-white doe Lord Ronald had brought
  Leapt up from where she lay,
Dropt her head in the maiden's hand,
  And followed her all the way.

Down stept Lord Ronald from his tower:
  " O Lady Clare, you shame your worth!
Why come you drest like a village maid,
  That are the flower of the earth?"

" If I come drest like a village maid,
  I am but as my fortunes are:

I am a beggar born," she said,
  " And not the Lady Clare."

" Play me no tricks," said Lord Ronald,
  " For I am yours in word and in deed.
Play me no tricks," said Lord Ronald,
  " Your riddle is hard to read."

O and proudly stood she up!
  Her heart within her did not fail:
She looked into Lord Ronald's eyes,
  And told him all her nurse's tale.

He laughed a laugh of merry scorn:
  He turned and kissed her where she stood:
" If you are not the heiress born,
  And I," said he, " the next in blood—

" If you are not the heiress born,
  And I," said he, " the lawful heir,
We two will wed to-morrow morn,
  And you shall still be Lady Clare."

ALFRED, LORD TENNYSON.

CURFEW MUST NOT RING TO-NIGHT.

SLOWLY England's sun was setting o'er the hill-
    tops far away,
Filling all the land with beauty at the close of one
    sad day,
And the last rays kissed the forehead of a man
    and maiden fair,—

He with footsteps slow and weary, she with sunny
    floating hair;
He with bowed head, sad and thoughtful, she with
    lips all cold and white,
Struggling to keep back the murmur,—
    " Curfew must not ring to-night."

" Sexton," Bessie's white lips faltered, pointing to
    the prison old,
With its turrets tall and gloomy, with its walls
    dark, damp, and cold,
" I 've a lover in that prison, doomed this very
    night to die,
At the ringing of the Curfew, and no earthly help
    is nigh;
Cromwell will not come till sunset," and her lips
    grew strangely white
As she breathed the husky whisper:—
    " Curfew must not ring to-night."

" Bessie," calmly spoke the sexton,—every word
    pierced her young heart
Like the piercing of an arrow, like a deadly poi-
    soned dart,—
" Long, long years I 've rung the Curfew from
    that gloomy, shadowed tower;
Every evening, just at sunset, it has told the twi-
    light hour;
I have done my duty ever, tried to do it just and
    right,
Now I 'm old I will not falter,—
    Curfew, it must ring to-night."

Wild her eyes and pale her features, stern and
    white her thoughtful brow,
As within her secret bosom Bessie made a solemn
    vow.
She had listened while the judges read without
    a tear or sigh:
" At the ringing of the Curfew, Basil Underwood
    must die."
And her breath came fast and faster, and her eyes
    grew large and bright;
In an undertone she murmured:—
    " Curfew must not ring to-night."

With quick step she bounded forward, sprung
    within the old church door,
Left the old man threading slowly paths so oft
    he 'd trod before;
Not one moment paused the maiden, but with eye
    and cheek aglow
Mounted up the gloomy tower, where the bell
    swung to and fro
As she climbed the dusty ladder on which fell no
    ray of light,
Up and up,—her white lips saying:—
    " Curfew must not ring to-night."

She has reached the topmost ladder; o'er her
    hangs the great dark bell;
Awful is the gloom beneath her, like the pathway
    down to hell.
Lo, the ponderous tongue is swinging,—'t is the
    hour of Curfew now,
And the sight has chilled her bosom, stopped her
    breath, and paled her brow.

20

Shall she let it ring?   No, never! flash her eyes
      with sudden light,
As she springs, and grasps it firmly,—
     " Curfew shall not ring to-night!"

Out she swung—far out; the city seemed a speck
      of light below,
There 'twixt heaven and earth suspended as the
      bell swung to and fro,
And the sexton at the bell-rope, old and deaf,
      heard not the bell,
Sadly thought, " That twilight Curfew rang young
      Basil's funeral knell."
Still the maiden clung more firmly, and with
      trembling lips so white,
Said to hush her heart's wild throbbing:—
     " Curfew shall not ring to-night!"

It was o'er, the bell ceased swaying, and the
      maiden stepped once more
Firmly on the dark old ladder where for hundred
      years before
Human foot had not been planted.   The brave
      deed that she had done
Should be told long ages after, as the rays of set-
      ting sun
Crimson all the sky with beauty; agèd sires, with
      heads of white,
Tell the eager, listening children,
     " Curfew did not ring that night."

O'er the distant hills came Cromwell; Bessie sees
      him, and her brow,

Lately white with fear and anguish, has no
    anxious traces now.
At his feet she tells her story, shows her hands all
    bruised and torn;
And her face so sweet and pleading, yet with
    sorrow pale and worn,
Touched his heart with sudden pity, lit his eyes
    with misty light:
" Go! your lover lives," said Cromwell,
    " Curfew shall not ring to-night."

Wide they flung the massive portal; led the
    prisoner forth to die,—
All his bright young life before him. 'Neath the
    darkening English sky
Bessie comes with flying footsteps, eyes aglow
    with love-light sweet;
Kneeling on the turf beside him, lays his pardon
    at his feet.
In his brave, strong arms he clasped her, kissed
    the face upturned and white,
Whispered, " Darling, you have saved me,—
    Curfew will not ring to-night! "

ROSE HARTWICK THORPE.

THE SLEEPING BEAUTY.

FROM " THE DAY DREAM."

YEAR after year unto her feet,
    She lying on her couch alone,
Across the purple coverlet,
    The maiden's jet-black hair has grown;

On either side her trancèd form
　Forth streaming from a braid of pearl;
The slumberous light is rich and warm,
　And moves not on the rounded curl.

The silk star-broidered coverlid
　Unto her limbs itself doth mould,
Languidly ever; and amid
　Her full black ringlets, downward rolled,
Glows forth each softly-shadowed arm,
　With bracelets of the diamond bright.
Her constant beauty doth inform
　Stillness with love, and day with light.

She sleeps: her breathings are not heard
　In palace chambers far apart.
The fragrant tresses are not stirred
　That lie upon her charmèd heart.
She sleeps; on either hand upswells
　The gold-fringed pillow lightly prest:
She sleeps, nor dreams, but ever dwells
　A perfect form in perfect rest.

THE ARRIVAL.

ALL precious things discovered late,
　To those that seek them issue forth;
For love in sequel works with fate,
　And draws the veil from hidden worth.
He travels far from other skies,
　His mantle glitters on the rocks—
A fairy prince, with joyful eyes,
　And lighter-footed than the fox.

The bodies and the bones of those
   That strove in other days to pass,
Are withered in the thorny close,
   Or scattered blanching in the grass.
He gazes on the silent dead:
   " They perished in their daring deeds."
This proverb flashes through his head:
   " The many fail; the one succeeds."

He comes, scarce knowing what he seeks.
   He breaks the hedge; he enters there;
The color flies into his cheeks;
   He trusts to light on something fair;
For all his life the charm did talk
   About his path, and hover near
With words of promise in his walk,
   And whispered voices in his ear.

More close and close his footsteps wind;
   The magic music in his heart
Beats quick and quicker, till he find
   The quiet chamber far apart.
His spirit flutters like a lark,
   He stoops, to kiss her, on his knee:
" Love, if thy tresses be so dark,
   How dark those hidden eyes must be!"

THE REVIVAL.

A touch, a kiss! the charm was snapt.
   There rose a noise of striking clocks,
And feet that ran, and doors that clapt,
   And barking dogs, and crowing cocks;
A fuller light illumined all,
   A breeze through all the garden swept,

A sudden hubbub shook the hall,
    And sixty feet the fountain leapt.

The hedge broke in, the banner blew,
    The butler drank, the steward scrawled,
The fire shot up, the martin flew,
    The parrot screamed, the peacock squalled,
The maid and page renewed their strife,
    The palace banged, and buzzed and clackt,
And all the long-pent stream of life
    Dashed downward in a cataract.

At last with these the king awoke,
    And in his chair himself upreared,
And yawned, and rubbed his face, and spoke,
    " By holy rood, a royal beard!
How say you? we have slept, my lords.
    My beard has grown into my lap."
The barons swore, with many words,
    'T was but an after-dinner's nap.

" Pardy," returned the king, " but still
    My joints are something stiff or so.
My lord, and shall we pass the bill
    I mentioned half an hour ago? "
The chancellor, sedate and vain,
    In courteous words returned reply :
But dallied with his golden chain,
    And, smiling, put the question by.

THE DEPARTURE.

And on her lover's arm she leant,
    And round her waist she felt it fold ;

And far across the hills they went
  In that new world which is the old.
Across the hills, and far away
  Beyond their utmost purple rim,
And deep into the dying day,
  The happy princess followed him.

" I 'd sleep another hundred years,
  O love, for such another kiss; "
" O wake forever, love," she hears,
  " O love, 't was such as this and this."
And o'er them many a sliding star,
  And many a merry wind was borne,
And, streamed through many a golden bar,
  The twilight melted into morn.

" O eyes long laid in happy sleep ! "
  " O happy sleep that lightly fled ! "
" O happy kiss, that woke thy sleep ! "
  " O love, thy kiss would wake the dead ! "
And o'er them many a flowing range
  Of vapor buoyed the crescent bark;
And, rapt thro' many a rosy change,
  The twilight died into the dark.

" A hundred summers ! can it be ?
  And whither goest thou, tell me where? "
" O, seek my father's court with me,
  For there are greater wonders there."
And o'er the hills, and far away
  Beyond their utmost purple rim,
Beyond the night, across the day,
  Thro' all the world she followed him.

                    ALFRED, LORD TENNYSON.

THE EVE OF SAINT AGNES.

SAINT AGNES' EVE,—ah, bitter chill it was!
The owl, for all his feathers, was a-cold;
The hare limped trembling through the frozen
    grass,
And silent was the flock in woolly fold:
Numb were the beadsman's fingers while he told
His rosary, and while his frosted breath,
Like pious incense from a censer old,
Seemed taking flight for heaven without a death,
Past the sweet virgin's picture, while his prayer
    he saith.

His prayer he saith, this patient, holy man;
Then takes his lamp and riseth from his knees,
And back returneth, meagre, barefoot, wan,
Along the chapel aisle by slow degrees;
The sculptured dead on each side seem to freeze,
Emprisoned in black, purgatorial rails;
Knights, ladies, praying in dumb orat'ries,
He passeth by; and his weak spirit fails
To think how they may ache in icy hoods and
    mails.

Northward he turneth through a little door,
And scarce three steps, ere music's golden tongue
Flattered to tears this aged man and poor;
But no,—already had his death-bell rung;
The joys of all his life were said and sung:
His was harsh penance on Saint Agnes' Eve:

Another way he went, and soon among
Rough ashes sat he for his soul's reprieve,
And all night kept awake, for sinners' sake to
    grieve.

That ancient beadsman heard the prelude soft:
And so it chanced, for many a door was wide,
From hurry to and fro. Soon, up aloft,
The silver, snarling trumpets 'gan to chide;
The level chambers, ready with their pride,
Were glowing to receive a thousand guests:
The carvèd angels, ever eager-eyed,
Stared, where upon their heads the cornice rests,
With hair blown back, and wings put crosswise
    on their breasts.

At length burst in the argent revelry,
With plume, tiara, and all rich array,
Numerous as shadows haunting fairily
The brain, new-stuffed, in youth, with triumphs
    gay
Of old romance. These let us wish away;
And turn, sole-thoughted, to one lady there,
Whose heart had brooded, all that wintry day,
On love, and winged Saint Agnes' saintly care,
As she had heard all dames full many times
    declare.

They told her how, upon Saint Agnes' Eve,
Young virgins might have visions of delight,
And soft adorings from their loves receive
Upon the honeyed middle of the night,
If ceremonies due they did aright;

As, supperless to bed they must retire,
And couch supine their beauties, lily white;
Nor look behind, nor sideways, but require
Of heaven with upward eyes for all that they
    desire.

Full of this whim was thoughtful Madeline;
The music, yearning like a god in pain,
She scarcely heard; her maiden eyes divine,
Fixed on the floor, saw many a sweeping train
Pass by,—she heeded not at all; in vain
Came many a tiptoe, amorous cavalier,
And back retired, not cooled by high disdain.
But she saw not; her heart was otherwhere;
She sighed for Agnes' dreams, the sweetest of the
    year.

She danced along with vague, regardless eyes,
Anxious her lips, her breathing quick and short;
The hallowed hour was near at hand; she sighs
Amid the timbrels, and the thronged resort
Of whisperers in anger or in sport;
Mid looks of love, defiance, hate, and scorn,
Hoodwinked with fairy fancy; all amort
Save to Saint Agnes and her lambs unshorn,
And all the bliss to be before to-morrow morn.

So purposing each moment to retire,
She lingered still. Meantime, across the moors,
Had come young Porphyro, with heart on fire
For Madeline. Beside the portal doors,
Buttressed from moonlight, stands he, and im-
    plores

All saints to give him sight of Madeline;
But for one moment in the tedious hours,
That he might gaze and worship all unseen;
Perchance speak, kneel, touch, kiss,—in sooth
    such things have been.

He ventures in: let no buzzed whisper tell:
All eyes be muffled, or a hundred swords
Will storm his heart, love's feverous citadel;
For him, those chambers held barbarian hordes,
Hyena foemen, and hot-blooded lords,
Whose very dogs would execrations howl
Against his lineage; not one breast affords
Him any mercy, in that mansion foul,
Save one old beldame, weak in body and in soul.

Ah, happy chance! the aged creature came,
Shuffling along with ivory-headed wand,
To where he stood, hid from the torch's flame,
Behind a broad hall-pillar, far beyond
The sound of merriment and chorus bland.
He startled her; but soon she knew his face,
And grasped his fingers in her palsied hand,
Saying, "Mercy, Porphyro! hie thee from this
    place;
They are all here to-night, the whole bloodthirsty
    race!

"Get hence! get hence! there's dwarfish Hilde-
    brand;
He had a fever late, and in the fit
He cursèd thee and thine, both house and land;
Then there's that old Lord Maurice, not a whit

More tame for his gray hairs—Alas me! flit!
Flit like a ghost away!" "Ah, gossip dear,
We 're safe enough; here in this arm-chair sit
And tell me how—" "Good saints, not here, not
    here;
Follow me, child, or else these stones will be thy
    bier."

He followed through a lowly archèd way,
Brushing the cobwebs with his lofty plume;
And as she muttered, "Well-a—well-a-day!"
He found him in a little moonlight room,
Pale, latticed, chill, and silent as a tomb.
"Now tell me where is Madeline," said he,
"O, tell me, Angela, by the holy loom
Which none but secret sisterhood may see,
When they Saint Agnes' wool are weaving
    piously."

"Saint Agnes! Ah! it is Saint Agnes' Eve,—
Yet men will murder upon holy days;
Thou must hold water in a witch's sieve,
And be liege-lord of all the elves and fays,
To venture so. It fills me with amaze
To see thee, Porphyro!—Saint Agnes' Eve!
God's help! my lady fair the conjurer plays
This very night; good angels her deceive!
But let me laugh awhile, I 've mickle time to
    grieve."

Feebly she laugheth in the languid moon,
While Porphyro upon her face doth look,
Like puzzled urchin on an aged crone
Who keepeth closed a wondrous riddle-book,

As spectacled she sits in chimney nook.
But soon his eyes grew brilliant, when she told
His lady's purpose; and he scarce could brook
Tears, at the thought of those enchantments cold,
And Madeline asleep in lap of legends old.

Sudden a thought came like a full-blown rose,
Flushing his brow, and in his painèd heart
Made purple riot; then doth he propose
A stratagem, that makes the beldame start:
"A cruel man and impious thou art!
Sweet lady, let her pray, and sleep and dream
Alone with her good angels, far apart
From wicked men like thee. Go, go! I deem
Thou canst not surely be the same that thou didst
    seem."

"I will not harm her, by all saints I swear!"
Quoth Porphyro; "O, may I ne'er find grace
When my weak voice shall whisper its last prayer,
If one of her soft ringlets I displace,
Or look with ruffian passion in her face:
Good Angela, believe me by these tears;
Or I will, even in a moment's space,
Awake, with horrid shout, my foemen's ears,
And beard them, though they be more fanged
    than wolves and bears."

"Ah! why wilt thou affright a feeble soul?
A poor, weak, palsy-stricken, churchyard thing,
Whose passing-bell may ere the midnight toll;
Whose prayers for thee, each morn and evening,
Were never missed." Thus plaining, doth she
    bring

A gentle speech from burning Porphyro;
So woful, and of such deep sorrowing,
That Angela gives promise she will do
Whatever he shall wish, betide her weal or woe.

Which was, to lead him, in close secrecy,
Even to Madeline's chamber, and there hide
Him in a closet, of such privacy
That he might see her beauty unespied,
And win perhaps that night a peerless bride,
While legioned fairies paced the coverlet,
And pale enchantment held her sleepy-eyed.
Never on such a night have lovers met,
Since Merlin paid his demon all the monstrous
     debt.

" It shall be as thou wishest," said the dame;
" All cates and dainties shall be storèd there
Quickly on this feast-night; by the tambour frame
Her own lute thou wilt see; no time to spare,
For I am slow and feeble, and scarce dare
On such a catering trust my dizzy head.
Wait here, my child, with patience kneel in prayer
The while. Ah! thou must needs the lady wed,
Or may I never leave my grave among the dead."

So saying, she hobbled off with busy fear.
The lover's endless minutes slowly passed:
The dame returned, and whispered in his ear
To follow her; with aged eyes aghast
From fright of dim espial. Safe at last,
Through many a dusky gallery, they gain
The maiden's chamber, silken, hushed and chaste;

Where Porphyro took covert, pleased amain.
His poor guide hurried back with agues in her
    brain.

Her faltering hand upon the balustrade,
Old Angela was feeling for the stair,
When Madeline, Saint Agnes' charmèd maid,
Rose, like a missioned spirit, unaware;
With silver taper's light, and pious care,
She turned, and down the aged gossip led
To a safe level matting. Now prepare,
Young Porphyro, for gazing on that bed!
She comes, she comes again, like ring-dove frayed
    and fled.

Out went the taper as she hurried in;
Its little smoke, in pallid moonshine, died;
She closed the door, she panted, all akin
To spirits of the air, and visions wide;
No uttered syllable, or, woe betide!
But to her heart, her heart was voluble,
Paining with eloquence her balmy side;
As though a tongueless nightingale should swell
Her throat in vain, and die, heart-stifled in her
    dell.

A casement high and triple-arched there was,
All garlanded with carven imageries
Of fruits, and flowers, and bunches of knot-grass,
And diamonded with panes of quaint device,
Innumerable of stains and splendid dyes,
As are the tiger-moth's deep-damasked wings;
And in the midst, 'mong thousand heraldries,

And twilight saints, and dim emblazonings,
A shielded scutcheon blushed with blood of queens
    and kings.

Full on this casement shone the wintry moon,
And threw warm gules on Madeline's fair breast,
As down she knelt for heaven's grace and boon;
Rose-bloom fell on her hands, together prest,
And on her silver cross soft amethyst,
And on her hair a glory, like a saint;
She seemed a splendid angel, newly drest,
Save wings, for heaven. Porphyro grew faint:
She knelt, so pure a thing, so free from mortal
    taint.

Anon his heart revives; her vespers done,
Of all its wreathèd pearls her hair she frees;
Unclasps her warmèd jewels one by one;
Loosens her fragrant bodice; by degrees
Her rich attire creeps rustling to her knees;
Half hidden, like a mermaid in sea-weed,
Pensive awhile she dreams awake, and sees,
In fancy, fair Saint Agnes in her bed,
But dares not look behind, or all the charm is
    fled.

Soon, trembling in her soft and chilly nest,
In sort of wakeful swoon, perplexed she lay,
Until the poppied warmth of sleep oppressed
Her soothèd limbs, and soul fatigued away;
Flown like a thought, until the morrow-day;
Blissfully havened both from joy and pain;
Clasped like a missal where swart Paynims
    pray;

Blinded alike from sunshine and from rain,
As though a rose should shut, and be a bud
   again.

Stolen to this paradise, and so entranced,
Porphyro gazed upon her empty dress,
And listened to her breathing, if it chanced
To wake into a slumberous tenderness;
Which when he heard, that minute did he bless,
And breathed himself; then from the closet
   crept,
Noiseless as fear in a wide wilderness,
And over the hushed carpet, silent, stept,
And 'tween the curtains peeped, where, lo!—
   how fast she slept.

Then by the bedside, where the faded moon
Made a dim, silver twilight soft he set
A table, and, half anguished, threw thereon
A cloth of woven crimson, gold, and jet:—
O for some drowsy Morphean amulet!
The boisterous, midnight, festival clarion,
The kettle-drum, and far-heard clarionet,
Affray his ears, though but in dying tone:—
The hall-door shuts again, and all the noise is
   gone.

And still she slept an azure-lidded sleep,
In blanchèd linen, smooth and lavendered;
While he from forth the closet brought a heap
Of candied apple, quince, and plum, and gourd;
With jellies soother than the creamy curd,
And lucent syrops, tinct with cinnamon;
  21

Manna and dates, in argosy transferred
From Fez; and spicèd dainties, every one,
From silken Samarc and to cedared Lebanon.

These delicates he heaped with glowing hand
On golden dishes and in baskets bright
Of wreathèd silver. Sumptuous they stand
In the retired quiet of the night,
Filling the chilly room with perfume light.—
"And now, my love, my seraph fair, awake!
Thou art my heaven, and I thine eremite;
Open thine eyes, for meek Saint Agnes' sake,
Or I shall drowse beside thee, so my soul doth
    ache."

Thus whispering, his warm, unnervèd arm
Sank in her pillow. Shaded was her dream
By the dusk curtains;—'t was a midnight charm
Impossible to melt as icèd stream:
The lustrous salvers in the moonlight gleam;
Broad golden fringe upon the carpet lies;
It seemed he never, never could redeem
From such a steadfast spell his lady's eyes;
So mused awhile, entoiled in woofèd phantasies.

Awakening up, he took her hollow lute,—
Tumultuous,—and, in chords that tenderest be,
He played an ancient ditty, long since mute,
In Provence called "La belle dame sans merci;"
Close to her ear touching the melody;—
Wherewith disturbed, she uttered a soft moan:
He ceased; she panted quick,—and suddenly

Her blue affrayèd eyes wide open shone:
Upon his knees he sank, pale as smooth-sculp-
    tured stone.

Her eyes were open, but she still beheld,
Now wide awake, the vision of her sleep.
There was a painful change, that nigh expelled
The blisses of her dream so pure and deep;
At which fair Madeline began to weep,
And moan forth witless words with many a
    sigh;
While still her gaze on Porphyro would keep;
Who knelt, with joinèd hands and piteous eye,
Fearing to move or speak, she looked so dream-
    ingly.

"Ah, Porphyro!" said she, "but even now
Thy voice was at sweet tremble in mine ear,
Made tunable with every sweetest vow;
And those sad eyes were spiritual and clear;
How changed thou art! how pallid, chill, and
    drear!
Give me that voice again, my Porphyro,
Those looks immortal, those complainings dear!
O, leave me not in this eternal woe,
For if thou diest, my love, I know not where to
    go."

Beyond a mortal man impassioned far
At these voluptuous accents, he arose,
Ethereal, flushed, and like a throbbing star
Seen mid the sapphire heaven's deep repose;
Into her dream he melted, as the rose

Blendeth its odor with the violet,—
Solution sweet; meantime the frost-wind blows
Like love's alarum pattering the sharp sleet
Against the window-panes: Saint Agnes' moon
    hath set.

'T is dark; quick pattereth the flaw-blown sleet:
" This is no dream, my bride, my Madeline! "
'T is dark; the icèd gusts still rave and beat:
" No dream? alas! alas! and woe is mine!
Porphyro will leave me here to fade and pine.
Cruel! what traitor could thee hither bring?
I curse not, for my heart is lost in thine,
Though thou forsakest a deceivèd thing;—
A dove forlorn and lost, with sick, unprunèd
    wing."

" My Madeline! sweet dreamer! lovely bride!
Say, may I be for aye thy vassal blest?
Thy beauty's shield, heart-shaped and vermeil
    dyed?
Ah, silver shrine, here will I take my rest
After so many hours of toil and quest,
A famished pilgrim,—saved by miracle.
Though I have found, I will not rob thy nest,
Saving of thy sweet self; if thou think'st well,
To trust, fair Madeline, to no rude infidel.

" Hark! 't is an elfin storm from faery land,
Of haggard seeming, but a boon indeed:
Arise, arise! the morning is at hand;—
The bloated wassailers will never heed:
Let us away, my love, with happy speed;

There are no ears to hear, or eyes to see,—
Drowned all in Rhenish and the sleepy mead:
Awake, arise, my love, and fearless be,
For o'er the southern moors I have a home for
    thee."

She hurried at his words, beset with fears,
For there were sleeping dragons all around,
At glaring watch, perhaps, with ready spears;
Down the wide stairs a darkling way they found,
In all the house was heard no human sound.
A chain-drooped lamp was flickering by each
    door;
The arras, rich with horseman, hawk, and hound,
Fluttered in the besieging wind's uproar;
And the long carpets rose along the gusty floor.

They glide, like phantoms, into the wide hall!
Like phantoms to the iron porch they glide,
Where lay the porter, in uneasy sprawl,
With a huge empty flagon by his side:
The wakeful bloodhound rose, and shook his hide,
But his sagacious eye an inmate owns;
By one, and one, the bolts full easy slide;
The chains lie silent on the footworn stones;
The key turns, and the door upon its hinges
    groans.

And they are gone! ay, ages long ago
These lovers fled away into the storm,
That night the baron dreamt of many a woe,
And all his warrior-guests, with shade and form
Of witch, and demon, and large coffin-worm,

Were long be-nightmared. Angela the old
Died palsy-twitched, with meagre face deform;
The beadsman, after thousand aves told,
For aye unsought-for slept among his ashes cold.

JOHN KEATS.

SO SWEET LOVE SEEMED.

So sweet love seemed that April morn,
When first we kissed beside the thorn,
So strangely sweet, it was not strange
We thought that love could never change.

But I can tell—let truth be told—
That love will change in growing old;
Though day by day is naught to see,
So delicate his motions be.

And in the end 't will come to pass
Quite to forget what once he was,
Nor even in fancy to recall
The pleasure that was all in all.

His little spring, that sweet we found,
So deep in summer floods is drowned,
I wonder, bathed in joy complete,
How love so young could be so sweet.

ROBERT SEYMOUR BRIDGES.

ECHOES.

How sweet the answer Echo makes
To Music at night
When, roused by lute or horn, she wakes,
And far away o'er lawns and lakes
Goes answering light!

Yet Love hath echoes truer far
And far more sweet
Than e'er, beneath the moonlight's star,
Of horn or lute or soft guitar
The songs repeat.

'T is when the sigh,—in youth sincere
And only then,
The sigh that 's breathed for one to hear—
Is by that one, that only Dear,
Breathed back again.

THOMAS MOORE.

LOVE'S YOUNG DREAM.

FROM " IRISH MELODIES."

O the days are gone when beauty bright
   My heart's chain wove!
When my dream of life, from morn till night,
   Was love, still love!
   New hope may bloom,
   And days may come,

Of milder, calmer beam,
But there 's nothing half so sweet in life
　As love's young dream!
O, there 's nothing half so sweet in life
　As love's young dream!

Though the bard to purer fame may soar,
　　　When wild youth 's past;
Though he win the wise, who frowned before,
　　　To smile at last;
　　　He 'll never meet
　　　A joy so sweet
　In all his noon of fame
As when first he sung to woman's ear
　　　His soul-felt flame,
And at every close she blushed to hear
　　　The one loved name!

O, that hallowed form is ne'er forgot,
　Which first love traced;
Still it lingering haunts the greenest spot
　On memory's waste!
　　　'T was odor fled
　　　As soon as shed;
　'T was morning's wingèd dream;
'T was a light that ne'er can shine again
　On life's dull stream!
O, 't was a light that ne'er can shine again
　On life's dull stream!

THOMAS MOORE.

VII.

LOVE'S POWER.

THE MIGHT OF ONE FAIR FACE.

THE might of one fair face sublimes my love,
 For it hath weaned my heart from low desires;
Nor death I heed, nor purgatorial fires.
Thy beauty, antepast of joys above,
 Instructs me in the bliss that saints approve;
For O, how good, how beautiful, must be
The God that made so good a thing as thee,
So fair an image of the heavenly Dove!
Forgive me if I cannot turn away
From those sweet eyes that are my earthly
      heaven,
For they are guiding stars, benignly given
To tempt my footsteps to the upward way;
And if I dwell too fondly in thy sight,
I live and love in God's peculiar light.

From the Italian of MICHAEL ANGELO.
Translation of J. E. TAYLOR.

MY TRUE–LOVE HATH MY HEART.

My true-love hath my heart, and I have his,
    By just exchange one to the other given:
I hold his dear, and mine he cannot miss,
    There never was a better bargain driven:
My true-love hath my heart, and I have his.

His heart in me keeps him and me in one;
    My heart in him his thoughts and senses guides:
He loves my heart, for once it was his own;
    I cherish his because in me it bides:
My true-love hath my heart, and I have his.

SIR PHILIP SIDNEY.

WERE I AS BASE AS IS THE LOWLY PLAIN.

Were I as base as is the lowly plain,
And you, my Love, as high as heaven above,
Yet should the thoughts of me your humble swain
Ascend to heaven, in honor of my Love.

Were I as high as heaven above the plain,
And you, my Love, as humble and as low
As are the deepest bottoms of the main,
    Wheresoe'er you were, with you my love should
        go.

Were you the earth, dear Love, and I the skies,
My love should shine on you like to the sun,

And look upon you with ten thousand eyes
Till heaven waxed blind, and till the world were
   done.

Wheresoe'er I am, below, or else above you,
Wheresoe'er you are, my heart shall truly love
   you.

JOSHUA SYLVESTER.

WHEN STARS ARE IN THE QUIET SKIES.

When stars are in the quiet skies,
   Then most I pine for thee;
Bend on me then thy tender eyes,
   As stars look on the sea!
For thoughts, like waves that glide by night,
   Are stillest when they shine;
Mine earthly love lies hushed in light
   Beneath the heaven of thine.

There is an hour when angels keep
   Familiar watch o'er men,
When coarser souls are wrapped in sleep—
   Sweet spirit, meet me then!
There is an hour when holy dreams
   Through slumber fairest glide;
And in that mystic hour it seems
   Thou shouldst be by my side.

My thoughts of thee too sacred are
   For daylight's common beam:

I can but know thee as my star,
My angel and my dream;
When stars are in the quiet skies,
Then most I pine for thee;
Bend on me then thy tender eyes,
As stars look on the sea!

EDWARD, LORD LYTTON.

COME, REST IN THIS BOSOM.

FROM " IRISH MELODIES."

COME, rest in this bosom, my own stricken deer,
Though the herd have fled from thee, thy home is
    still here;
Here still is the smile, that no cloud can o'ercast,
And a heart and a hand all thy own to the last.

Oh! what was love made for, if 't is not the same
Through joy and through torment, through glory
    and shame?
I know not, I ask not, if guilt's in that heart,
I but know that I love thee, whatever thou art.

Thou hast called me thy Angel in moments of
    bliss,
And thy Angel I'll be, mid the horrors of this,
Through the furnace, unshrinking, thy steps to
    pursue,
And shield thee, and save thee,—or perish there
    too!

THOMAS MOORE.

THE GILLYFLOWER OF GOLD.

A GOLDEN gillyflower to-day
I wore upon my helm alway,
And won the prize of this tourney.
　Hah! hah! la belle jaune giroflée.

However well Sir Giles might sit,
His sun was weak to wither it,
Lord Miles's blood was dew on it:
　Hah! hah! la belle jaune giroflée.

Although my spear in splinters flew
From John's steel-coat, my eye was true;
I wheeled about, and cried for you,
　Hah! hah! la belle jaune giroflée.

Yea, do not doubt my heart was good,
Though my sword flew like rotten wood,
To shout, although I scarcely stood,
　Hah! hah! la belle jaune giroflée.

My hand was steady, too, to take
My axe from round my neck, and break
John's steel-coat up for my love's sake.
　Hah! hah! la belle jaune giroflée.

When I stood in my tent again,
Arming afresh, I felt a pain
Take hold of me, I was so fain—
　Hah! hah! la belle jaune giroflée.

To hear: " *Honneur aux fils des preux!* "
Right in my ears again, and shew
The gillyflower blossomed new.
    Hah! hah! la belle jaune giroflée.

The Sieur Guillaume against me came,
His tabard bore three points of flame
From a red heart: with little blame—
    Hah! hah! la belle jaune giroflée.

Our tough spears crackled up like straw;
He was the first to turn and draw
His sword, that had no speck nor flaw,—
    Hah! hah! la belle jaune giroflée.

But I felt weaker than a maid,
And my brain, dizzied and afraid,
Within my helm a fierce tune play'd,—
    Hah! hah! la belle jaune giroflée.

Until I thought of your dear head,
Bowed to the gillyflower bed,
The yellow flowers stained with red;—
    Hah! hah! la belle jaune giroflée.

Crash! how the swords met, " *giroflée!* "
The fierce tune in my helm would play,
" *La belle! la belle jaune giroflée!* "
    Hah! hah! la belle jaune giroflée.

Once more the great swords met again,
    " *La belle! la belle!* " but who fell then?
Le Sieur Guillaume, who struck down ten;—
    Hah! hah! la belle jaune giroflée.

And as, with mazed and unarmed face,
Toward my own crown and the Queen's place
They led me at a gentle pace,—
  Hah! hah! la belle jaune giroflée.

I almost saw your quiet head
Bowed o'er the gillyflower bed,
The yellow flowers stained with red,—
  Hah! hah! la belle jaune giroflée.

                    WILLIAM MORRIS.

THE LANDLADY'S DAUGHTER.

THREE students were travelling over the Rhine;
They stopped when they came to the landlady's
      sign;
"Good landlady, have you good beer and wine?
And where is that dear little daughter of thine?"

"My beer and wine are fresh and clear;
My daughter she lies on the cold death-bier!"
And when to the chamber they made their way,
There, dead, in the coal-black shrine, she lay.

The first he drew near, and the veil gently raised,
And on her pale face he mournfully gazed:
"Ah! wert thou but living yet," he said,
"I 'd love thee from this time forth, fair maid!"

The second he slowly put back the shroud,
And turned him away and wept aloud:
"Ah! that thou liest in the cold death-bier!
Alas! I have loved thee for many a year!"

The third he once more uplifted the veil,
And kissed her upon her mouth so pale:
" Thee loved I always; I love still but thee;
And thee will I love through eternity!"

From the German of UHLAND.
Translation of J. S. DWIGHT.

BELIEVE ME, IF ALL THOSE ENDEAR- ING YOUNG CHARMS.

BELIEVE me, if all those endearing young charms,
　Which I gaze on so fondly to-day,
Were to change by to-morrow, and fleet in my
　　arms,
　Like fairy-gifts fading away,
Thou wouldst still be adored, as this moment thou
　　art,
　Let thy loveliness fade as it will,
And around the dear ruin each wish of my heart
　Would entwine itself verdantly still.

It is not while beauty and youth are thine own,
　And thy cheeks unprofaned by a tear,
That the fervor and faith of a soul may be known,
　To which time will but make thee more dear!
No, the heart that has truly loved never forgets,
　But as truly loves on to the close,
As the sunflower turns to her god when she sets
　The same look which she turned when he rose!

THOMAS MOORE.

FORGET THEE?

" Forget thee? "—If to dream by night, and muse
 on thee by day,
If all the worship, deep and wild, a poet's heart
 can pay,
If prayers in absence breathed for thee to Heav-
 en's protecting power,
If wingèd thoughts that flit to thee—a thousand
 in an hour,
If busy Fancy blending thee with all my future
 lot,—
If this thou call'st " forgetting," thou indeed shalt
 be forgot!

" Forget thee? "—Bid the forest-birds forget their
 sweetest tune;
" Forget thee? "—Bid the sea forget to swell beneath the moon;
Bid the thirsty flowers forget to drink the eve's
 refreshing dew;
Thyself forget thine " own dear land," and its
 " mountains wild and blue; "
Forget each old familiar face, each long-remem-
 bered spot;—
When these things are forgot by thee, then thou
 shalt be forgot!

Keep, if thou wilt, thy maiden peace, still calm
 and fancy-free,
For God forbid thy gladsome heart should grow
 less glad for me;
22

Yet, while that heart is still unwon, O, bid not
    mine to rove,
But let it nurse its humble faith and uncomplain-
    ing love;
If these, preserved for patient years, at last avail
    me not,
Forget me then;—but ne'er believe that thou
    canst be forgot!

                    JOHN MOULTRIE.

RENOUNCEMENT.

I MUST not think of thee; and, tired yet strong,
I shun the thought that lurks in all delight—
The thought of thee—and in the blue Heaven's
    height,
And in the sweetest passage of a song.
Oh, just beyond the fairest thoughts that throng
This breast, the thought of thee waits, hidden yet
    bright;
But it must never, never come in sight;
I must stop short of thee the whole day long.
But when sleep comes to close each difficult day,
When night gives pause to the long watch I keep,
And all my bonds I needs must loose apart,
Must doff my will as raiment laid away,—
With the first dream that comes with the first
    sleep
I run, I run, I am gathered to thy heart.

                  ALICE MEYNELL.

LOVE.

Such a starved bank of moss
　Till, that May morn,
Blue ran the flash across:
　Violets were born!

Sky—what a scowl of cloud
　Till, near and far,
Ray on ray split the shroud:
　Splendid, a star!

World—how it walled about
　Life with disgrace
Till God's own smile came out;
　That was thy face!

ROBERT BROWNING.

LAST NIGHT.

Last night the nightingale waked me,
　Last night when all was still;
It sang in the golden moonlight
　From out the woodland hill.
I opened the window gently,
　And all was dreamy dew—
And oh! the bird, my darling,
　Was singing, singing of you!

I think of you in the day-time;
　I dream of you by night—

I wake—would you were near me,
  And hot tears blind my sight.
I hear a sigh in the lime-tree,
  The wind is floating through,
And oh! the night, my darling,
  Is longing, longing for you.

Nor think I can forget you!
  I could not though I would!
I see you in all around me,—
  The stream, the night, the wood;
The flowers that sleep so gently,
  The stars above the blue,
Oh! heaven itself, my darling,
  Is praying, praying for you.

From the Swedish.
Translation of THÉOPHILE MARZIALS.

MINSTRELS' MARRIAGE-SONG.

FROM " ŒLLA : A TRAGICAL INTERLUDE."

First Minstrel.

THE budding floweret blushes at the light:
  The meads are sprinkled with the yellow hue;
In daisied mantles is the mountain dight;
  The slim young cowslip bendeth with the dew;
The trees enleafèd, into heaven straught,
When gentle winds do blow, to whistling din are
      brought.

The evening comes and brings the dew along;
  The ruddy welkin sheeneth to the eyne;

Around the ale-stake minstrels sing the song;
  Young ivy round the doorpost doth entwine;
I lay me on the grass; yet, to my will,
Albeit all is fair, there lacketh something still.

Second Minstrel.

So Adam thought, what time, in Paradise,
  All heaven and earth did homage to his mind.
In woman and none else man's pleasaunce lies,
  As instruments of joy are kind with kind.
Go, take a wife unto thine arms, and see
Winter and dusky hills will have a charm for thee.
                THOMAS CHATTERTON.

SUMMER DAYS.

  In summer, when the days were long,
We walked together in the wood:
  Our heart was light, our steps were strong;
Sweet flutterings were there in our blood,
  In summer, when the days were long.

  We strayed from morn till evening came;
We gathered flowers, and wove us crowns;
  We walked mid poppies red as flame,
Or sat upon the yellow downs;
  And always wished our life the same.

  In summer, when the days were long,
We leaped the hedge-row, crossed the brook;
  And still her voice flowed forth in song,
Or else she read some graceful book,
  In summer, when the days were long.

And then we sat beneath the trees,
With shadows lessening in the noon;
　And in the sunlight and the breeze,
We feasted many a gorgeous June,
　While larks were singing o'er the leas.

　In summer, when the days were long,
On dainty chicken, snow-white bread,
　We feasted, with no grace but song;
We plucked wild strawberries, ripe and red,
　In summer, when the days were long.

　We loved, and yet we knew it not,—
For loving seemed like breathing then;
　We found a heaven in every spot;
Saw angels, too, in all good men;
　And dreamed of God in grove and grot.

　In summer, when the days are long,
Alone I wander, muse alone.
　I see her not; but that old song
Under the fragrant wind is blown,
　In summer, when the days are long.

　Alone I wander in the wood:
But one fair spirit hears my sighs;
　And half I see, so glad and good,
The honest daylight of her eyes,
　That charmed me under earlier skies.

　In summer, when the days are long,
I love her as we loved of old.
　My heart is light, my step is strong;

For love brings back those hours of gold,
In summer, when the days are long.
WATHEN MARKS WILKS CALL.

FLY TO THE DESERT, FLY WITH ME.

SONG OF NOURMAHAL IN " THE LIGHT OF THE
HAREM."

" FLY to the desert, fly with me,
Our Arab tents are rude for thee;
But oh! the choice what heart can doubt
Of tents with love or thrones without?

" Our rocks are rough, but smiling there
The acacia waves her yellow hair,
Lonely and sweet, nor loved the less
For flowering in the wilderness.

" Our sands are bare, but down their slope
The silvery-footed antelope
As gracefully and gayly springs
As o'er the marble courts of kings.

" Then come,—thy Arab maid will be
The loved and lone acacia-tree,
The antelope, whose feet shall bless
With their light sound thy loneliness.

" Oh! there are looks and tones that dart
An instant sunshine through the heart,
As if the soul that minute caught
Some treasure it through life had sought;

" As if the very lips and eyes
Predestined to have all our sighs,
And never be forgot again,
Sparkled and spoke before as then!

" So came thy every glance and tone,
When first on me they breathed and shone;
New, as if brought from other spheres,
Yet welcome as if loved for years!

" Then fly with me, if thou hast known
No other flame, nor falsely thrown
A gem away, that thou hadst sworn
Should ever in thy heart be worn.

" Come, if the love thou hast for me
Is pure and fresh as mine for thee,—
Fresh as the fountain underground,
When first 't is by the lapwing found.

" But if for me thou dost forsake
Some other maid, and rudely break
Her worshipped image from its base,
To give to me the ruined place;

" Then, fare thee well!—I 'd rather make
My bower upon some icy lake
When thawing suns begin to shine,
Than trust to love so false as thine!"

There was a pathos in this lay,
　That even without enchantment's art

Would instantly have found its way
  Deep into Selim's burning heart;
But breathing, as it did, a tone
To earthly lutes and lips unknown;
With every chord fresh from the touch
Of music's spirit, 't was too much!
Starting, he dashed away the cup,—
  Which, all the time of this sweet air,
His hand had held, untasted, up,
  As if 't were fixed by magic there,
And naming her, so long unnamed,
So long unseen, wildly exclaimed,
" O Nourmahal! O Nourmahal!
  Hadst thou but sung this witching strain,
I could forget—forgive thee all,
  And never leave those eyes again."

The mask is off,—the charm is wrought,—
And Selim to his heart has caught,
In blushes, more than ever bright,
His Nourmahal, his Harem's Light!
And well do vanished frowns enhance
The charm of every brightened glance;
And dearer seems each dawning smile
For having lost its light awhile;
And, happier now for all her sighs,
  As on his arm her head reposes,
She whispers him, with laughing eyes,
  " Remember, love, the Feast of Roses!"

THOMAS MOORE.

IN A GONDOLA.

He sings.

I send my heart up to thee, all my heart
   In this my singing.
For the stars help me, and the sea bears part;
   The very night is clinging
Closer to Venice' streets to leave one space
   Above me, whence thy face
May light my joyous heart to thee its dwelling-
    place.

She speaks.

Say after me, and try to say
My very words, as if each word
Came from you of your own accord,
In your own voice, in your own way:
" This woman's heart and soul and brain
Are mine as much as this gold chain
She bids me wear; which " (say again)
" I choose to make by cherishing
A precious thing, or choose to fling
Over the boat-side, ring by ring."
And yet once more say . . . no word more!
Since words are only words. Give o'er!

Unless you call me, all the same,
Familiarly by my pet name,
Which if the Three should hear you call,
And me reply to, would proclaim
At once our secret to them all.

Ask of me, too, command me, blame—
Do, break down the partition-wall
'Twixt us, the daylight world beholds
Curtained in dusk and splendid folds!
What 's left but—all of me to take?
I am the Three's: prevent them, slake
Your thirst! 'T is said the Arab sage,
In practising with gems, can loose
Their subtle spirit in his cruce
And leave but ashes: so, sweet mage,
Leave them my ashes when thy use
Sucks out my soul, thy heritage!

He sings.

Past we glide, and past, and past!
  What 's that poor Agnesè doing
  Where they make the shutters fast?
  Gray Zanobi 's just a-wooing
To his couch the purchased bride:
  Past we glide!

Past we glide, and past, and past!
  Why 's the Pucci Palace flaring
Like a beacon to the blast?
  Guests by hundreds, not one caring
If the dear host's neck were wried:
  Past we glide!

She sings.

The moth's kiss, first!
Kiss me as if you made believe
You were not sure, this eve,

How my face, your flower, had pursed
Its petals up; so, here and there
You brush it, till I grow aware
Who wants me, and wide ope I burst.

The bee's kiss, now!
Kiss me as if you entered gay
My heart at some noonday,—
A bud that dares not disallow
The claim, so, all is rendered up,
And passively its shattered cup
Over your head to sleep I bow.

He sings.

What are we two?
I am a Jew,
And carry thee, farther than friends can pursue,
To a feast of our tribe;
Where they need thee to bribe
The devil that blasts them unless he imbibe
Thy . . . Scatter the vision for ever! And now,
As of old, I am I, thou art thou!
Say again, what we are?
The sprite of a star,
I lure thee above where the destinies bar
My plumes their full play
Till a ruddier ray
Than my pale one announce there is withering
　　away
Some . . . Scatter the vision for ever!
　　And now,
As of old, I am I, thou art thou!

He muses.

Oh, which were best, to roam or rest?
The land's lap or the water's breast?
To sleep on yellow millet-sheaves,
Or swim in lucid shallows, just
Eluding water-lily leaves,
An inch from Death's black fingers, thrust
To lock you, whom release he must;
Which life were best on Summer eves?

He speaks, musing.

Lie back: could thought of mine improve you?
From this shoulder let there spring
A wing; from this, another wing;
Wings, not legs and feet, shall move you!
Snow-white must they spring, to blend
With your flesh, but I intend
They shall deepen to the end,
Broader, into burning gold,
Till both wings crescent-wise enfold
Your perfect self, from 'neath your feet
To o'er your head, where, lo, they meet
As if a million sword-blades hurled
Defiance from you to the world!
Rescue me thou, the only real!
And scare away this mad ideal
That came, nor motions to depart!
Thanks! Now, stay ever as thou art!

Still he muses.

What if the Three should catch at last
Thy serenader? While there's cast,

Paul's cloak about my head, and fast
Gian pinions me, Himself has past
His stylet through my back; I reel;
And . . . is it thou I feel?

They trail me, these three godless knaves,
Past every church that saints and saves,
Nor stop till, where the cold sea raves
By Lido's wet accursèd graves,
They scoop mine, roll me to its brink,
And . . . on thy breast I sink!

She replies, musing.

Dip your arm o'er the boat side, elbow-deep,
As I do: thus: were death so unlike sleep,
Caught this way?   Death 's to fear from flame or
        steel,
Or poison doubtless; but from water—feel!

Go   find   the   bottom!   Would   you   stay   me?
        There!
Now pluck a great blade of that ribbon-grass
To plait in where the foolish jewel was,
I flung away: since you have praised my hair,
'T is proper to be choice in what I wear.

He speaks.

Row home? must we row home? too surely
Know I where its front 's demurely
Over the Guidecca piled;
Window just with window mating,
Door on door exactly waiting,

All 's the set face of a child:
But behind it, where 's a trace
Of the staidness and reserve,
And formal lines without a curve,
In the same child's playing-face?
No two windows look one way
O'er the small sea-water thread
Below them. Ah, the autumn day
I, passing, saw you overhead!
First, out a cloud of curtain blew,
Then a sweet cry, and last came you—
To catch your lory that must needs
Escape just then, of all times then,
To peck a tall plant's fleecy seeds
And make me happiest of men.
I scarce could breathe to see you reach
So far back o'er the balcony,
To catch him ere he climbed too high
Above you in the Smyrna peach,
That quick the round smooth cord of gold,
This coiled hair on your head, unrolled,
Fell down you like a gorgeous snake
The Roman girls were wont, of old,
When Rome there was, for coolness' sake
To let lie curling o'er their bosoms.
Dear lory, may his beak retain
Ever its delicate rose stain,
As if the wounded lotus-blossoms
Had marked their thief to know again.
Stay longer yet, for others' sake
Than mine! What should your chamber do?
—With all its rarities that ache
In silence while day lasts, but wake

At night-time and their life renew,
Suspended just to pleasure you
Who brought against their will together
These objects, and, while day lasts, weave
Around them such a magic tether
That dumb they look: your harp, believe,
With all the sensitive tight strings
Which dare not speak, now to itself
Breathes slumberously, as if some elf
Went in and out the chords,—his wings
Make murmur, wheresoe'er they graze,
As an angel may, between the maze
Of midnight palace-pillars, on
And on, to sow God's plagues, have gone
Through guilty glorious Babylon.
And while such murmurs flow, the nymph
Bends o'er the harp-top from her shell
As the dry limpet for the lymph
Come with a tune he knows so well.
And how your statues' hearts must swell!
And how your pictures must descend
To see each other, friend with friend!
Oh, could you take them by surprise,
You'd find Schidone's eager Duke
Doing the quaintest courtesies
To that prim saint by Haste-thee-Luke!
And, deeper into her rock den,
Bold Castelfranco's Magdalen
You'd find retreated from the ken
Of that robed counsel-keeping Ser—
As if the Tizian thinks of her,
And is not, rather, gravely bent
On seeing for himself what toys

Are these his progeny invent,
What litter now the board employs
Whereon he signed a document
That got him murdered! Each enjoys
Its night so well, you cannot break
The sport up: so, indeed must make
More stay with me, for others' sake.

She speaks.

To-morrow, if a harp-string, say,
Is used to tie the jasmine back
That overfloods my room with sweets,
Contrive your Zorzi somehow meets
My Zanze! If the ribbon 's black,
The Three are watching: keep away!

Your gondola—let Zorzi wreathe
A mesh of water-weeds about
Its prow, as if he unaware
Had struck some quay or bridge-foot stair!
That I may throw a paper out
As you and he go underneath.

There 's Zanze's vigilant taper; safe are we.
Only one minute more to-night with me?
Resume your past self of a month ago!
Be you the bashful gallant, I will be
The lady with the colder breast than snow.
Now bow you, as becomes, nor touch my hand
More than I touch yours when I step to land.
Just say, " All thanks, Siora!"—
                     Heart to heart
And lips to lips! yet once more, ere we part,
Clasp me and make me thine, as mine thou art!
  23

He is surprised, and stabbed.

It was ordained to be so, sweet!—and best
Comes now, beneath thine eyes, upon thy breast.
Still kiss me! Care not for the cowards! Care
Only to put aside thy beauteous hair
My blood will hurt! The Three, I do not scorn
To death, because they never lived: but I
Have lived indeed, and so—(yet one more kiss)—
    can die!

ROBERT BROWNING.

CLEOPATRA.

HERE Charmian, take my bracelets:
    They bar with a purple stain
My arms; turn over my pillows—
    They are hot where I have lain:
Open the lattice wider,
    A gauze o'er my bosom throw,
And let me inhale the odors
    That over the garden blow.

I dreamed I was with my Antony,
    And in his arms I lay;
Ah, me! the vision has vanished—
    The music has died away.
The flame and the perfume have perished—
    As this spiced aromatic pastille
That wound the blue smoke of its odor
    Is now but an ashy hill.

Scatter upon me rose leaves,
    They cool me after my sleep,

And with sandal odors fan me
  Till into my veins they creep;
Reach down the lute, and play me
  A melancholy tune,
To rhyme with the dream that has vanished
  And the slumbering afternoon.

There, drowsing in golden sunlight,
  Loiters the slow smooth Nile,
Through slender papyri, that cover
  The wary crocodile.
The lotus lolls on the water,
  And opens its heart of gold,
And over its broad leaf pavement
  Never a ripple is rolled.
The twilight breeze is too lazy
  Those feathery palms to wave,
And yon little cloud is motionless
  As a stone above a grave.

Ah, me! this lifeless nature
  Oppresses my heart and brain!
Oh! for a storm and thunder—
  For lightning and wild fierce rain!
Fling down that lute—I hate it!
  Take rather his buckler and sword,
And crash them and clash them together
  Till this sleeping world is stirred.

Hark! to my Indian beauty—
  My cockatoo, creamy white,
With roses under his feathers—
  That flashes across the light.

Look! listen! as backward and forward
  To his hoop of gold he clings,
How he trembles, with crest uplifted,
  And shrieks as he madly swings!
Oh, cockatoo, shriek for Antony!
  Cry, " Come, my love, come home!"
Shriek, " Antony! Antony! Antony!"
  Till he hears you even in Rome.

There—leave me, and take from my chamber
  That stupid little gazelle,
With its bright black eyes so meaningless,
  And its silly tinkling bell!
Take him,—my nerves he vexes—
  The thing without blood or brain,
Or, by the body of Isis,
  I 'll snap his thin neck in twain!

Leave me to gaze at the landscape
  Mistily stretching away,
Where the afternoon's opaline tremors
  O'er the mountains quivering play;
Till the fiercer splendor of sunset
  Pours from the west its fire,
And melted, as in a crucible,
  Their earthly forms expire;
And the bald blear skull of the desert
  With glowing mountains is crowned,
That burning like molten jewels
  Circle its temples round.

I will lie and dream of the past time,
  Æons of thought away,

And through the jungle of memory
  Loosen my fancy to play;
When, a smooth and velvety tiger,
  Ribbed with yellow and black,
Supple and cushion-footed
  I wandered, where never the track
Of a human creature had rustled
  The silence of mighty woods,
And, fierce in a tyrannous freedom,
  I knew but the law of my moods.
The elephant, trumpeting, started,
  When he heard my footstep near,
And the spotted giraffes fled wildly
  In a yellow cloud of fear.
I sucked in the noontide splendor,
  Quivering along the glade,
Or yawning, panting, and dreaming,
  Basked in the tamarisk shade,
Till I heard my wild mate roaring,
  As the shadows of night came on
To brood in the trees' thick branches,
  And the shadow of sleep was gone;
Then I roused, and roared in answer,
  And unsheathed from my cushioned feet
My curving claws, and stretched me,
  And wandered my mate to greet.
We toyed in the amber moonlight,
  Upon the warm flat sand,
And struck at each other our massive arms—
  How powerful he was and grand!
His yellow eyes flashed fiercely
  As he crouched and gazed at me,
And his quivering tail, like a serpent,
  Twitched curving nervously.

Then like a storm he seized me,
  With a wild triumphant cry,
And we met, as two clouds in heaven
  When the thunder before them fly.
We grappled and struggled together,
  For his love like his rage was rude;
And his teeth in the swelling folds of my neck
  At times, in our play, drew blood.

Often another suitor—
  For I was flexile and fair—
Fought for me in the moonlight,
  While I lay couching there,
Till his blood was drained by the desert;
  And, ruffled with triumph and power,
He licked me and lay beside me
  To breathe him a vast half-hour.
Then down to the fountain we loitered,
  Where the antelopes came to drink;
Like a bolt we sprang upon them,
  Ere they had time to shrink.
We drank their blood and crushed them,
  And tore them limb from limb,
And the hungriest lion doubted
  Ere he disputed with him.

That was a life to live for!
  Not this weak human life,
With its frivolous bloodless passions,
  Its poor and petty strife!

Come to my arms, my hero!
  The shadows of twilight grow,

And the tiger's ancient fierceness
  In my veins begins to flow.
Come not cringing to sue me!
  Take me with triumph and power,
As a warrior storms a fortress!
  I will not shrink or cower.
Come, as you came in the desert,
  Ere we were women and men,
When the tiger passions were in us,
  And love as you loved me then!

WILLIAM WETMORE STORY.

LOVE.

THERE are who say the lover's heart
  Is in the loved one's merged;
O, never by love's own warm art
  So cold a plea was urged!
No!—hearts that love hath crowned or crossed
  Love fondly knits together;
But not a thought or hue is lost
  That made a part of either.

   .   .   .   .   .

It is an ill-told tale that tells
  Of " hearts by love made one; "
He grows who near another's dwells
  More conscious of his own;
In each spring up new thoughts and powers
  That mid love's warm, clear weather,
Together tend like climbing flowers,
  And, turning, grow together.

Such fictions blink love's better part,
  Yield up its half of bliss;
The wells are in the neighbor heart
  When there is thirst in this:
There findeth love the passion-flowers
  On which it learns to thrive,
Makes honey in another's bowers,
  But brings it home to hive.

Love's life is in its own replies,—
  To each low beat it beats,
Smiles back the smiles, sighs back the sighs,
  And every throb repeats.
Then, since one loving heart still throws
  Two shadows in love's sun,
How should two loving hearts compose
  And mingle into one?

                    THOMAS KIBBLE HERVEY.

KEATS'S LAST SONNET.

BRIGHT star! would I were steadfast as thou art
Not in lone splendor hung aloft the night,
And watching, with eternal lids apart,
Like Nature's patient sleepless Eremite,
The moving waters at their priestlike task
Of pure ablution round earth's human shores,
Or gazing on the new soft fallen mask
Of snow upon the mountains and the moors.—
No—yet still steadfast, still unchangeable,
Pillowed upon my fair love's ripening breast,
To feel for ever its soft fall and swell,

Awake for ever in a sweet unrest;
Still, still to hear her tender-taken breath,
And so live ever—or else swoon to death.

JOHN KEATS.

STANZAS.

WRITTEN ON THE ROAD BETWEEN FLORENCE AND PISA.

OH, talk not to me of a name great in story;
The days of our youth are the days of our glory,
And the myrtle and ivy of sweet two-and-twenty
Are worth all your laurels, though ever so plenty.

What are garlands and crowns to the brow that is
      wrinkled?
'T is but as a dead flower with May-dew be-
      sprinkled.
Then away with all such from the head that is
      hoary!
What care I for the wreaths that can only give
      glory?

O, Fame! if I e'er took delight in thy praises,
'T was less for the sake of thy high-sounding
      phrases
Than to see the bright eyes of the dear one dis-
      cover
She thought that I. was not unworthy to love
      her.

There chiefly I sought thee, there only I found
      thee;

Her glance was the best of the rays that surround
    thee;
When it sparkled o'er aught that was bright in my
    story,
I knew it was love and I felt it was glory.

LORD BYRON.

THE SONG OF THE CAMP.

" GIVE us a song!" the soldiers cried,
    The outer trenches guarding,
When the heated guns of the camps allied
    Grew weary of bombarding.

The dark Redan, in silent scoff,
    Lay grim and threatening under;
And the tawny mound of the Malakoff
    No longer belched its thunder.

There was a pause. A guardsman said:
    " We storm the forts to-morrow;
Sing while we may, another day
    Will bring enough of sorrow."

They lay along the battery's side,
    Below the smoking cannon:
Brave hearts from Severn and from Clyde,
    And from the banks of Shannon.

They sang of love, and not of fame;
    Forgot was Britain's glory:

Each heart recalled a different name,
  But all sang " Annie Laurie."

Voice after voice caught up the song,
  Until its tender passion
Rose like an anthem, rich and strong,—
  Their battle-eve confession.

Dear girl, her name he dared not speak,
  But as the song grew louder,
Something upon the soldier's cheek
  Washed off the stains of powder.

Beyond the darkening ocean burned
  The bloody sunset's embers,
While the Crimean valleys learned
  How English love remembers.

And once again a fire of hell
  Rained on the Russian quarters,
With scream of shot, and burst of shell,
  And bellowing of the mortars!

And Irish Nora's eyes are dim
  For a singer dumb and gory;
And English Mary mourns for him
  Who sang of " Annie Laurie."

Sleep, soldiers! still in honored rest
  Your truth and valor wearing:
The bravest are the tenderest,—
  The loving are the daring.

                BAYARD TAYLOR.

TO FIDESSA.

Tongue! never cease to sing Fidessa's praise;
Heart! howe'er she deserve, conceive the best;
Eyes! stand amazed to see her beauty's rays;
Lips! steal one kiss and be for ever blessed;
 Hands! touch that hand wherein your life is
  closed;
Breast! lock up fast in thee thy life's sole
  treasure;
Arms! still embrace, and never be disclosed;
Feet! run to her without or pace or measure,
Tongue! heart! eyes! lips! hands! breast! arms!
  feet!
Consent to do true homage to your Queen:
Lovely, fair, gent, wise, virtuous, sober, sweet,
Whose like shall never be, hath never been!
O that I were all tongue her praise to show!
Then surely my poor heart were freed from woe.

BARTHOLOMEW GRIFFIN.

MEETING AT NIGHT.

The gray sea, and the long black land;
And the yellow half-moon large and low;
And the startling little waves, that leap
In fiery ringlets from their sleep,
As I gain the cove with pushing prow,
And quench its speed in the slushy sand.

Then a mile of warm, sea-scented beach;
Three fields to cross, till a farm appears:

A tap at the pane, the quick sharp scratch
And blue spurt of a lighted match,
And a voice less loud, through its joys and fears,
Than the two hearts, beating each to each.

ROBERT BROWNING.

CHARLIE MACHREE.

COME over, come over
The river to me,
If ye are my laddie,
Bold Charlie machree.

Here's Mary McPherson
And Susy O'Linn,
Who say ye're faint-hearted,
And darena plunge in.

But the dark rolling water,
Though deep as the sea,
I know willna scare ye,
Nor keep ye frae me;

For stout is yer back,
And strong is yer arm,
And the heart in yer bosom
Is faithful and warm.

Come over, come over
The river to me,
If ye are my laddie,
Bold Charlie machree!

I see him, I see him!
He's plunged in the tide,
His strong arms are dashing
The big waves aside.

O, the dark rolling water
Shoots swift as the sea,
But blithe is the glance
Of his bonny blue ee.

And his cheeks are like roses,
Twa buds on a bough;
Who says ye're faint-hearted,
My brave Charlie, now?

Ho, ho, foaming river,
Ye may roar as ye go,
But ye canna bear Charlie
To the dark loch below!

Come over, come over
The river to me,
My true-hearted laddie,
My Charlie machree!

He's sinking, he's sinking,
O, what shall I do!
Strike out, Charlie, boldly,
Ten strokes and ye're thro'!

He's sinking, O Heaven!
Ne'er fear, man, ne'er fear;

I 've a kiss for ye, Charlie,
As soon as ye 're here!

He rises, I see him,—
Five strokes, Charlie, mair,—
He 's shaking the wet
From his bonny brown hair;

He conquers the current,
He gains on the sea,—
Ho, where is the swimmer
Like Charlie machree?

Come over the river,
But once come to me,
And I 'll love ye forever,
Dear Charlie machree!

He 's sinking, he 's gone,—
O God! it is I,
It is I, who have killed him—
Help, help!—he must die!

Help, help!—ah, he rises,—
Strike out and ye 're free!
Ho, bravely done, Charlie,
Once more now, for me!

Now cling to the rock,
Now gie us yer hand,—
Ye 're safe, dearest Charlie,
Ye 're safe on the land!

Come rest in my bosom,
If *there* ye can sleep;
I canna speak to ye,
I only can weep.

Ye 've crossed the wild river,
Ye 've risked all for me,
And I 'll part frae ye never,
Dear Charlie machree!

WILLIAM J. HOPPIN.

HOPE DEFERRED.

His hand at last! By his own fingers writ,
I catch my name upon the wayworn sheet:
His hand—oh, reach it to me quick! And yet,
Scarce can I hold, so fast my pulses beat.

O feast of soul! O banquet richly spread!
O passion-lettered scroll from o'er the sea!
Like a fresh burst of life to one long dead,
Joy, strength, and bright content come back
with thee,

Long prayed and waited for through months so
drear;
Each day methought my waiting heart must
break;
Why is it that our loved ones grow more dear
The more we suffer for their sweetest sake?

His hand at last! each simple word aglow
With truthful tenderness and promise sweet.

Now to my daily tasks I 'll singing go,
  Fed by the music of this wayworn sheet.
ANONYMOUS.

THE OLD MAID.

SHE gave her life to love. She never knew
  What other women give their all to gain.
Others were fickle. She was passing true.
  She gave pure love, and faith without a stain.

She never married. Suitors came and went:
  The dark eyes flashed their love on one alone.
Her life was passed in quiet and content.
  The old love reigned. No rival shared the
    throne.

Think you her life was wasted? Vale and hill
  Blossomed in summer, and white winter came;
The blue ice stiffened on the silenced rill;
  All times and seasons found her still the same.

Her heart was full of sweetness till the end.
  What once she gave, she never took away.
Through all her youth she loved one faithful
    friend:
  She loves him now her hair is growing gray.
GEORGE BARLOW.

24

THE LOVELINESS OF LOVE.

It is not Beauty I demand,
    A crystal brow, the moon's despair,
Nor the snow's daughter, a white hand,
    Nor mermaid's yellow pride of hair:

Tell me not of your starry eyes,
    Your lips that seem on roses fed,
Your breasts, where Cupid tumbling lies
    Nor sleeps for kissing of his bed,—

A bloomy pair of vermeil cheeks
    Like Hebe's in her ruddiest hours,
A breath that softer music speaks
    Than summer winds a-wooing flowers;—

These are but gauds: nay, what are lips?
    Coral beneath the ocean-stream,
Whose brink when your adventurer slips
    Full oft he perisheth on them.

And what are cheeks, but ensigns oft
    That wave hot youth to fields of blood?
Did Helen's breast, though ne'er so soft,
    Do Greece or Ilium any good?

Eyes can with baleful ardor burn;
    Poison can breath, that erst perfumed;
There 's many a white hand holds an urn
    With lovers' hearts to dust consumed.

For crystal brows there 's naught within;
  They are but empty cells for pride;
He who the Siren's hair would win
  Is mostly strangled in the tide.

Give me, instead of Beauty's bust,
  A tender heart, a loyal mind,
Which with temptation I would trust,
  Yet never linked with error find,—

One in whose gentle bosom I
  Could pour my secret heart of woes,
Like the care-burdened honey-fly
  That hides his murmurs in the rose,—

My earthly Comforter! whose love
  So indefeasible might be
That, when my spirit wonned above,
  Hers could not stay, for sympathy.

GEORGE DARLEY.

TO ONE IN PARADISE.

Thou wast all that to me, love,
  For which my soul did pine:
A green isle in the sea, love,
  A fountain and a shrine
All wreathed with fairy fruits and flowers,
  And all the flowers were mine.

Ah, dream too bright to last!
  Ah, starry Hope, that didst arise

But to be overcast!
  A voice from out the Future cries,
"On! on!"—but o'er the Past
  (Dim gulf!) my spirit hovering lies
Mute, motionless, aghast.

For, alas! alas! with me
  The light of Life is o'er!
No more—no more—no more—
(Such language holds the solemn sea
  To the sands upon the shore)
Shall bloom the thunder-blasted tree,
  Or the stricken eagle soar.

And all my days are trances,
  And all my nightly dreams
Are where thy gray eye glances,
  And where thy footstep gleams—
In what ethereal dances,
  By what eternal streams.

                              EDGAR ALLAN POE.

AN OLD SWEETHEART OF MINE.

As one who cons at evening o'er an album all
    alone,
And muses on the faces of the friends that he has
    known,
So I turn the leaves of fancy, till in shadowy
    design
I find the smiling features of an old sweetheart of
    mine.

The lamplight seems to glimmer with a flicker of
    surprise,
As I turn it low to rest me of the dazzle in my
    eyes,
And light my pipe in silence, save a sigh that
    seems to yoke
Its fate with my tobacco, and to vanish with the
    smoke.

'T is a fragrant retrospection—for the loving
    thoughts that start
Into being are like perfume from the blossom of
    the heart;
And to dream the old dreams over is a luxury
    divine—
When my truant fancy wanders with that old
    sweetheart of mine.

Though I hear, beneath my study, like a fluttering
    of wings,
The voices of my children, and the mother as she
    sings,
I feel no twinge of conscience to deny me any
    theme
When Care has cast her anchor in the harbor of a
    dream.

In fact, to speak in earnest, I believe it adds a
    charm
To spice the good a trifle with a little dust of
    harm—
For I find an extra flavor in Memory's mellow
    wine
That makes me drink the deeper to that old
    sweetheart of mine.

A face of lily-beauty, with a form of airy grace,
Floats out of my tobacco as the genii from the
    vase;
And I thrill beneath the glances of a pair of azure
    eyes
As glowing as the summer and as tender as the
    skies.

I can see the pink sunbonnet and the little check-
    ered dress
She wore when first I kissed her and she answered
    the caress
With the written declaration that, " as surely as
    the vine
Grew round the stump," she loved me—that old
    sweetheart of mine.

And again I feel the pressure of her slender little
    hand,
As we used to talk together of the future we had
    planned—
When I should be a poet, and with nothing else
    to do
But write the tender verses that she set the
    music to:

When we should live together in a cosy little cot,
Hid in a nest of roses, with a fairy garden-spot,
Where the vines were ever fruited, and the
    weather ever fine,
And the birds were ever singing for that old
    sweetheart of mine:

When I should be her lover forever and a day,
And she my faithful sweetheart till the golden
hair was gray;
And we should be so happy that when either's lips
were dumb
They would not smile in Heaven till the other's
kiss had come.

.   .   .   .   .

But, ah! my dream is broken by a step upon the
stair,
And the door is softly opened, and—my wife is
standing there;
Yet with eagerness and rapture all my visions I
resign
To greet the living presence of that old sweetheart of mine.

JAMES WHITCOMB RILEY.

ROSE AYLMER.

Ah what avails the sceptred race,
Ah what the form divine!
What every virtue, every grace!
Rose Aylmer, all were thine.
Rose Aylmer, whom these wakeful eyes
May weep, but never see,
A night of memories and of sighs
I consecrate to thee.

WALTER SAVAGE LANDOR.

VIII.

WEDDED LOVE.

LET ME NOT TO THE MARRIAGE OF TRUE MINDS.

SONNET CXVI.

LET me not to the marriage of true minds
Admit impediments: love is not love,
Which alters when it alteration finds,
Or bends with the remover to remove;
O, no! it is an ever-fixèd mark,
That looks on tempests, and is never shaken;
It is the star to every wandering bark,
Whose worth's unknown, although his height be
    taken.
Love's not Time's fool, though rosy lips and
    cheeks
Within his bending sickle's compass come;
Love alters not with his brief hours and weeks,
But bears it out even to the edge of doom.
  If this be error, and upon me proved,
  I never writ, nor no man ever loved.

SHAKESPEARE.

SONNETS FROM THE PORTUGUESE.

VI.

Go from me. Yet I feel that I shall stand
Henceforward in thy shadow. Nevermore
Alone upon the threshold of my door
Of individual life, I shall command
The uses of my soul, nor lift my hand
Serenely in the sunshine as before,
Without the sense of that which I forbore, . . .
Thy touch upon the palm. The widest land
Doom takes to part us, leaves thy heart in mine
With pulses that beat double. What I do
And what I dream include thee, as the wine
Must taste of its own grapes. And when I sue
God for myself, he hears that name of thine,
And sees within my eyes the tears of two.

XIV.

If thou must love me, let it be for naught
Except for love's sake only. Do not say
" I love her for her smile . . . her look . . . her
    way
Of speaking gently,—for a trick of thought
That falls in well with mine, and certes brought
A sense of pleasant ease on such a day."
For these things in themselves, belovèd, may
Be changed, or change for thee,—and love so
    wrought,
May be unwrought so. Neither love me for
Thine own dear pity's wiping my cheeks dry,—

A creature might forget to weep, who bore
Thy comfort long, and lose thy love thereby.
But love me for love's sake, that evermore
Thou mayst love on, through love's eternity.

XVIII.

I NEVER gave a lock of hair away
To a man, Dearest, except this to thee,
Which now upon my fingers thoughtfully
I ring out to the full brown length and say
"Take it." My day of youth went yesterday;
My hair no longer bounds to my foot's glee.
Nor plant I it from rose or myrtle tree,
As girls do, any more. It only may
Now shade on two pale cheeks, the mark of tears,
Taught drooping from the head that hangs aside
Through sorrow's trick. I thought the funeral
    shears
Would take this first, but Love is justified,—
Take it thou, . . . finding pure, from all those
    years,
The kiss my mother left here when she died.

XXI.

SAY over again, and yet once over again,
That thou dost love me. Though the word re-
    peated
Should seem a " cuckoo-song," as thou dost treat
    it,
Remember never to the hill or plain,
Valley and wood, without her cuckoo-strain,
Comes the fresh spring in all her green completed.
Beloved, I, amid the darkness greeted

By a doubtful spirit-voice, in that doubt's pain
Cry: "Speak once more—thou lovest!" Who
    can fear
Too many stars, though each in heaven shall
    roll,—
Too many flowers, though each shall crown the
    year?
Say thou dost love me, love me, love me,—toll
The silver iterance!—only minding, dear,
To love me also in silence, with thy soul.

XXVIII.

My letters! all dead paper, . . . mute and
    white!—
And yet they seem alive and quivering
Against my tremulous hands which loose the
    string
And let them drop down on my knee to-night.
This said, . . . he wished to have me in his sight
Once, as a friend: this fixed a day in spring
To come and touch my hand . . . a simple thing,
Yet I wept for it! this, . . . the paper's light . . .
Said, *Dear, I love thee;* and I sank and quailed
As if God's future thundered on my past.
This said, *I am thine.*—and so its ink has paled
With lying at my heart that beat too fast.
And this . . . O Love, thy words have ill availed,
If what this said, I dared repeat at last!

XXXV.

If I leave all for thee, wilt thou exchange
And be all to me? Shall I never miss
Home-talk and blessing and the common kiss

That comes to each in turn, nor count it strange,
When I look up, to drop on a new range
Of walls and floors, another home than this?
Nay, wilt thou fill that place by me which is
Filled by dead eyes too tender to know change
That's hardest? If to conquer love, has tried,
To conquer grief, tries more, as all things prove,
For grief indeed is love and grief beside.
Alas, I have grieved so I am hard to love.
Yet love me—wilt thou? Open thine heart wide,
And fold within the wet wings of thy dove.

XXXVIII.

First time he kissed me, he but only kissed
The fingers of this hand wherewith I write;
And, ever since, it grew more clean and white,
Slow to world-greetings, quick with its "O list!"
When the angels speak. A ring of amethyst
I could not wear here, plainer to my sight
Than that first kiss. The second passed in height
The first, and sought the forehead, and half
      missed,
Half falling on the hair. O, beyond meed!
That was the chrism of love, which love's own
      crown,
With sanctifying sweetness, did precede.
The third upon my lips was folded down
In perfect, purple state; since when, indeed,
I have been proud, and said, "My love, my own!"

XXXIX.

Because thou hast the power and own'st the grace
To look through and behind this mask of me,

(Against which, years have beat thus blanchingly
With their rains,) and behold my soul's true face,
The dim and weary witness of life's race,—
Because thou hast the faith and love to see,
Through that same soul's distracting lethargy,
The patient angel waiting for a place
In the new Heavens,—because nor sin nor woe,
Nor God's infliction, nor death's neighborhood,
Nor all which others viewing, turn to go,
Nor all which makes me tired of all, self-viewed,—
Nothing repels thee, . . . Dearest, teach me so
To pour out gratitude, as thou dost, good!

XLIII.

How do I love thee? Let me count the ways.
I love thee to the depth and breadth and height
My soul can reach, when feeling out of sight
For the ends of Being and ideal Grace.
I love thee to the level of every day's
Most quiet need, by sun and candle-light.
I love thee freely, as men strive for Right;
I love thee purely, as they turn from Praise.
I love thee with the passion put to use
In my old griefs, and with my childhood's faith.
I love thee with a love I seemed to lose
With my lost saints,—I love thee with the breath,
Smiles, tears, of all my life!—and, if God
    choose,
I shall but love thee better after death.

ELIZABETH BARRETT BROWNING.

SONNETS.

My Love, I have no fear that thou shouldst die;
Albeit I ask no fairer life than this,
Whose numbering-clock is still thy gentle kiss,
While Time and Peace with hands unlockèd fly,—
Yet care I not where in Eternity
We live and love, well knowing that there is
No backward step for those who feel the bliss
Of Faith as their most lofty yearnings high:
Love hath so purified my being's core,
Meseems I scarcely should be startled, even,
To find, some morn, that thou hadst gone before;
Since, with thy love, this knowledge too was
    given,
Which each calm day doth strengthen more and
    more,
That they who love are but one step from Heaven.

Our love is not a fading, earthly flower:
Its wingèd seed dropped down from Paradise,
And, nursed by day and night, by sun and shower,
Doth momently to fresher beauty rise:
To us the leafless autumn is not bare,
Nor winter's rattling boughs lack lusty green,
Our summer hearts make summer's fulness,
    where
No leaf, or bud, or blossom may be seen:
For nature's life in love's deep life doth lie,
Love,—whose forgetfulness is beauty's death,

Whose mystic key these cells of Thou and I
Into the infinite freedom openeth,
And makes the body's dark and narrow grate
The wind-flung leaves of Heaven's palace-gate.

————

I THOUGHT our love at full, but I did err;
Joy's wreath drooped o'er mine eyes; I could not
     see
That sorrow in our happy world must be
Love's deepest spokesman and interpreter.
But, as a mother feels her child first stir
Under her heart, so felt I instantly
Deep in my soul another bond to thee
Thrill with that life we saw depart from her;
O mother of our angel child! twice dear!
Death knits as well as parts, and still, I wis,
Her tender radiance shall infold us here,
Even as the light, borne up by inward bliss,
Threads the void glooms of space without a fear,
To print on farthest stars her pitying kiss.

JAMES RUSSELL LOWELL.

————

MY LOVE.

NOT as all other women are
    Is she that to my soul is dear;
Her glorious fancies come from far,
Beneath the silver evening-star,
    And yet her heart is ever near.

Great feelings hath she of her own,
    Which lesser souls may never know;

God giveth them to her alone,
And sweet they are as any tone
   Wherewith the wind may choose to blow.

Yet in herself she dwelleth not,
  Although no home were half so fair;
No simplest duty is forgot;
Life hath no dim and lowly spot
   That doth not in her sunshine share.

She doeth little kindnesses,
  Which most leave undone, or despise;
For naught that sets one heart at ease,
And giveth happiness or peace,
   Is low-esteemèd in her eyes.

She hath no scorn of common things;
  And, though she seem of other birth,
Round us her heart entwines and clings,
And patiently she folds her wings
   To tread the humble paths of earth.

Her glorious fancies come from far,
  And deeds of week-day holiness
Fall from her noiseless as the snow;
Nor hath she ever chanced to know
   That aught were easier than to bless.

She is most fair, and thereunto
  Her life doth rightly harmonize;
Feeling or thought that was not true
Ne'er made less beautiful the blue
   Unclouded heaven of her eyes.

She is a woman—one in whom
  The spring-time of her childish years
Hath never lost its fresh perfume,
Though knowing well that life hath room
  For many blights and many tears.

I love her with a love as still
  As a broad river's peaceful might,
Which, by high tower and lowly mill,
Goes wandering at its own will,
  And yet doth ever flow aright.

And, on its full, deep breast serene,
  Like quiet isles my duties lie;
It flows around them and between,
And makes them fresh and fair and green—
  Sweet homes wherein to live and die.

JAMES RUSSELL LOWELL.

ADAM DESCRIBING EVE.

FROM "PARADISE LOST," BOOK VIII.

MINE eyes he closed, but open left the cell
Of fancy, my internal sight, by which
Abstract, as in a trance, methought I saw,
Though sleeping, where I lay, and saw the shape
Still glorious before whom awake I stood;
Who, stooping, opened my left side, and took
From thence a rib, with cordial spirits warm,
And life-blood streaming fresh; wide was the
    wound,
But suddenly with flesh filled up and healed:
25

The rib he formed and fashioned with his hands;
Under his forming hands a creature grew,
Manlike, but different sex, so lovely fair,
That what seemed fair in all the world seemed
    now
Mean, or in her summed up, in her contained,
And in her looks, which from that time infused
Sweetness into my heart, unfelt before,
And into all things from her air inspired
The spirit of love and amorous delight.
She disappeared, and left me dark; I waked
To find her, or forever to deplore
Her loss, and other pleasures all abjure:
When out of hope, behold her, not far off,
Such as I saw her in my dream, adorned
With what all earth or Heaven could bestow
To make her amiable. On she came,
Led by her heavenly Maker, though unseen,
And guided by his voice, nor uninformed
Of nuptial sanctity and marriage rites:
Grace was in all her steps, Heaven in her eye,
In every gesture dignity and love.
I, overjoyed, could not forbear aloud:
  " This turn hath made amends; thou hast ful-
    filled
Thy words, Creator bounteous and benign,
Giver of all things fair, but fairest this
Of all thy gifts, nor enviest. I now see
Bone of my bone, flesh of my flesh, myself
Before me; Woman is her name, of man
Extracted: for this cause he shall forego
Father and mother, and to his wife adhere;
And they shall be one flesh, one heart, one soul."

She heard me thus, and though divinely
    brought,
Yet innocence and virgin modesty,
Her virtue and the conscience of her worth,
That would be wooed, and not unsought be won,
Not obvious, not obtrusive, but retired,
The more desirable; or, to say all,
Nature herself, though pure of sinful thought,
Wrought in her so, that, seeing me, she turned;
I followed her; she what was honor knew,
And with obsequious majesty approved
My pleaded reason. To the nuptial bower
I led her blushing like the morn: all Heaven,
And happy constellations on that hour
Shed their selectest influence; the earth
Gave sign of gratulation, and each hill;
Joyous the birds; fresh gales and gentle airs
Whispered it to the woods, and from their wings
Flung rose, flung odors from the spicy shrub,
Disporting, till the amorous bird of night
Sung spousal, and bid haste the evening star
On his hill-top, to light the bridal lamp.

.   .   .   .

                       When I approach
Her loveliness, so absolute she seems,
And in herself complete, so well to know
Her own, that what she wills to do or say
Seems wisest, virtuousest, discreetest, best;
All higher knowledge in her presence falls
Degraded, wisdom in discourse with her
Loses discountenanced, and like folly shows;
Authority and reason on her wait,
As one intended first, not after made

Occasionally; and, to consummate all,
Greatness of mind and nobleness their seat
Build in her loveliest, and create an awe
About her, as a guard angelic placed,

.   .   .   .   .   .

Neither her outside formed so fair, nor aught

.   .   .   .   .   .

So much delights me, as those graceful acts,
Those thousand decencies that daily flow
From all her words and actions, mixed with love
And sweet compliance, which declare unfeigned
Union of mind, or in us both one soul;
Harmony to behold in wedded pair
More grateful than harmonious sound to the ear.

MILTON.

ADAM TO EVE.

FROM "PARADISE LOST," BOOK IX.

O FAIREST of creation, last and best
Of all God's works, creature in whom excelled
Whatever can to sight or thought be formed,
Holy, divine, good, amiable, or sweet!
How art thou lost, how on a sudden lost,
Defaced, deflowered, and now to death devote!
Rather, how hast thou yielded to transgress
The strict forbiddance, how to violate
The sacred fruit forbidden! Some cursèd fraud
Of enemy hath beguiled thee, yet unknown,
And me with thee hath ruined, for with thee
Certain my resolution is to die.

How can I live without thee, how forego
Thy sweet converse, and love so dearly joined,
To live again in these wild woods forlorn?
Should God create another Eve, and I
Another rib afford, yet loss of thee
Would never from my heart; no, no, I feel
The link of nature draw me: flesh of flesh,
Bone of my bone thou art, and from thy state
Mine never shall be parted, bliss or woe.

  . . . . . .

However, I with thee have fixed my lot,
Certain to undergo like doom; if death
Consort with thee, death is to me as life;
So forcible within my heart I feel
The bond of nature draw me to my own,
My own in thee, for what thou art is mine;
Our state cannot be severed, we are one,
One flesh; to lose thee were to lose myself

          MILTON.

BRUTUS AND PORTIA.

FROM " JULIUS CÆSAR," ACT II. SC. 1

Enter PORTIA.

PORTIA.—   Brutus, my lord!
BRUTUS.—Portia, what mean you? Wherefore
  rise you now?
It is not for your health thus to commit
Your weak condition to the raw cold morning.
  PORTIA.—Nor for yours neither. You 've un-
  gently, Brutus,

Stole from my bed; and yesternight, at supper,
You suddenly arose and walked about,
Musing and sighing, with your arms across;
And, when I asked you what the matter was,
You stared upon me with ungentle looks.
I urged you further; then you scratched your
    head,
And too impatiently stamped with your foot.
Yet I insisted, yet you answered not,
But with an angry wafture of your hand
Gave sign for me to leave you. So I did;
Fearing to strengthen that impatience
Which seemed too much enkindled, and withal
Hoping it was but an effect of humor,
Which sometime hath his hour with every man.
It will not let you eat, nor talk, nor sleep,
And, could it work so much upon your shape
As it hath much prevailed on your condition,
I should not know you, Brutus. Dear my lord,
Make me acquainted with your cause of grief.

    BRUTUS.—I am not well in health, and that is
      all.

    PORTIA.—Brutus is wise, and, were he not in
      health,
He would embrace the means to come by it.

    BRUTUS.—Why, so I do.—Good Portia, go to
      bed.

    PORTIA.—Is Brutus sick? and is it physical
To walk unbraced and suck up the humors
Of the dank morning? What! is Brutus sick,
And will he steal out of his wholesome bed,
To dare the vile contagion of the night,
And tempt the rheumy and unpurgèd air

To add unto his sickness? No, my Brutus;
You have some sick offence within your mind,
Which by the right and virtue of my place
I ought to know of: and, upon my knees,
I charm you, by my once commended beauty,
By all your vows of love and that great vow
Which did incorporate and make us one,
That you unfold to me, yourself, your half,
Why you are heavy, and what men to-night
Have had resort to you; for here have been
Some six or seven, who did hide their faces
Even from darkness.

    BRUTUS.—   Kneel not, gentle Portia.

    PORTIA.—I should not need, if you were gentle
       Brutus.
Within the bond of marriage, tell me, Brutus,
Is it excepted I should know no secrets
That appertain to you? Am I yourself
But, as it were, in sort of limitation,
To keep with you at meals, comfort your bed,
And talk to you sometimes? Dwell I but in the
       suburbs
Of your good pleasure? If it be no more,
Portia is Brutus' harlot, not his wife.

    BRUTUS.—You are my true and honorable wife,
As dear to me as are the ruddy drops
That visit my sad heart.

    PORTIA.—If this were true, then should I know
       this secret.
I grant I am a woman, but withal
A woman that Lord Brutus took to wife;
I grant I am a woman, but withal
A woman well reputed, Cato's daughter.

Think you I am no stronger than my sex,
Being so fathered and so husbanded?
Tell me your counsels, I will not disclose 'em:
I have made strong proof of my constancy,
Giving myself a voluntary wound
Here in the thigh; can I bear that with patience,
And not my husband's secrets?

BRUTUS.—   O, ye gods,
Render me worthy of this noble wife!—
            (*Knocking within.*)
Hark, hark! one knocks. Portia, go in a while;
And by and by thy bosom shall partake
The secrets of my heart.
All my engagements I will cónstrue to thee,
All the charáctery of my sad brows.
Leave me with haste.—   (*Exit Portia.*)

                              SHAKESPEARE.

LORD WALTER'S WIFE.

" BUT why do you go? " said the lady, while both
    sate under the yew,
And her eyes were alive in their depth, as the
    kraken beneath the sea-blue.

" Because I fear you," he answered;—"because
    you are far too fair,
And able to strangle my soul in a mesh of your
    gold-colored hair."

" Oh, that," she said, " is no reason! Such knots
    are quickly undone,
And too much beauty, I reckon, is nothing but
    too much sun."

"Yet farewell so," he answered;—"the sun-
    stroke's fatal at times.
I value your husband, Lord Walter, whose gallop
    rings still from the limes."

"O, that," she said, "is no reason. You smell a
    rose through a fence:
If two should smell it, what matter? who grum-
    bles, and where's the pretence?"

"But I," he replied, "have promised another,
    when love was free,
To love her alone, alone, who alone and afar loves
    me."

"Why, that," she said, "is no reason. Love's
    always free, I am told.
Will you vow to be safe from the headache on
    Tuesday, and think it will hold?"

"But you," he replied, "have a daughter, a young
    little child, who was laid
In your lap to be pure; so I leave you: the angels
    would make me afraid."

"O, that," she said, "is no reason. The angels
    keep out of the way;
And Dora, the child, observes nothing, although
    you should please me and stay."

At which he rose up in his anger,—"Why, now,
    you no longer are fair!
Why, now, you no longer are fatal, but ugly and
    hateful, I swear."

At which she laughed out in her scorn,—" These
    men! O, these men overnice,
Who are shocked if a color not virtuous is frankly
    put on by a vice."

Her eyes blazed upon him—" And *you!* You
    bring us your vices so near
That we smell them! you think in our presence a
    thought 't would defame us to hear!

" What reason had you, and what right,—I appeal
    to your soul from my life,—
To find me too fair as a woman? Why, sir, I am
    pure, and a wife.

" Is the day-star too fair up above you? It burns
    you not. Dare you imply
I brushed you more close than the star does,
    when Walter had set me as high?

" If a man finds a woman too fair, he means sim-
    ply adapted too much
To uses unlawful and fatal. The praise!—shall
    I thank you for such?

" Too fair?—not unless you misuse us! and surely
    if, once in a while,
You attain to it, straightway you call us no longer
    too fair, but too vile.

" A moment,—I pray your attention!—I have a
    poor word in my head

I must utter, though womanly custom would set it
    down better unsaid.

" You grew, sir, pale to impertinence, once when I
    showed you a ring.
You kissed my fan when I dropped it. No mat-
    ter! I 've broken the thing.

" You did me the honor, perhaps, to be moved at
    my side now and then
In the senses,—a vice, I have heard, which is com-
    mon to beasts and some men.

" Love 's a virtue for heroes!—as white as the
    snow on high hills,
And immortal as every great soul is that strug-
    gles, endures, and fulfils.

" I love my Walter profoundly,—you, Maude,
    though you faltered a week,
For the sake of . . . what was it? an eyebrow?
    or, less still, a mole on a cheek?

" And since, when all 's said, you 're too noble to
    stoop to the frivolous cant
About crimes irresistible, virtues that swindle, be-
    tray, and supplant,

" I determined to prove to yourself that, what-
    e'er you might dream or avow
By illusion, you wanted precisely no more of me
    than you have now.

"There! Look me full in the face!—in the face.
    Understand, if you can,
That the eyes of such women as I am are clean as
    the palm of a man.

"Drop his hand, you insult him. Avoid us for
    fear we should cost you a scar,—
You take us for harlots, I tell you, and not for the
    women we are.

"You wrong me: but then I consider . . .
    there's Walter! And so at the end,
I vowed that he should not be mulcted, by me,
    in the hand of a friend.

"Have I hurt you indeed? We are quits then.
    Nay, friend of my Walter, be mine!
Come, Dora, my darling, my angel, and help me
    to ask him to dine."

ELIZABETH BARRETT BROWNING.

PAULINA'S APPEAL.

FROM "POLYEUCTE."

SEVERUS—   I stand agaze,
Rooted, confounded, in sheer wonderment.
Such blind resolve is so unparalleled,
I scarce may trust the witness of mine ears.
A heart that loves you—and what heart so poor
That knowing, loves you not?—one loved of you,
To leave regretless so much bliss just won!

Nay, more—as though it were a fatal prize—
To his corrival straight to yield it up!
Truly, or wondrous manias Christians have,
Or their self-happiness must be sans bourn,
Since to attain it they will cast away
What others at an empire's cost would win.
For me, had fate, a little sooner kind,
Blessed my true service with your hand's reward,
The glory of your eyes had been my worship;
My twin kings had they reigned—kings? nay, my
    gods!
To dust, to powder, had I grinded been
E'er I had—
    PAULINA —Hold! let me not hear too much;
Let not the smoldering embers of old time
Relume to speech unworthy of us both.
Severus, know Paulina utterly:
His latest hour my Polyeuctus nears;
Nay, scarce a minute has he yet to live.
You all unwittingly have been the cause
Of this his death. I know not if your thoughts,
Their portals opening to your wish's knock,
Have dared to some wild hope give harboring,
Based upon his undoing; but know well,
No death so cruel I would not boldly front,
Hell hath no tortures I would not endure,
Or e'er my stainless honor I would spot,
My hand bestowing upon any man
Who any wise were his death's instrument.
And could you for such madness deem me apt,
Hate would replace my erstwhile tender love.
You 're generous—still be so, to the end:
My father fears you; is in mood to grant

All you might ask; ay, I e'en dare aver
That if my husband he do sacrifice,
'T will be to you.   Save then your hapless victim;
Bestir yourself; stretch him your helping hand!
That this is much to claim of you, I know,
But more the effort 's great, the more the glory!
To save a rival 'spite of rivalry
Were greatness all particular to you.
And—be that not enough for your renown—
'T were much to let a woman erst so loved,
And haply who may yet be somewhat dear,
Her greatest treasure owe to your great heart.
In fine, remember that you are Severus!
Adieu! alone determine of your course;
For if you be not all I think you are,
I 'd still, not knowing it, believe you such.

From the French of PIERRE CORNEILLE.
Translation of W. F. NOKES.

THE WIFE OF LOKI.

CURSED by the gods and crowned with shame,
    Fell father of a direful brood,
Whose crimes have filled the heaven with flame
    And drenched the earth with blood;

Loki, the guileful Loki, stands
    Within a rocky mountain-gorge;
Chains gird his body, feet, and hands,
    Wrought in no mortal forge.

Coiled on the rock, a mighty snake
    Above him, day and night, is hung,

With dull malignant eyes awake,
  And poison-dropping tongue.

Drop follows drop in ceasless flow,
  Each falling where the other fell,
To lay upon his blistered brow
  The liquid fire of hell.

But lo, beside the howling wretch
  A woman stands, devoid of dread,
And one pale arm is seen to stretch
  Above his tortured head!

All through the day is lifted up,
  And all the weary night-time through,
One patient hand that holds a cup
  To catch the poison-dew.

Sometimes the venom overfills
  The cup, and she must pour it forth;
With Loki's curses then the hills
  Are rent from south to north.

But she in answer only sighs,
  And lays her lips upon his face,
And, with love's anguish in her eyes,
  Resumes her constant place.

LADY CHARLOTTE ELLIOT.

LIKE A LAVEROCK IN THE LIFT.

It 's we two, it 's we two for aye,
All the world, and we two, and Heaven be our
   stay!

Like a laverock* in the lift,† sing, O bonny
　　bride!
All the world was Adam once, with Eve by his
　　side.
What's the world, my lass, my love!—what can
　　it do?
I am thine, and thou art mine; life is sweet and
　　new.
If the world have missed the mark, let it stand
　　by;
For we two have gotten leave, and once more will
　　try.

Like a laverock in the lift, sing, O bonny bride!
It's we two, it's we two, happy side by side.
Take a kiss from me, thy man; now the song
　　begins:
" All is made afresh for us, and the brave heart
　　wins."

When the darker days come, and no sun will
　　shine,
Thou shalt dry my tears, lass, and I'll dry thine.
It's we two, it's we two, while the world's away,
Sitting by the golden sheaves on our wedding day.

JEAN INGELOW.

WERE I BUT HIS OWN WIFE.

WERE I but his own wife, to guard and to guide
　　him,
　　'T is little of sorrow should fall on my dear;

* Lark.　　† Cloud.

I 'd chant my low love-verses, stealing beside him,
  So faint and so tender his heart would but
      hear;
I 'd pull the wild blossoms from valley and high-
      land;
  And there at his feet I would lay them all down;
I 'd sing him the songs of our poor stricken island,
  Till his heart was on fire with a love like my
      own.

There 's a rose by his dwelling—I 'd tend the lone
      treasure,
  That he might have flowers when the summer
      would come;
There 's a harp in his hall—I would wake its
      sweet measure,
  For he must have music to brighten his home.
Were I but his own wife, to guide and to guard
      him,
  'T is little of sorrow should fall on my dear;
For every kind glance my whole life would award
      him—
  In sickness I 'd soothe and in sadness I 'd cheer.

My heart is a fount welling upward for ever,
  When I think of my true-love, by night or by
      day;
That heart keeps its faith like a fast-flowing river
  Which gushes for ever and sings on its way.
I have thoughts full of peace for his soul to repose
      in,
  Were I but his own wife, to win and to woo—
Oh, sweet, if the night of misfortune were closing,
  To rise like the morning star, darling for you!
                                    MARY DOWNING.

26

TWO LOVERS.

Two lovers by a moss-grown spring:
They leaned soft cheeks together there,
Mingled the dark and sunny hair,
And heard the wooing thrushes sing.
    O budding time!
    O love's blest prime!

Two wedded from the portal stept:
The bells made happy carolings,
The air was soft as fanning wings,
White petals on the pathway slept.
    O pure-eyed bride!
    O tender pride!

Two faces o'er a cradle bent:
Two hands above the head were locked;
These pressed each other while they rocked,
Those watched a life that love had sent.
    O solemn hour!
    O hidden power!

Two parents by the evening fire:
The red light fell about their knees
On heads that rose by slow degrees
Like buds upon the lily spire.
    O patient life!
    O tender strife!

The two still sat together. there,
The red light shone about their knees;
But all the heads by slow degrees

Had gone and left that lonely pair.
  O voyage fast!
  O vanished past!

The red light shone upon the floor
And made the space between them wide;
They drew their chairs up side by side,
Their pale cheeks joined, and said,
  "Once more!"
  O memories!
  O past that is!
   MARIAN EVANS LEWES CROSS (*George Eliot*).

IN TWOS.

SOMEWHERE in the world there hide
Garden-gates that no one sees
Save they come in happy twos,—
Not in one, nor yet in threes.

But from every maiden's door
Leads a pathway straight and true;
Map and survey know it not, —
He who finds, finds room for two!

Then they see the garden-gates!
Never skies so blue as theirs,
Never flowers so many-sweet,
As for those who come in pairs.

Round and round the alleys wind:
Now a cradle bars the way,

Now a little mound, behind,—
So the two go through the day.

When no nook in all the lanes
But has heard a song or sigh,
Lo! another garden-gate
Opens as the two go by.

In they wander, knowing not;
"Five and twenty!" fills the air
With a silvery echo low,
All about the startled pair.

Happier yet these garden-walks:
Closer, heart to heart, they lean;
Stiller, softer, falls the light;
Few the twos, and far between.

Till, at last, as on they pass
Down the paths so well they know,
Once again at hidden gates
Stand the two: they enter slow.

Golden Gates of "Fifty Years,"
May our two your latchet press!
Garden of the Sunset Land,
Hold their dearest happiness!

Then a quiet walk again:
Then a wicket in the wall:
Then one, stepping on alone,—
Then two at the Heart of All!

WILLIAM CHANNING GANNETT.

HEBREW WEDDING.

FROM "THE FALL OF JERUSALEM."

To the sound of timbrels sweet
Moving slow our solemn feet,
We have borne thee on the road
To the virgin's blest abode;
With thy yellow torches gleaming,
And thy scarlet mantle streaming,
And the canopy above
Swaying as we slowly move.
Thou hast left the joyous feast,
And the mirth and wine has ceased;
And now we set thee down before
The jealously unclosing door,
That the favored youth admits
Where the veilèd virgin sits
In the bliss of maiden fear,
Waiting our soft tread to hear,
And the music's brisker din
At the bridegroom's entering in,
Entering in, a welcome guest,
To the chamber of his rest.

CHORUS OF MAIDENS.

Now the jocund song is thine,
Bride of David's kingly line;
How thy dove-like bosom trembleth,
And thy shrouded eye resembleth
Violets, when the dews of eve
A moist and tremulous glitter leave

On the bashful sealèd lid!
Close within the bride-veil hid,
Motionless thou sitt'st and mute;
Save that at the soft salute
Of each entering maiden friend,
Thou dost rise and softly bend.

Hark! a brisker, merrier glee!
The door unfolds,—'t is he! 't is he!
Thus we lift our lamps to meet him,
Thus we touch our lutes to greet him.
Thou shalt give a fonder meeting,
Thou shalt give a tenderer greeting.

HENRY HART MILMAN.

THE WEDDING-DAY.

FROM " EPITHALAMION."

. . . . .

Now is my love all ready forth to come:
Let all the virgins therefore well awayt:
And ye fresh boyes, that tend upon her groome,
Prepare yourselves; for he is coming strayt.
Set all your things in seemely good array,
Fit for so joyfull day:
The joyfulst day that ever sunne did see,
Faire Sun! shew forth thy favourable ray,
And let thy lifull heat not fervent be,
For feare of burning her sunshyny face,
Her beauty to disgrace.
O fayrest Phœbus! father of the Muse!
If ever I did honour thee aright,

Or sing the thing that mote thy mind delight,
Doe not thy servant's simple boone refuse;
But let this day, let this one day, be myne;
Let all the rest be thine.
Then I thy soverayne prayses loud will sing,
That all the woods shal answer, and theyr eccho
    ring.

   .   .   .   .   .

Loe! where she comes along with portly pace,
Lyke Phœbe, from her chamber of the East.
Arysing forth to run her mighty race,
Clad all in white, that seemes a virgin best.
So well it her beseemes that ye would weene
Some angell she had beene.
Her long, loose, yellow locks lyke golden wyre,
Sprinckled with perle, and perling flowres
    atweene,
Doe like a golden mantle her attyre;
And, being crownèd with a garland greene,
Seeme lyke some mayden Queene.
Her modest eyes abashèd to behold
So many gazers as on her do stare,
Upon the lowly ground affixèd are;
Ne dare lift up her countenance too bold,
But blush to heare her prayses sung so loud,
So farre from being proud.
Nathlesse doe ye still loud her prayses sing,
That all the woods may answer, and your eccho
    ring.

Tell me, ye merchants' daughters, did ye see
So fayre a creature in your towne before?
So sweet, so lovely, and so mild as she,

Adorned with beauty's grace and vertue's store?
Her goodly eyes lyke saphyres shining bright;
Her forehead ivory white;
Her cheekes lyke apples which the sun hath
    rudded;
Her lips lyke cherries charming men to byte;
Her brest lyke to a bowl of cream uncrudded;
Her paps lyke lyllies budded;
Her snowie necke lyke to a marble towre;
And all her body like a pallace fayre,
Ascending up with many a stately stayre,
To honour's seat and chastity's sweet bowre.
Why stand ye still, ye virgins, in amaze
Upon her so to gaze,
Whiles ye forget your former lay to sing,
To which the woods did answer, and your echo
    ring?

But if ye saw that which no eyes can see,
The inward beauty of her lively spright,
Garnisht with heavenly gifts of high degree,
Much more then would ye wonder at that sight,
And stand astonisht, lyke to those which red
Meduses mazeful hed.
There dwels sweet love, and constant chastity,
Unspotted fayth, and comely womanhood,
Regard of honour, and mild modesty;
There vertue raynes as Queene in royal throne,
And giveth lawes alone,
The which the base affections doe obay,
And yeeld theyr services unto her will;
Ne thought of thing uncomely ever may
Thereto approch to tempt her mind to ill.

Had ye once seene these her celestial threasures,
And unrevealèd pleasures,
Then would ye wonder, and her prayses sing,
That al the woods should answer, and your eccho
    ring.

.   .   .   .   .

Behold, whiles she before the altar stands,
Hearing the holy priest that to her speakes,
And blesseth her with his two happy hands,
How the red roses flush up in her cheekes,
And the pure snow, with goodly vermill stayne,
Like crimson dyde in grayne:
That even the Angels, which continually
About the sacred Altare do remaine,
Forget their service and about her fly,
Ofte peeping in her face, that seemes more fayre
The more they on it stare.
But her sad eyes, still fastened on the ground,
Are governèd with goodly modesty,
That suffers not one looke to glaunce awry
Which may let in a little thought unsownd.
Why blush ye, love, to give to me your hand,
The pledge of all our band!
Sing, ye sweet Angels, Alleluya sing,
That all the woods may answer, and your eccho
    ring.

Now al is done: bring home the bride againe—
Bring home the triumph of our victory;
Bring home with you the glory of her gaine—
With joyance bring her and with jollity.
Never had man more joyful day than this,
Whom heaven would heape with blis,

Make feast therefore now all this live-long day;
This day for ever to me holy is.

. . . . .

EDMUND SPENSER.

THE BRIDE.

FROM " A BALLAD UPON A WEDDING."

. . . . .

THE maid, and thereby hangs a tale,
For such a maid no Whitsun-ale
   Could ever yet produce :
No grape that 's kindly ripe could be
So round, so plump, so soft as she,
   Nor half so full of juice.

Her finger was so small, the ring
Would not stay on which they did bring,—
   It was too wide a peck;
And, to say truth,—for out it must,—
It looked like the great collar—just—
   About our young colt's neck.

Her feet beneath her petticoat,
Like little mice, stole in and out,
   As if they feared the light;
But O, she dances such a way!
No sun upon an Easter-day
   Is half so fine a sight.

. . . .

Her cheeks so rare a white was on,
No daisy makes comparison;
   Who sees them is undone;

For streaks of red were mingled there,
Such as are on a Kath'rine pear,
    The side that's next the sun.

Her lips were red; and one was thin,
Compared to that was next her chin.
    Some bee had stung it newly;
But, Dick, her eyes so guard her face,
I durst no more upon them gaze,
    Than on the sun in July.

Her mouth so small, when she does speak,
Thou 'dst swear her teeth her words did break,
    That they might passage get;
But she so handled still the matter,
They came as good as ours, or better,
    And are not spent a whit.

   .   .   .   .   .

                SIR JOHN SUCKLING.

SONG.

FROM AN OLD SONG, " WOO'D AND MARRIED
AND A'."

THE bride she is winsome and bonny,
    Her hair it is snooded sae sleek,
And faithfu' and kind is her Johnny,
    Yet fast fa' the tears on her cheek.
New pearlins* are cause of her sorrow,
    New pearlins and plenishing too;

      * finery, lace.

The bride that has a' to borrow
  Has e'en right mickle ado.
    Woo'd and married and a'!
    Woo'd and married and a'!
  Is na' she very weel aff
    To be woo'd and married at a'?

Her mither then hastily spak,
  " The lassie is glaikit * wi' pride;
In my pouch I had never a plack
  On the day when I was a bride.
E'en tak to your wheel and be clever,
  And draw out your thread in the sun;
The gear that is gifted it never
    Will last like the gear that is won.
    Woo'ed and married and a'!
    Wi' havins and tocher † sae sma'!
  I think ye are very weel aff
    To be woo'd and married at a'."

" Toot, toot," quo' her grey-headed faither,
  " She's less o' a bride than a bairn,
She's ta'en like a cout ‡ frae the heather,
  Wi' sense and discretion to learn.
Half husband, I trow, and half daddy,
  As humour inconstantly leans,
The chiel maun be patient and steady
    That yokes wi' a mate in her teens.
    A kerchief sae douce § and sae neat
    O'er her locks that the wind used to blaw!
  I 'm baith like to laugh and to greet
    When I think of her married at a'!"

---

* silly.   † dowry and manners.   ‡ colt.   § grave, sober.

Then out spak the wily bridegroom,
  Weel waled * were his wordies, I ween,
" I 'm rich, though my coffer be toom,†
  Wi' the blinks o' your bonny blue een.
I 'm prouder o' thee by my side
  Though thy ruffles or ribbons be few,
Than if Kate o' the Croft were my bride
  Wi' purfles and pearlins enow.
    Dear and dearest of ony!
    Ye' re woo'd and buikit and a'!
  And do ye think scorn o' your Johnny,
    And grieve to be married at a'?"

She turned, and she blushed, and she smiled,
  And she looked sae bashfully down;
The pride o' her heart was beguiled,
  And she played wi' the sleeves o' her gown.
She twirled the tag o' her lace,
  And she nipped her boddice sae blue,
Syne ‡ blinket sae sweet in his face,
  And aff like a maukin § she flew.
    Woo'd and married and a'!
    Wi' Johnny to roose her and a' !
  She thinks hersel very weel aff
    To be woo'd and married at a'!

JOANNA BAILLIE.

THE NEWLY-WEDDED.

Now the rite is duly done,
  Now the word is spoken,
And the spell has made us one
  Which may ne'er be broken;

---

* chosen.   † empty.   ‡ then.   § hare.

Rest we, dearest, in our home,
  Roam we o'er the heather:
We shall rest, and we shall roam,
  Shall we not? together.

From this hour the summer rose
  Sweeter breathes to charm us;
From this hour the winter snows
  Lighter fall to harm us:
Fair or foul—on land or sea—
  Come the wind or weather,
Best and worst whate'er they be,
  We shall share together.

Death, who friend from friend can part,
  Brother rend from brother,
Shall but link us, heart and heart,
  Closer to each other:
We will call his anger play,
  Deem his dart a feather,
When we meet him on our way
  Hand in hand together.

WINTHROP MACKWORTH PRAED.

THE POET'S BRIDAL-DAY SONG.

O, MY love's like the steadfast sun,
Or streams that deepen as they run;
Nor hoary hairs, nor forty years,
Nor moments between sighs and tears,
Nor nights of thought, nor days of pain,
Nor dreams of glory dreamed in vain,

Nor mirth, nor sweetest song that flows
To sober joys and soften woes,
Can make my heart or fancy flee,
One moment, my sweet wife, from thee.

Even while I muse, I see thee sit
In maiden bloom and matron wit;
Fair, gentle as when first I sued,
Ye seem, but of sedater mood;
Yet my heart leaps as fond for thee
As when, beneath Arbigland tree,
We stayed and wooed, and thought the moon
Set on the sea an hour too soon;
Or lingered mid the falling dew,
When looks were fond and words were few.

Though I see smiling at thy feet
Five sons and ae fair daughter sweet,
And time, and care, and birthtime woes
Have dimmed thine eye and touched thy rose,
To thee, and thoughts of thee, belong
Whate'er charms me in tale or song.
When words descend like dews, unsought,
With gleams of deep, enthusiast thought,
And Fancy in her heaven flies free,
They come, my love, they come from thee.

O, when more thought we gave, of old,
To silver than some give to gold,
'T was sweet to sit and ponder o'er
How we should deck our humble bower;
'T was sweet to pull, in hope, with thee,
The golden fruit of fortune's tree;

And sweeter still to choose and twine
A garland for that brow of thine,—
A song-wreath which may grace my Jean,
While rivers flow, and woods grow green.

At times there come, as come there ought,
Grave moments of sedater thought,
When Fortune frowns, nor lends our night
One gleam of her inconstant light;
And Hope, that decks the peasant's bower,
Shines like a rainbow through the shower;
O, then I see, while seated nigh,
A mother's heart shine in thine eye,
And proud resolve and purpose meek,
Speak of thee more than words can speak.
I think this wedded wife of mine
The best of all that 's not divine.

ALLAN CUNNINGHAM.

THOU HAST SWORN BY THY GOD, MY JEANIE.

THOU hast sworn by thy God, my Jeanie,
  By that pretty white hand o' thine,
And by a' the lowing stars in heaven,
  That thou wad aye be mine!
And I hae sworn by my God, my Jeanie,
  And by that kind heart o' thine,
By a' the stars sown thick owre heaven,
  That thou shalt aye be mine!

Then foul fa' the hands that wad loose sic
      bands,
  And the heart that wad part sic luve!

But there's nae hand can loose the band,
  But the finger o' God abuve.
Though the wee, wee cot maun be my bield,
  An' my claithing ne'er sae mean,
I wad lap me up rich i' the faulds o' luve,—
  Heaven's armfu' o' my Jean!

Her white arm wad be a pillow to me,
  Fu' safter than the down;
An' Luve wad winnow owre us his kind, kind
    wings
  An' sweetly I'd sleep, an' soun'.
Come here to me, thou lass o' my luve!
  Come here and kneel wi' me!
The morn is fu' o' the presence o' God,
  An' I canna pray without thee.

The morn-wind is sweet 'mang the beds o' new
    flowers,
  The wee birds sing kindlie an' hie;
Our gudeman leans owre his kail-yard dike,
  And a blythe auld bodie is he.
The Book maun be ta'en whan the carle comes
    hame,
  Wi' the holie psalmodie;
And thou maun speak o' me to thy God,
  And I will speak o' thee.

ALLAN CUNNINGHAM.

27

POSSESSION.

" It was our wedding-day
A month ago," dear heart, I hear you say.
If months, or years, or ages since have passed,
I know not: I have ceased to question Time.
I only know that once there pealed a chime
Of joyous bells, and then I held you fast,
And all stood back, and none my right denied,
And forth we walked: the world was free and
    wide
Before us. Since that day
I count my life: the Past is washed away.

It was no dream, that vow:
It was a voice that woke me from a dream;—
A happy dream, I think; but I am waking now,
And drink the splendor of a sun supreme
That turns the mist of former tears to gold.
With these arms I hold
The fleeting promise, chased so long in vain:
Ah, weary bird! thou wilt not fly again:
Thy wings are clipped, thou canst no more de-
    part,—
Thy nest is builded in my heart!

I was the crescent; thou
The silver phantom of the perfect sphere,
Held in its bosom: in one glory now
Our lives united shine, and many a year—
Not the sweet moon of bridal only—we

One lustre, ever at the full, shall be:
One pure and rounded light, one planet whole,
One life developed, one completed soul!
For I in thee, and thou in me,
Unite our cloven halves of destiny.

God knew his chosen time.
He bade me slowly ripen to my prime,
And from my boughs withheld the promised
    fruit,
Till storm and sun gave vigor to the root.
Secure, O Love! secure
Thy blessing is: I have thee day and night:
Thou art become my blood, my life, my light:
God's mercy thou, and therefore shalt endure.

BAYARD TAYLOR.

MY AIN WIFE.

I WADNA gi'e my ain wife
    For ony wife I see;
I wadna gi'e my ain wife
    For ony wife I see;
A bonnier yet I 've never seen,
    A better canna be—
I wadna gi'e my ain wife
    For ony wife I see!

O couthie is my ingle-cheek,
    An' cheerie is my Jean;
I never see her angry look,
    Nor hear her word on ane.

She 's gude wi' a' the neebours roun'
　　An' aye gude wi' me—
I wadna gi'e my ain wife
　　For ony wife I see.

An' O her looks sae kindlie,
　　They melt my heart outright,
When o'er the baby at her breast
　　She hangs wi' fond delight;
She looks intil its bonnie face,
　　An' syne looks to me—
I wadna gi'e my ain wife
　　For ony wife I see.

ALEXANDER LAING.

———

MY WIFE 'S A WINSOME WEE THING.

She is a winsome wee thing,
She is a handsome wee thing,
She is a bonnie wee thing,
This sweet wee wife o' mine.

I never saw a fairer,
I never lo'ed a dearer,
And neist my heart I 'll wear her,
For fear my jewel tine.

She is a winsome wee thing,
She is a handsome wee thing,
She is a bonnie wee thing,
This sweet wife o' mine.

The warld's wrack we share o't,
The wrastle and the care o't:
Wi' her I 'll blythely bear it,
And think my lot divine.

ROBERT BURNS.

THE POET'S SONG TO HIS WIFE.

How many summers, love,
  Have I been thine?
How many days, thou dove,
  Hast thou been mine?
Time, like the wingèd wind
  When 't bends the flowers,
Hath left no mark behind,
  To count the hours!

Some weight of thought, though loath,
  On thee he leaves;
Some lines of care round both
  Perhaps he weaves;
Some fears,—a soft regret
  For joys scarce known;
Sweet looks we half forget;—
  All else is flown!

Ah!—With what thankless heart
  I mourn and sing!
Look, where our children start,
  Like sudden spring!
With tongues all sweet and low
  Like a pleasant rhyme,

They tell how much I owe
To thee and time!
BRYAN WALLER PROCTER (*Barry Cornwall*).

THE DAY RETURNS, MY BOSOM BURNS.

THE day returns, my bosom burns;
　The blissful day we twa did meet;
Though winter wild in tempest toiled,
　Ne'er summer sun was half sae sweet.
Than a' the pride that loads the tide,
　And crosses o'er the sultry line,—
Than kingly robes, and crowns and globes,
　Heaven gave me more; it made thee mine.

While day and night can bring delight,
　Or nature aught of pleasure give,—
While joys above my mind can move,
　For thee and thee alone I live;
When that grim foe of life below
　Comes in between to make us part,
The iron hand that breaks our band,
　It breaks my bliss,—it breaks my heart.
ROBERT BURNS.

SHE WAS A PHANTOM OF DELIGHT.

SHE was a phantom of delight
When first she gleamed upon my sight;
A lovely apparition, sent
To be a moment's ornament;

Her eyes as stars of twilight fair;
Like Twilight's, too, her dusky hair;
But all things else about her drawn
From May-time and the cheerful dawn;
A dancing shape, an image gay,
To haunt, to startle, and waylay.

I saw her upon nearer view,
A spirit, yet a woman too!
Her household motions light and free,
And steps of virgin-liberty;
A countenance in which did meet
Sweet records, promises as sweet;
A creature not too bright or good
For human nature's daily food,
For transient sorrows, simple wiles,
Praise, blame, love, kisses, tears, and smiles.

And now I see with eye serene
The very pulse of the machine;
A being breathing thoughtful breath,
A traveller between life and death:
The reason firm, the temperate will,
Endurance, foresight, strength, and skill;
A perfect woman, nobly planned
To warn, to comfort, and command;
And yet a spirit still, and bright
With something of an angel-light.

WILLIAM WORDSWORTH.

POSSESSION.

A POET loved a Star,
And to it whispered nightly,
"Being so fair, why art thou, love, so far?
Or why so coldly shine, who shin'st so brightly?
O Beauty wooed and unpossest!
  O, might I to this beating breast
  But clasp thee once and then die blest!"
That Star her Poet's love,
So wildly warm, made human;
And leaving, for his sake, her heaven above,
His Star stooped earthward, and became a
    Woman.
"Thou who hast wooed and hast possest,
My lover, answer: Which was best,
The Star's beam or the Woman's breast?"
"I miss from heaven," the man replied,
"A light that drew my spirit to it."
And to the man the woman sighed,
"I miss from earth a poet."
      ROBERT BULWER, LORD LYTTON (*Owen Meredith*).

MY HEART IS A LUTE.

Alas, that my heart is a lute,
  Whereon you have learned to play!
For a many years it was mute,
  Until one summer's day
You took it, and touched it, and made it thrill,
And it thrills and throbs, and quivers still!

I had known you, dear, so long!
Yet my heart did not tell me why
It should burst one morn into song,
And wake to new life with a cry,
Like a babe that sees the light of the sun,
And for whom this great world has just begun.

Your lute is enshrined, cased in,
Kept close with love's magic key,
So no hand but yours can win
And wake it to minstrelsy;
Yet leave it not silent too long, nor alone,
Lest the strings should break, and the music
be done.

LADY LINDSAY.

REUNITED LOVE.

" I DREAMED that we were lovers still,
As tender as we used to be
When I brought you the daffodil,
And you looked up and smiled at me."

" True sweethearts were we then, indeed,
When youth was budding into bloom;
And now the flowers are gone to seed,
And breezes have left no perfume."

" Because you ever, ever will
Take such a crooked view of things,
Distorting this and that, until
Confusion ends in cavillings."

" Because you never, never will
    Perceive the force of what I say;
As if I always reasoned ill—
    Enough to take one's breath away!"

" But what if riper love replace
    The vision that enchanted me,
When all you did was perfect grace,
    And all you said was melody?"

" And what if loyal heart renew
    The image never quite foregone,
Combining, as of yore, in you
    A Samson and a Solomon?"

" Then to the breezes will I toss
The straws we split with temper's loss;
Then seal upon your lips anew
The peace that gentle hearts ensue."

" Oh, welcome then, ye playful ways,
And sunshine of the early days;
And banish to the clouds above
Dull reason, that bedarkens love!"

                    RICHARD DODDRIDGE BLACKMORE.

A WOMAN'S COMPLAINT.

I KNOW that deep within your heart of hearts
    You hold me shrined apart from common
        things,

And that my step, my voice, can bring to you
  A gladness that no other presence brings.

And yet, dear love, through all the weary days
  You never speak one word of tenderness,
Nor stroke my hair, nor softly clasp my hand
  Within your own in loving, mute caress.

You think, perhaps, I should be all content
  To know so well the loving place I hold
Within your life, and so you do not dream
  How much I long to hear the story told.

You cannot know, when we two sit alone,
  And tranquil thoughts within your mind are
     stirred,
My heart is crying like a tired child
  For one fond look, one gentle, loving word.

It may be when your eyes look into mine
  You only say, " How dear she is to me!"
Oh, could I read it in your softened glance,
  How radiant this plain old world would be!

Perhaps, sometimes, you breathe a secret prayer
  That choicest blessings unto me be given;
But if you said aloud, " God bless thee, dear!"
  I should not ask a greater boon from Heaven.

I weary sometimes of the rugged way;
  But should you say, " Through thee my life is
     sweet,"

The dreariest desert that our path could cross
   Would suddenly grow green beneath my feet.

'T is not the boundless waters ocean holds
   That give refreshment to the thirsty flowers,
But just the drops that, rising to the skies,
   From thence descend in softly falling showers.

What matter that our granaries are filled
   With all the richest harvest's golden stores,
If we who own them cannot enter in,
   But famished stand before the close-barred
     doors?

And so 't is sad that those who should be rich
   In that true love that crowns our earthly lot,
Go praying with white lips from day to day
   For love's sweet tokens, and receive them not.

ANONYMOUS.

LOVE LIGHTENS LABOR.

A GOOD wife rose from her bed one morn,
   And thought, with a nervous dread,
Of the piles of clothes to be washed, and more
   Than a dozen mouths to be fed.
" There 's the meals to get for the men in the
     field,
   And the children to fix away
To school, and the milk to be skimmed and
     churned;
   And all to be done this day."

It had rained in the night, and all the wood
  Was wet as it could be;
There were puddings and pies to bake, besides a
    loaf of cake for tea.
And the day was hot, and her aching head
  Throbbed wearily as she said,
" If *maidens* but knew what *good wives* know,
  They would not be in haste to *wed!* "

"Jennie, what do you think I told Ben Brown?"
  Called the farmer from the well;
And a flush crept up to his bronzèd brow,
  And his eyes half-bashfully fell.
" It was this," he said, and coming near
  He smiled, and stooping down,
Kissed her cheek,—" 't was this, that you were
    the best
  And the *dearest* wife in town! "

The farmer went back to the field, and the wife,
  In a smiling, absent way,
Sang snatches of tender little songs
  She 'd not sung for many a day.
And the pain in her head was gone, and the
    clothes
  Were white as the foam of the sea;
Her bread was light, and her butter was sweet,
  And as golden as it could be.

" Just think," the children all called in a breath,
  " Tom Wood has run off to sea!
He wouldn't, I know, if he 'd only had
  As happy a home as we."

The night came down, and the good wife smiled
　To herself, as she softly said:
" 'T is so sweet to labor for those we love,—
　It 's *not* strange that *maids will wed!* "

ANONYMOUS.

CONNUBIAL LIFE.

FROM " THE SEASONS: SPRING."

BUT happy they! the happiest of their kind!
Whom gentler stars unite, and in one fate
Their hearts, their fortunes, and their beings
　　blend.
'T is not the coarser tie of human laws,
Unnatural oft, and foreign to the mind,
That binds their peace, but harmony itself,
Attuning all their passions into love;
Where friendship full-exerts her softest power,
Perfect esteem enlivened by desire
Ineffable, and sympathy of soul;
Thought meeting thought, and will preventing
　　will,
With boundless confidence: for naught but love
Can answer love, and render bliss secure.
Meantime a smiling offspring rises round,
And mingles both their graces. By degrees,
The human blossom blows; and every day,
Soft as it rolls along, shows some new charm,
The father's lustre and the mother's bloom.
Then infant reason grows apace, and calls
For the kind hand of an assiduous care.

Delightful task! to rear the tender thought,
To teach the young idea how to shoot,
To pour the fresh instruction o'er the mind,
To breathe the enlivening spirit, and to fix
The generous purpose in the glowing breast.
O, speak the joy! ye whom the sudden fear
Surprises often, while you look around,
And nothing strikes your eye but sights of bliss,
All various nature pressing on the heart;
An elegant sufficiency, content,
Retirement, rural quiet, friendships, books,
Ease and alternate labor, useful life,
Progressive virtue, and approving Heaven.
These are the matchless joys of virtuous love;
And thus their moments fly. The Seasons thus,
As ceaseless round a jarring world they roll,
Still find them happy; and consenting Spring
Sheds her own rosy garlands on their heads:
Till evening comes at last, serene and mild;
When after the long vernal day of life,
Enamored more, as more remembrance swells
With many a proof of recollected love,
Together down they sink in social sleep;
Together freed, their gentle spirits fly
To scenes where love and bliss immortal reign.

JAMES THOMSON.

THE RETORT.

Old Birch, who taught the village school,
    Wedded a maid of homespun habit;
He was as stubborn as a mule,
    And she as playful as a rabbit.

Poor Kate had scarce become a wife
  Before her husband sought to make her
The pink of country polished life,
  And prim and formal as a Quaker.

One day the tutor went abroad,
  And simple Katie sadly missed him,
When he returned, behind her lord
  She shyly stole, and fondly kissed him.
The husband's anger rose, and red
  And white his face alternate grew:
" Less freedom, ma'am!" Kate sighed and said,
  " O, dear! I *didn't know 't was you!* "

GEORGE POPE MORRIS.

THE EGGS AND THE HORSES.

A MATRIMONIAL EPIC.

JOHN DOBBINS was so captivated
By Mary Trueman's fortune, face, and cap,
(With near two thousand pounds the hook was
      baited,)
  That in he popped to matrimony's trap.

One small ingredient towards happiness,
It seems, ne'er occupied a single thought;
      For his accomplished bride
      Appearing well supplied
With the three charms of riche   y, dress,
      He did not, as he ought,
      Think of aught else; so no inquiry made he
      As to the temper of the lady.

And here was certainly a great omission;
None should accept of Hymen's gentle fetter,
"For worse or better,"
Whatever be their prospect or condition,
Without acquaintance with each other's nature;
For many a mild and quiet creature
Of charming disposition,
Alas! by thoughtless marriage has destroyed it.
So take advice; let girls dress e'er so tastily,
Don't enter into wedlock hastily
Unless you can't avoid it.

Week followed week, and, it must be confest,
The bridegroom and the bride had both been
blest;
Month after month had languidly transpired,
Both parties became tired:
Year after year dragged on;
Their happiness was gone.

Ah! foolish pair!
"Bear and forbear"
Should be the rule for married folks to take.
But blind mankind (poor discontented elves!)
Too often make
The misery of themselves.

At length the husband said, "This will not do!
Mary, I never will be ruled by you;
So, wife, d' ye see?
To live together as we can't agree.
therefore we part!"
With woman's pride,
Mary replied,
"With all my heart!"

John Dobbins then to Mary's father goes,
And gives the list of his imagined woes.

" Dear son-in-law!" the father said, " I see
All is quite true that you 've been telling me;
Yet there in marriage is such strange fatality,
    That when as much of life
    You shall have seen
    As it has been
My lot to see, I think you 'll own your wife
As good or better than the generality.

" An interest in your case I really take,
And therefore gladly this agreement make:
An hundred eggs within this basket lie,
With which your luck, to-morrow, you shall try;
Also my five best horses, with my cart;
And from the farm at dawn you shall depart.
    All round the country go,
    And be particular, I beg;
   Where husbands rule, a horse bestow,
   But where the wives an egg.
And if the horses go before the eggs,
I 'll ease you of your wife,—I will,—I' fegs!"

   Away the married man departed,
     Brisk and light-hearted:
    Not doubting that, of course,
The first five houses each would take a horse.
    At the first house he knocked,
    He felt a little shocked,
  To hear a female voice, with angry roar,
    Scream out,—" Hullo!
    Who's there below?

Why, husband, are you deaf? go to the door,
    See who it is, I beg."
        Our poor friend John
        Trudged quickly on,
  But first laid at the door an egg.

    I will not all this journey through
    The discontented traveller pursue;
      Suffice it here to say
That when his first day's task was nearly done,
He 'd seen an hundred husbands, minus one,
And eggs just ninety-nine had given away.
" Ha! there 's a house where he I seek must
        dwell,"
At length cried John; " I 'll go and ring the
        bell."

    The servant came,—John asked him, " Pray,
    Friend, is your master in the way? "
      " No," said the man, with smiling phiz,
    " My master is not, but my mistress is;
    Walk in that parlor, sir, my lady 's in it:
    Master will be himself there—in a minute."
The lady said her husband then was dressing,
And, if his business was not very pressing,
She would prefer that he should wait until
    His toilet was completed;
    Adding, " Pray, sir, be seated."
      " Madam, I will,"
Said John, with great politeness; " but I own
      That you alone
    Can tell me all I wish to know;
      Will you do so?

Pardon my rudeness,
And just have the goodness
(A wager to decide) to tell me—do—
Who governs in this house,—your spouse or
    you?"

"Sir," said the lady, with a doubting nod,
    "Your question is very odd;
But as I think none ought to be
Ashamed to do their duty (do you see?)
On that account I scruple not to say
It always is my pleasure to obey.
But here's my husband (always sad with-
    out me);
Take not my word, but ask him, if you doubt
    me."

"Sir," said the husband, "'t is most true;
    I promise you,
A more obedient, kind, and gentle woman
Does not exist."
    "Give us your fist,"
Said John, "and, as the case is something more
    than common,
Allow me to present you with a beast
Worth fifty guineas at the very least.

"There's Smiler, sir, a beauty, you must own,
    There's Prince, that handsome black,
Ball the gray mare, and Saladin the roan,
    Besides old Dunn;
    Come, sir, choose one;
    But take advice from me,
    Let Prince be he;
Why, sir, you'll look the hero on his back."

I 'll take the black, and thank you too."
  "Nay, husband, that will never do;
  You know, you 've often heard me say
  How much I long to have a gray;
  And this one will exactly do for me."
        "No, no," said he;
    "Friend, take the four others back,
    And only leave the black."
"Nay, husband, I declare
I must have the gray mare;"
    Adding (with gentle force),
"The gray mare is, I 'm sure, the better horse."

  "Well, if it must be so,—good sir,
    The gray mare *we* prefer;
So we accept your gift."   John made a leg:
"Allow me to present you with an egg;
    'T is my last egg remaining,
    The cause of my regaining,
I trust, the fond affection of my wife,
Whom I will love the better all my life.
  "Home to content has her kind father brought
        me;
I thank him for the lesson he has taught me."

ANONYMOUS.

WOMAN'S WILL.

AN EPIGRAM.

MEN, dying, make their wills, but wives
  Escape a work so sad;
Why should they make what all their lives
  The gentle dames have had?

JOHN GODFREY SAXE.

THE WORN WEDDING-RING.

YOUR wedding-ring wears thin, dear wife; ah,
  summers not a few,
Since I put it on your finger first, have passed o'er
  me and you;
And, love, what changes we have seen,—what cares
  and pleasures, too,—
Since you became my own dear wife, when this old
  ring was new!

O, blessings on that happy day, the happiest of my
  life,
When, thanks to God, your low, sweet "Yes"
  made you my loving wife!
Your heart will say the same, I know; that day's
  as dear to you,—
That day that made me yours, dear wife, when
  this old ring was new.

How well do I remember now your young sweet
  face that day!
How fair you were, how dear you were, my tongue
  could hardly say;
Nor how I doated on you; O, how proud I was of
  you!
But did I love you more than now, when this old
  ring was new?

No—no! no fairer were you then than at this hour
  to me;
And, dear as life to me this day, how could you
  dearer be?
As sweet your face might be that day as now it
  is, 't is true;
But did I know your heart as well when this old
  ring was new?

O partner of my gladness, wife, what care, what
  grief is there
For me you would not bravely face, with me you
  would not share?
O, what a weary want had every day, if wanting
  you,
Wanting the love that God made mine when this
  old ring was new!

Years bring fresh links to bind us, wife,—young
  voices that are here;
Young faces round our fire that make their
  mother's yet more dear;
Young loving hearts your care each day makes yet
  more like to you,

More like the loving heart made mine when this
 old ring was new.

And blessed be God! all he has given are with us
 yet; around
Our table every precious life lent to us still is
 found.
Though cares we've known, with hopeful hearts
 the worst we've struggled through;
Blessed be his name for all his love since this old
 ring was new!

The past is dear, its sweetness still our memories
 treasure yet;
The griefs we've borne, together borne, we would
 not now forget.
Whatever, wife, the future brings, heart unto
 heart still true,
We'll share as we have shared all else since this
 old ring was new.

And if God spare us 'mongst our sons and daughters to grow old,
We know his goodness will not let your heart or
 mine grow cold.
Your aged eyes will see in mine all they've still
 shown to you,
And mine and yours all they have seen since this
 old ring was new!

And O, when death shall come at last to bid me
 to my rest,
May I die looking in those eyes, and resting on
 that breast;

O, may my parting gaze be blessed with the dear
    sight of you,
Of those fond eyes,—fond as they were when this
    old ring was new!

WILLIAM COX BENNETT.

IF THOU WERT BY MY SIDE, MY LOVE.

LINES WRITTEN TO HIS WIFE, WHILE ON A VISIT TO UPPER INDIA.

If thou wert by my side, my love!
    How fast would evening fail
In green Bengala's palmy grove,
    Listening the nightingale!

If thou, my love, wert by my side,
    My babies at my knee,
How gayly would our pinnace glide
    O'er Gunga's mimic sea!

I miss thee at the dawning gray,
    When, on our deck reclined,
In careless ease my limbs I lay
    And woo the cooler wind.

I miss thee when by Gunga's stream
    My twilight steps I guide,
But most beneath the lamp's pale beam
    I miss thee from my side.

I spread my books, my pencil try,
  The lingering noon to cheer,
But miss thy kind, approving eye,
  Thy meek, attentive ear.

But when at morn and eve the star
  Beholds me on my knee,
I feel, though thou art distant far,
  Thy prayers ascend for me.

Then on! then on! where duty leads,
  My course be onward still,
O'er broad Hindostan's sultry meads,
  O'er bleak Almorah's hill.

That course nor Delhi's kingly gates,
  Nor mild Malwah detain;
For sweet the bliss us both awaits
  By yonder western main.

Thy towers, Bombay, gleam bright, they say,
  Across the dark blue sea;
But never were hearts so light and gay
  As then shall meet in thee!

REGINALD HEBER.

THERE'S NAE LUCK ABOUT THE HOUSE.

AND are ye sure the news is true?
  And are ye sure he's weel?
Is this a time to think of wark?
  Ye jauds, fling by your wheel.

Is this a time to think of wark,
  When Colin 's at the door?
Gie me my cloak! I 'll to the quay
  And see him come ashore.

For there 's nae luck about the house,
  There 's nae luck ava;
There 's little pleasure in the house,
  When our gudeman 's awa'.

Rise up and mak' a clean fireside;
  Put on the muckle pot;
Gi'e little Kate her cotton gown,
  And Jock his Sunday coat:
And mak' their shoon as black as slaes,
  Their hose as white as snaw;
It 's a' to please my ain gudeman,
  For he 's been long awa'.

There 's twa fat hens upo' the bank,
  Been fed this month and mair;
Mak' haste and thraw their necks about,
  That Colin weel may fare;
And mak' the table neat and clean,
  Gar ilka thing look braw;
It 's a' for love of my gudeman,
  For he 's been long awa'.

O gi'e me down my bigonet,
  My bishop satin gown,
For I maun tell the bailie's wife
  That Colin 's come to town.

My Sunday's shoon they maun gae on,
  My hose o' pearly blue;
'T is a' to please my ain gudeman,
  For he 's baith leal and true.

Sae true his words, sae smooth his speech,
  His breath 's like caller air!
His very foot has music in 't,
  As he comes up the stair.
And will I see his face again?
  And will I hear him speak?
I 'm downright dizzy wi' the thought,—
  In troth, I 'm like to greet.

The cauld blasts o' the winter wind,
  That thrillèd through my heart,
They 're a' blown by; I ha'e him safe,
  Till death we 'll never part:
But what puts parting in my head?
  It may be far awa';
The present moment is our ain,
  The neist we never saw.

Since Colin 's weel, I 'm weel content,
  I ha'e nae more to crave,
Could I but live to mak' him blest,
  I 'm blest above the lave:
And will I see his face again?
  And will I hear him speak?
I 'm downright dizzy wi' the thought,—
  In troth, I 'm like to greet.

For there 's nae luck about the house,
  There 's nae luck ava;

There's little pleasure in the house,
  When our gudeman's awa'.

JEAN ADAM.

DOLCINO TO MARGARET.

THE world goes up and the world goes down,
  And the sunshine follows the rain;
And yesterday's sneer, and yesterday's frown,
  Can never come over again,
      Sweet wife,
No, never come over again.

For woman is warm, though man be cold,
  And the night will hallow the day;
Till the heart which at even was weary and old
  Can rise in the morning gay,
      Sweet wife,
To its work in the morning gay.

CHARLES KINGSLEY.

O LAY THY HAND IN MINE, DEAR!

O LAY thy hand in mine, dear!
  We're growing old;
But Time hath brought no sign, dear,
  That hearts grow cold.
'T is long, long since our new love
  Made life divine;
But age enricheth true love,
  Like noble wine.

And lay thy cheek to mine, dear,
    And take thy rest;
Mine arms around thee twine, dear,
    And make thy nest.
A many cares are pressing
    On this dear head;
But Sorrow's hands in blessing
    Are surely laid.

O, lean thy life on mine, dear!
    'T will shelter thee.
Thou wert a winsome vine, dear,
    On my young tree:
And so, till boughs are leafless,
    And songbirds flown,
We 'll twine, then lay us, griefless,
    Together down.

                GERALD MASSEY.

FAITH AND HOPE.

O, DON'T be sorrowful, darling!
    Now, don't be sorrowful, pray;
For, taking the year together, my dear,
    There isn't more night than day.
It 's rainy weather, my loved one;
    Time's wheels they heavily run;
But taking the year together, my dear,
    There isn't more cloud than sun.

We 're old folks now, companion,—
    Our heads they are growing gray;

But taking the year all round, my dear,
  You always will find the May.
We 've had our May, my darling,
  And our roses, long ago;
And the time of the year is come, my dear,
  For the long dark nights, and the snow.

But God is God, my faithful,
  Of night as well as of day;
And we feel and know that we can go
  Wherever he leads the way.
Ay, God of night, my darling!
  Of the night of death so grim;
And the gate that from life leads out, good wife,
  Is the gate that leads to Him.

                              REMBRANDT PEALE.

DARBY AND JOAN.

  DARBY, dear, we are old and gray,
  Fifty years since our wedding day,
  Shadow and sun for every one
  As the years roll on;
  Darby, dear, when the world went wry,
  Hard and sorrowful then was I—
  Ah! lad, how you cheered me then,
  Things will be better, sweet wife again!
  Always the same, Darby, my own,
  Always the same to your old wife Joan.

  Darby, dear, but my heart was wild
  When we buried our baby child,

Until you whispered " Heav'n knows best!"
And my heart found rest;
Darby, dear, 't was your loving hand
Showed the way to the better land—
Ah! lad, as you kissed each tear,
Life grew better, and Heaven more near.
Alwas the same, Darby, my own,
Always the same to your old wife Joan.

Hand in hand when our life was May,
Hand in hand when our hair is gray,
Shadow and sun for every one,
As the years roll on;
Hand in hand when the long night-tide
Gently covers us side by side—
Ah! lad, though we know not when,
Love will be with us forever then:
Always the same, Darby, my own,
Always the same to your old wife Joan.

FREDERIC EDWARD WEATHERLY.

THE GOLDEN WEDDING.

O LOVE, whose patient pilgrim feet
    Life's longest path have trod,
Whose ministry hath symbolled sweet
    The dearer love of God,—
The sacred myrtle wreathes again
    Thine altar, as of old;
And what was green with summer then,
    Is mellowed, now, to gold.

Not now, as then, the Future's face
  Is flushed with fancy's light;
But Memory, with a milder grace,
  Shall rule the feast to-night.
Blest was the sun of joy that shone,
  Nor less the blinding shower—
The bud of fifty years agone
  Is Love's perfected flower.

O Memory, ope thy mystic door!
  O dream of youth, return!
And let the lights that gleamed of yore
  Beside this altar burn!
The past is plain; 't was Love designed
  E'en Sorrow's iron chain,
And Mercy's shining thread has twined
  With the dark warp of Pain.

So be it still. O thou who hast
  That younger bridal blest,
Till the May-morn of love has passed
  To evening's golden west,
Come to this later Cana, Lord,
  And, at thy touch divine,
The water of that earlier board
  To-night shall turn to wine.

DAVID GRAY.

THE FIRE OF LOVE.

FROM THE " EXAMEN MISCELLANEUM," 1708.

THE fire of love in youthful blood,
Like what is kindled in brushwood,
  But for a moment burns;

Yet in that moment makes a mighty noise;
It crackles, and to vapor turns,
    And soon itself destroys.

But when crept into agèd veins
It slowly burns, and then long remains,
    And with a silent heat,
Like fire in logs, it glows and warms 'em long,
And though the flame be not so great,
    Yet is the heat as strong.

        CHARLES SACKVILLE, EARL OF DORSET.

NOT OURS THE VOWS.

Not ours the vows of such as plight
    Their troth in sunny weather,
While leaves are green and skies are bright,
    To walk on flowers together.

But we have loved as those who tread
    The thorny path of sorrow,
With clouds above, and cause to dread
    Yet deeper gloom to-morrow.

That thorny path, those stormy skies,
    Have drawn our spirits nearer;
And rendered us, by sorrow's ties,
    Each to the other dearer.

Love, born in hours of joy and mirth,
    With mirth and joy may perish;
That to which darker hours gave birth
    Still more and more we cherish.

It looks beyond the clouds of time,
   And through death's shadowy portal;
Made by adversity sublime,
   By faith and hope immortal.

BERNARD BARTON.

LAODAMIA.

" WITH sacrifice, before the rising morn,
   Vows have I made by fruitless hope inspired;
And from th' infernal gods, 'mid shades forlorn
   Of night, my slaughtered lord have I required;
Celestial pity I again implore;
Restore him to my sight—great Jove, restore! "

So speaking, and by fervent love endowed
   With faith, the suppliant heavenward lifts her
      hands;
While, like the sun emerging from a cloud,
   Her countenance brightens and her eye ex-
      pands;
Her bosom heaves and spreads, her stature grows;
And she expects the issue in repose.

Oh terror! what hath she perceived?—oh joy!
   What doth she look on?—whom doth she be-
      hold?
Her hero slain upon the beach of Troy?
   His vital presence? his corporeal mould?
It is—if sense deceive her not—'t is he!
And a god leads him—wingèd Mercury!

Mild Hermes spake—and touched her with his
   wand

That calms all fear: " Such grace hath crowned
    thy prayer,
Laodamia! that at Jove's command
  Thy husband walks the paths of upper air;
He comes to tarry with thee three hours' space;
Accept the gift, behold him face to face!"

Forth sprang the impassioned queen her lord to
    clasp;
  Again that consummation she essayed;
But unsubstantial form eludes her grasp
  As often as that eager grasp was made.
The phantom parts—but parts to reunite,
And reässume his place before her sight.

" Protesilaus, lo! thy guide is gone!
  Confirm, I pray, the vision with thy voice:
This is our palace,—yonder is thy throne!
  Speak! and the floor thou tread'st on will re-
    joice.
Not to appal me have the gods bestowed
This precious boon, and blest a sad abode."

" Great Jove, Laodamia, doth not leave
  His gifts imperfect: spectre though I be,
I am not sent to scare thee or deceive;
  But in reward of thy fidelity.
And something also did my worth obtain;
For fearless virtue bringeth boundless gain.

" Thou know'st, the Delphic oracle foretold
  That the first Greek who touched the Trojan
    strand

Should die; but me the threat could not with-
    hold—
  A generous cause a victim did demand;
And forth I leapt upon the sandy plain;
A self-devoted chief, by Hector slain."

" Supreme of heroes! bravest, noblest, best!
  Thy matchless courage I bewail no more,
Which then, when tens of thousands were deprest
  By doubt, propelled thee to the fatal shore;
Thou found'st—and I forgive thee—here thou
    art—
A nobler counsellor than my poor heart.

" But thou, though capable of sternest deed,
  Wert kind as resolute, and good as brave;
And he whose power restores thee hath decreed
  Thou shouldst elude the malice of the grave;
Redundant are thy locks, thy lips as fair
As when their breath enriched Thessalian air.

" No spectre greets me,—no vain shadow this;
  Come, blooming hero, place thee by my side!
Give, on this well-known couch, one nuptial kiss
  To me, this day a second time thy bride!"
Jove frowned in heaven; the conscious Parcæ
    threw
Upon those roseate lips a Stygian hue.

" This visage tells thee that my doom is past;
  Nor should the change be mourned, even if the
    joys

Of sense were able to return as fast
   And surely as they vanish. Earth destroys
Those raptures duly—Erebus disdains;
Calm pleasures there abide—majestic pains.

" Be taught, O faithful consort, to control
   Rebellious passion : for the gods approve
The depth, and not the tumult, of the soul;
   A fervent, not ungovernable, love.
Thy transports moderate; and meekly mourn
When I depart, for brief is my sojourn—"

" Ah, wherefore?   Did not Hercules by force
   Wrest from the guardian monster of the tomb
Alcestis, a reanimated corse,
   Given back to dwell on earth in vernal bloom?
Medea's spells dispersed the weight of years,
And Æson stood a youth 'mid youthful peers.

" The gods to us are merciful, and they
   Yet further may relent; for mightier far
Than strength of nerve and sinew, or the sway
   Of magic potent over sun and star,
Is love, though oft to agony distrest,
And though its favorite seat be feeble woman's
     breast.

" But if thou goest, I follow—"   " Peace ! " he
     said;
   She looked upon him and was calmed and
     cheered;
The ghastly color from his lips had fled;
   In his deportment, shape, and mien appeared

Elysian beauty, melancholy grace,
Brought from a pensive, though a happy place.

He spake of love, such love as spirits feel
    In worlds whose course is equable and pure;
No fears to beat away—no strife to heal—
    The past unsighed for, and the future sure;
Spake of heroic arts in graver mood
Revived, with finer harmony pursued;

Of all that is most beauteous, imaged there
    In happier beauty; more pellucid streams,
An ampler ether, a diviner air,
    And fields invested with purpureal gleams;
Climes which the sun, who sheds the brightest day
Earth knows, is all unworthy to survey.

Yet there the soul shall enter which hath earned
    That privilege by virtue—" Ill," said he,
" The end of man's existence I discerned,
    Who from ignoble games and revelry
Could draw, when we had parted, vain delight,
While tears were thy best pastime, day and night;

" And while my youthful peers before my eyes
    (Each hero following his peculiar bent)
Prepared themselves for glorious enterprise
    By martial sports,—or, seated in the tent,
Chieftains and kings in council were detained,
What time the fleet at Aulis lay enchained.

" The wished-for wind was given; I then revolved
    The oracle, upon the silent sea;

And, if no worthier led the way, resolved
    That, of a thousand vessels, mine should be
The foremost prow in pressing to the strand—
Mine the first blood that tinged the Trojan sand.

" Yet bitter, ofttimes bitter, was the pang
    When of thy loss I thought, belovèd wife!
On thee too fondly did my memory hang,
    And on the joys we shared in mortal life—
The paths which we had trod—these fountains,
        flowers—
My new-planned cities, and unfinished towers.

" But should suspense permit the foe to cry,
   ' Behold they tremble!—haughty their array,
Yet of their number no one dares to die '?
    In soul I swept th' indignity away.
Old frailties then recurred; but lofty thought,
In acts embodied, my deliverance wrought.

" And thou, though strong in love, art all too weak
    In reason, in self-government too slow;
I counsel thee by fortitude to seek
    Our blest reunion in the shades below.
The invisible world with thee hath sympathized;
Be thy affections raised and solemnized.

" Learn, by a mortal yearning, to ascend,
    Seeking a higher object. Love was given,
Encouraged, sanctioned, chiefly for that end;
    For this the passion to excess was driven,
That self might be annulled—her bondage prove
The fetters of a dream, opposed to love."

Aloud she shrieked! for Hermes reappears!
　Round the dear shade she would have clung,—
　　't is vain;
The hours are past,—too brief had they been
　　years;
　And him no mortal effort can detain.
Swift, toward the realms that know not earthly
　　day,
He through the portal takes his silent way,
And on the palace floor a lifeless corse she lay.

Thus, all in vain exhorted and reproved,
　She perished; and, as for a wilful crime,
By the just gods, whom no weak pity moved,
　Was doomed to wear out her appointed time,
Apart from happy ghosts, that gather flowers
Of blissful quiet 'mid unfading bowers.

—Yet tears to human suffering are due;
　And mortal hopes defeated and o'erthrown
　Are mourned by man, and not by man alone,
As fondly he believes.—Upon the side
Of Hellespont (such faith was entertained)
　A knot of spiry trees for ages grew
From out the tomb of him for whom she died;
And ever, when such stature they have gained
　That Ilium's walls were subject to their view,
The trees' tall summits withered at the sight
A constant interchange of growth and blight!
　　　　　　　WILLIAM WORDSWORTH.

"TILL DEATH US PART."

"Till death us part,"
Thus speaks the heart
When each to each repeats the words of doom;
For better and for worse,
Through blessing and through curse,
We shall be one, till life's last hour shall come.

Life with its myriad grasp
Our yearning souls shall clasp
By ceaseless love and still expectant wonder;
In bonds that shall endure
Indissolubly sure
Till God in death shall part our paths asunder.

Till death us join!
Oh, word yet more divine,
Which to the breaking heart breathes hope sub-
lime!
Through wasted hours,
And shattered powers,
We still are one, despite the change and time.

Death with his healing hand
Shall knit once more the band,
Which needs but that one link that none may
sever;
Till, through the only Good,
Seen, felt, and understood,
The life in God shall make us one forever.

ARTHUR PENRHYN STANLEY.

THE OLD MAN DREAMS.

O FOR one hour of youthful joy!
　　Give back my twentieth spring!
I 'd rather laugh a bright-haired boy
　　Than reign a gray-beard king!

Off with the spoils of wrinkled age!
　　Away with learning's crown!
Tear out life's wisdom-written page,
　　And dash its trophies down!

One moment let my life-blood stream
　　From boyhood's fount of flame!
Give me one giddy, reeling dream
　　Of life all love and fame!

My listening angel heard the prayer,
　　And, calmly smiling, said,
" If I but touch thy silvery hair,
　　Thy hasty wish has sped.

" But is there nothing in thy track
　　To bid thee fondly stay,
While the swift seasons hurry back
　　To find the wished-for day?"

Ah! truest soul of womankind!
　　Without thee what were life?
One bliss I cannot leave behind:
　　I 'll take—my—precious—wife!

The angel took a sapphire pen
  And wrote in rainbow dew,
" The man would be a boy again,
  And be a husband, too ! "

" And is there nothing yet unsaid
  Before the change appears?
Remember, all their gifts have fled
  With those dissolving years ! "

" Why, yes ; for memory would recall
  My fond paternal joys ;
I could not bear to leave them all :
  I' ll take—my—girl—and—boys ! "

The smiling angel dropped his pen—
  " Why, this will never do ;
The man would be a boy again,
  And be a father, too ! "

And so I laughed—my laughter woke
  The household with its noise—
And wrote my dream, when morning broke,
  To please the gray-haired boys.

OLIVER WENDELL HOLMES.

JOHN ANDERSON, MY JO.

JOHN ANDERSON, my jo, John,
  When we were first acquent,
Your locks were like the raven,
  Your bonnie brow was brent ;

But now your brow is beld, John,
  Your locks are like the snaw;
But blessings on your frosty pow,
  John Anderson, my jo.

John Anderson, my jo, John,
  We clamb the hill thegither;
And monie a canty day, John,
  We've had wi' ane anither.
Now we maun totter down, John,
  But hand in hand we'll go:
And sleep thegither at the foot,
  John Anderson, my jo.

ROBERT BURNS.

INDEX: AUTHORS AND TITLES.

463

INDEX OF AUTHORS AND TITLES.

For occupation, nativity, etc., of Authors, and the American publishers of American poetical works, see General Index of Authors, Volume X.